Psychology of Coaching: Theory and Application

Jack H. Llewellyn
Judy A. Blucker

Florida International University
Miami, Florida

Burgess Publishing Company
Minneapolis, Minnesota

Editorial: Wayne Schotanus, Anne Heller, Elisabeth Sövik
Copy Editing: Sandra Chizinsky
Art: Judy Vicars
Production: Morris Lundin, Pat Barnes

Cover design by Don Pulver

©1982 by Burgess Publishing Company
Printed in the United States of America
Library of Congress Catalog Card Number 81-52344
ISBN 0-8087-1243-8

Burgess Publishing Company
7108 Ohms Lane
Minneapolis, Minnesota 55435

J I H G F E D C B A

To my folks—*JHL*

To my first coach, Hazel B. Albin—*JAB*

Dr. Jack H. Llewellyn is an associate professor at Florida International University, and serves as director of the International Institute for the Study of Sport. He teaches courses in sport psychology, psychology of coaching, children in sport, and motor learning. He also travels extensively, lecturing on the topics of motivation and performance, and competition and children.

Years of experience in the field have earned Dr. Llewellyn a number of national positions, among them editor of the *Journal of Sport Behavior* for the United States Sports Academy and director of youth sport programs for the National Football League Alumni Association. Producer of a series of films on children in sport, he is also the author of many published research articles on sport psychology and youth, and has edited a handbook on sports skills.

Dr. Llewellyn's background in sport psychology has led to positions as sport psychology consultant for the Houston Astros Minor League Organization, the Montreal Expos Minor League System, Pepsi Cola Youth Sport Programs, the United States International Shooting Teams, and various youth sport organizations. With the aid of research grants, he has conducted studies in such areas as personality traits of professional athletes and college athletes.

Dr. Judy A. Blucker is assistant dean for professional studies at Florida International University's School of Education. She has received numerous honors in her discipline, notably recognition for outstanding contributions to women's athletics at FIU for five years, and the honor award from the Florida Association for Health, Physical Education and Recreation.

Dr. Blucker brings to this book fifteen years of coaching experience in basketball, volleyball, softball, and track, and she has proved her skill as coach of two Florida AIAW State Championship Volleyball teams. Her knowledge of the sports she coaches is grounded in years of her own playing experience, including two ASA National Slowpitch Softball Championships and an All-American selection for slowpitch softball.

Dr. Blucker is the published author of articles appearing in the *Florida Journal of Health, Physical Education and Recreation* and the *NAGWS Softball Guide*. She has served as a speaker and clinician at athletic clinics, conferences, and workshops in her home state and across the country. Her list of professional offices includes a current position as chairperson for the Rules Standard Committee for the Association for Intercollegiate Athletics for Women.

Contents

Foreword   vii

Preface   ix

1   Introduction   1

2   Growth and Development   9

3   Personality Defined   23

4   Personality and Performance   35

5   Motivation   49

6   Techniques of Motivation   63

7   Anxiety and Performance   77

8   Information Processing   89

9   Aggression and Performance   97

10   Mental Preparation and Performance   107

11   Practice Factors   117

12   The Coach as Counselor   127

13   Coaching Girls and Women   133

14   Coaching Youth Sport   143

15   Coaching High School Athletes   153

16   Coaching College Athletes   167

Index   177

Foreword

Medicine, the sciences, and education are becoming more involved in the athletic world in a harmonious way. The net result should be improved athletic achievement, and indeed, we are witnessing ever-improving accomplishment in all sports.

Psychology as a behavioral science has made its contribution in this regard. It has helped coaches coach more effectively and athletes perform more proficiently. Psychology is also concerned with the total well-being and personal adjustment of those involved in sports. In this book, Jack Llewellyn and Judy Blucker demonstrate the importance of both aspects of psychology to sport.

Psychologists are concerned with behavior—understanding, explaining, and even predicting it. Since so many factors influence and are related to behavior, it is no easy task to decide on the most relevant topics to include in a book dealing with the psychology of, and psychology in, sport. Weaving research findings with practical concerns, Drs. Llewellyn and Blucker have carefully selected important and contemporary topics. The chapters help clarify many of the misunderstandings about what is known in psychology, especially as it applies to sport. Another benefit is that the authors draw from personal experience in sport as participants, scientists, and educators.

Drs. Llewellyn and Blucker are dedicated to improving the sport experience for all kinds of participants in all kinds of athletic programs. Coaches, as they point out in the book, have to be "psychologists" in addition to their many other responsibilities. The prospective or present coach should benefit immensely from the material presented in this book—it was prepared not only to help the reader learn more about sport psychology but also to offer practical guidelines for conducting athletic programs.

My experience has been that coaches are among the most dedicated workers in this country. They spend an incredible number of hours learning what they need to know to be more effective. Until recently, little organized material was available in this country in the area of the psychology of coaching. This book is a much needed contribution to such material. After a careful review of this book, the coach's ever-expanding knowledge and understanding of preparing and training athletes will be expanded even more.

Robert N. Singer
Professor and Director
Motor Behavior Resource Center
Florida State University
Tallahassee

Preface

The importance of psychology and mental preparation to all levels of sport is rapidly gaining acceptance both in the United States and abroad. Since the 1976 Olympic Games, several European programs for the psychological assessment and preparation of athletes have been publicized. In the United States, however, the use of practical sport psychology programs conducted by professional clinicians has been limited. Until more sport psychologists begin to apply their theories to the task of training athletes, coaches must continue to be sport psychologists to their teams.

Given these recent developments in sport, it is clear that coaches must be as familiar with sport psychology as they are with team strategies and techniques. The primary purpose of this text is to educate prospective coaches in the psychology of sport. The first twelve chapters of the text cover subjects such as growth and development, personality, motivation, anxiety, aggression, and the role of the coach as counselor.

Coaches from the little league to the collegiate level should look at physical ability from a developmental perspective. An athlete must be viewed not only in comparison to other athletes of the same age, but in relation to his or her individual rate of development. Aspects of growth and development are extensively discussed in Chapter 2.

No one would dispute that a coach should know about the development of strength, endurance, power, flexibility, and coordination. Once he or she understands the role of physiological variables in sport, the coach should learn about the role of psychological variables. Chapters 3 through 7 and 9 deal with emotional factors that can affect athletic performance. The discussion begins with a definition of personality and a description of its development. The relation of particular traits to the performance of coaches and athletes is examined.

Chapter 5 focuses on an often-discussed and more often misunderstood concept: motivation, both its definition and use. Whether in athletics, business, education, or the home, we all see ourselves as motivators of someone or something. Motivation is a particularly complex issue in sport.

Anxiety and aggression, two emotions whose influence on performance has received a great deal of attention, are the subjects of Chapters 7 and 9. Both chapters are designed to help the coach understand the anxieties and aggressive tendencies of athletes. All athletes seem to have a degree of anxiety and aggression. The coach's task is to help the athlete channel these emotions to enhance performance.

A coach who understands the role of emotions in performance is prepared to use the material on learning and development in Chapters 8, 10, 11, and 12. Chapter 8 analyzes the process by which athletes receive and process information. Specific techniques of instruction are discussed. To obtain the best performance, coaches should use techniques tailored to individual athletes.

Chapter 10 describes methods of hypnosis that have been found effective in reducing anxiety and enhancing the ability of athletes to concentrate during sport performance. Chapter 11 covers the topic of practice; Chapter 12 examines the coach's role as a counselor. Suggestions for improving the coach's skills in these two areas are offered.

Following the largely theoretical material presented in the first twelve chapters, there are four chapters that provide practical suggestions for applying sport psychology to humanistic coaching. The application of theory is an important topic that has been either omitted or covered only superficially in sport psychology texts. Although most coaches will be working with high school athletes, we felt that every prospective coach should also be familiar with the psychology of coaching young children and college athletes. We offer techniques for coaching athletes of various ages. The chapters on coaching also examine the similarities and differences between coaching men and coaching women.

In order to enhance the book's usefulness as a text for a college coaching class, there are suggested learning activities at the end of most chapters. These learning activities can supplement any other assignments the teacher may give the students in such a class.

The text should provide the prospective coach with both a theoretical knowledge of the psychology of coaching and practical suggestions for applying the material to coaching situations. We believe the text will assist in filling a need that exists in the training of coaches at all levels. It is intended as a guide for humanistic coaches who wish to promote and carry out educational athletic programs.

Jack H. Llewellyn
Judy A. Blucker

Chapter 1

Introduction

Why play sport? What benefits does it afford to athletes, coaches, spectators, and parents? How can athletes get the most from their talents? Assuming an athlete has the physical talent to perform, what are the psychological determinants of success or failure? Such questions are asked daily by many people interested in sport. There are other people involved in sport who have never paid serious attention to anything but the role of physical training in athletic performance.

Professional sport, until recent years, has been dominated by "old school" management. Evaluation of an athlete's potential was based almost entirely on his or her demonstration of physical talent. In baseball, for example, if a player did not run, hit, and throw on every required occasion, he was released. No apparent attention was paid to psychological variables that might have influenced performance. Baseball was not the only professional sport to ignore the role of psychology in athletics.

Professional sport has had an enormous influence on college, high school, and youth sport programs. Such programs have adopted the teaching and coaching techniques used at the professional level. Until recently, physical talent alone was considered an adequate recommendation for a player. Today the number of talented players is greater than ever. The growth of sport technology has made available additional techniques for the assessment of a player's potential and performance.

Sport has undergone a tremendous change in consequence. Although there are still holdouts from the "old school," sport is now dominated by a new breed of coach. The new coach is interested in a combination of physical talent with other qualities—qualities that not only influence performance, but help sustain the athlete in his or her commitment to sport.

The psychological aspects of sport are gaining attention at meetings of sport administrators representing all levels of competition. Administrators are aware that sport is no longer the only choice for young people. Their interests have broadened, and they often choose forms of recreation other than sport. To help make sport more attractive to prospective athletes, coaches need to learn about the psychology of coaching and sport.

Mastery of the various aspects of coaching psychology is not a simple task. The discipline of sport psychology has grown tremendously during recent years. Most subjects encompassed by sport psychology have come to coaching and physical education from psychological research. Table 1.1, proposed by Singer, provides an overview of the many facets of sport psychology [1].

It is probably unreasonable to expect coaches to become experts in sport psychology. They can, however, learn enough about the topics outlined in Table 1.1 to understand their importance in coaching and sport. A brief discussion of each subject follows.

Table 1.1. Facets of Sport Psychology

DEVELOPMENTAL	PERSONALITY	LEARNING AND TRAINING	SOCIAL	PSYCHOMETRICS
Optimal learning & performance years	Adjustment problems	Learning processes & variables	Group & organizational dynamics	Measurement
Heredity & experience	Self-concept	Factors influencing skill acquisition	Competition & co-operation	Individual differences
Maturational processes	Motivation: Persistence, direction, effort	Administration of practice sessions		Group differences
Childhood, adolescence, maturity & aging	Psychological attributes & success	Performance variables	Leadership & management	Abilities, aptitudes, & skills
Disabilities		Ergonomics	Spectator effects	Personnel selection, prediction of success
		Instructional design	Peer & culture effects	
		Systems models, media usage, individualized learning approaches	Communication	
			Social dimensions	

From Robert Singer, "Overview of Sport Psychology," *Journal of Physical Education and Recreation* (September 1976), p. 25.

DEVELOPMENTAL PSYCHOLOGY

Knowledge of developmental psychology is important to every coach. Whatever the level of competition, coaches need to recognize the role of heredity in performance. To be most effective, they must also understand the relation of critical learning periods to motivation and readiness.

PERSONALITY

Personality and psychometrics have traditionally been more closely associated with clinical work than have the other topics in the table. Coaches should recognize the role of personality in performance, and understand the importance of give-and-take in communication. Coaches who can communicate effectively with athletes can provide an environment that is conducive to motivated performances and the development of favorable self-concepts.

LEARNING AND TRAINING

The third heading in the sport psychology model, learning and training, is one that is often neglected in sport psychology texts. Athletes must receive, process, and retain information for subsequent use. The coach is responsible for creating an environment in which information can be efficiently received. He or she should take time to prepare for practice: topics should be arranged in a logical sequence and spaced so that the athletes can think over each subject before the next one is covered.

SOCIAL PSYCHOLOGY

The study of group dynamics, including participation in sport, is an important aspect of the discipline of social psychology. Most coaches are aware that some players possess leadership qualities, and that others are significant contributors or good followers. To accommodate the needs of athletes with various levels of skill, coaches should also be familiar with various teaching methods. Each member of the team must learn the correct techniques of execution, but not everyone responds to the same techniques of instruction. The coach must not only be aware of the social dimensions of performance, but must be technically proficient in sport execution.

PSYCHOMETRICS

Psychometrics, the last area encompassed by sport psychology, is primarily concerned with measurement. Even though coaches are not often involved in psychological measurement, they should be aware that such measurement is possible and that it can be a valuable guide to the selection of personnel and the prediction of performance.

Knowledge of the areas encompassed by sport psychology and an understanding of physiology and mechanical analysis should enable coaches to get the most out of athletes at every performance. But this has not been the case. Perhaps because the research has not substantiated certain claims made by the profession, sport psychology has not been accepted at every level of sport participation.

With the exception of motivation, few aspects of sport psychology have been studied by coaches. Although this is the case in the United States, it is not so in other parts of the world. In many European countries, sport psychology plays a significant role in the preparation of athletes.

INTERNATIONAL SPORT PSYCHOLOGY

The United States has had only one official sport psychology consultant. Richard M. Suinn has acted as consultant for both the winter and summer Olympic Games. He has worked primarily with skiers and participants in women's track-and-field, using relaxation and mental rehearsal techniques. During the past five years several researchers and sport psychology practitioners have become active both regionally and nationally.

It has been no surprise to sport psychologists that European nations such as East Germany have improved their performance in international sport competition. These countries have recognized the importance of mental development as an accompaniment to physiological training. The Soviet Union and Czechoslovakia are examples of countries in which psychological training has become an essential part of the athletic conditioning regimen for all athletes. Psychological training has been used to improve performance in international shooting meets. Before each World Shooting Championship all participating nations have the opportunity to attend a symposium on the psychology of shooting. Although a review of all the techniques employed by other countries is beyond the scope of our text, most of them do use the relaxation and mental rehearsal techniques discussed in Chapter 10.

The United States is now beginning to follow the lead of European nations. In 1978, the United States Olympic Committee appointed a special committee on sport medicine to investigate techniques that will provide our athletes with the optimum in training procedures. Sport psychology is one of the areas under study by the committee. This is the first step in instituting psychological training for our finest athletes. The recommendations offered by this committee will undoubtedly spread to all levels of sport competition in the United States.

SPORT PSYCHOLOGY IN THE UNITED STATES

To discuss international developments before discussing national trends might seem illogical. In this case, however, the work of other nations has helped foster an interest in sport psychology in the United States. Even though our research is highly respected in Europe, American sport psychologists have not communicated their findings to the practicing professionals, the coaches. But this does seem to be changing.

One of the first attempts at sport psychology in the United States was made as early as 1938 by Philip K. Wrigley, president of the Chicago Cubs [2]. He tried to determine the psychological profiles of champion baseball players. He hoped the profiles would help him decide whether to sign certain players. The major resistance he encountered was from the athletes themselves. They were afraid information about their mental abilities would be made public. Wrigley eventually abandoned the project.

Since Wrigley's early attempt, several projects in sport psychology have probably been conducted but unreported. Recently, however, there have been several instances of sport psychology consultants working with athletic teams. One psychologist spent a great deal of time with the San Diego Chargers. After his work with the team, he published several controversial articles describing the psychological makeup of professional football players.

As an example on the level of professional sport, Jack Llewellyn has been with the Montreal Expos Minor League Baseball Organization since 1975, working as a sport psychology consultant. His duties include administering psychological inventories to the players, observing both players and management, and writing a report on each player. It would ordinarily take months for management to get to know the team. The reports, which delineate the traits of each player, help speed up this process. The reports are intended to aid communication between players and management. The consultant makes no attempt to predict physical performance; that job is left to the management, which is more qualified to evaluate physical talent. Thomas Tutko and Bruce Ogilvie are other sport psychologists who have worked as consultants for professional baseball players.

On the basis of his work as a consultant to the Olympics, Richard Suinn has documented the productive use of mental preparation by downhill skiers. According to Suinn, "Jean-Claude Killy, a three-time winner of Olympic gold medals, reported that his only preparation for one race was to ski [the course] mentally. He reports that the race turned out to be one of his best" [3]. Suinn uses several techniques of sport psychology to enhance performance. The methods are tailored to meet the needs of each athlete.

Both popular and scientific literature on sport offer numerous examples of athletes and coaches using psychology to improve performance. In swimming, for example, college coaches have reported the successful use of rewards as a psychological ploy to improve performance [4]. During the spring of 1979 at Florida International University, an oustanding baseball player was having trouble hitting a certain kind of pitch. He was so good at hitting every other kind of pitch that opponents eventually began to throw to his weakness—low and inside. Using relaxation and mental rehearsal techniques (to be discussed in Chapter 10), the player overcame his inability to hit a low and inside pitch [5].

The athletes we have used as examples all had the ability to achieve the desired level of skill. An athlete cannot use psychological training to improve physical performance unless the potential for physical performance is present.

Like many other training techniques initiated in professional sport, sport psychology has begun to occupy a prominent place in the design of high school, college, and even youth sport programs. The services provided by sport psychologists are in demand by national youth sport associations. The American Youth Soccer Organization, for example, has made a concentrated effort to incorporate sport psychology into its structure and operation.

As prospective coaches review the material in this text, they should keep in mind the implications for coaches at all levels of sport. To make organized athletic programs better and more attractive to students, the psychological aspects of sport must be studied in as conscientious and constructive a manner as the physical aspects of training.

STUDENT LEARNING ACTIVITIES

1. Ask a number of people in the community to identify ten famous people (five in sport, five in politics). The results of this activity can prompt class discussion on the importance and value of sport in our society. Sport heroes are usually more well known than national or international political figures.
2. Review and report on current newspaper and magazine articles about athletes to see whether their success in sport can be linked to psychological preparation.
3. Assign special topic reports to compare the use of sport psychology in foreign countries such as East and West Germany and the Soviet Union.
4. Compile a list of the number of sport associations or professional teams that use sport psychologists. The class could write letters to obtain the necessary information.

NOTES

1. Robert Singer, "Overview of Sport Psychology," *Journal of Physical Education and Recreation* (September 1976), p. 25.
2. William Barry Furlong, "Psychology on the Playing Fields," *Psychology Today* (July 1976): 40.
3. Richard Suinn, "Body Thinking: Psychology for the Olympic Champs," *Psychology Today* (July 1976): 38.
4. Based on the work of "Doc" Counsilman, swimming coach at the University of Indiana, who has been successful in motivating his athletes by unusual rewards.
5. Personal knowledge and experience of Jack L. Llewellyn in his work with baseball athletes at Florida International University.

Chapter 2
Growth and Development

Perhaps because of the availability of subjects, researchers in sport psychology have usually chosen male athletes of college age—often the better athletes—as the focus for their work. Their investigations have covered topics such as personality, motivation, and aggression. The subject of growth and development, however, has been largely ignored, perhaps because the growth and development process is near completion by the time the athlete is in the later years of college.

The results of psychological inventories have been interpreted with little or no consideration of the physiological characteristics of the subjects. This approach might have been justified when sport psychology was in its infancy. But sport has become more important than ever in the lower elementary grades. Children begin to participate in athletics during the years when they are growing and developing, both physiologically and psychologically. Sport psychology can no longer afford to ignore the physiological factors that can affect the child's development and maturation.

It seems appropriate to include in the initial section of this text a chapter concerned primarily with physiological and psychological growth and development. The following concepts accent the importance of such a chapter:

1. Our psychological makeup is influenced tremendously by our physical structure. When educators refer to children's self-concept, they are referring in part to the way children perceive their physical abilities. Children often assess their value to the peer group on the basis of whether they are successful in physical endeavors. Children's self-concepts can be partly determined by their degree of physical skill.
2. Children grow and mature at different rates. Not all eight-year-olds are prepared to be proficient in baseball or hockey, but they may be prepared when they are nine years old. Some seven-year-olds have better motor skills than some nine-year-olds. Coaches, parents, or parent-coaches do not always know how to handle develop-

mental differences. A child who is not yet skilled in a particular sport may be ignored by the coach and be permanently turned off to that sport. Some children, in response to parental pressure, remain in competition for team membership and after repeated failure develop poor self-concepts. In order to ensure success when they reach team age, parents sometimes force their children to learn sport skills as early as possible. But "as early as possible" may be too early for the child.

3. Coaches are now working with such young children that a knowledge of developmental processes is a necessity. Coaches who understand the relationship of physiological development to psychological development will be better prepared to work effectively with youngsters.

4. Both boys and girls are now competing on the same teams, at least on the little league level. Coaches should be familiar with the growth and developmental trends of both boys and girls.

5. Coaches must be aware that it is almost impossible to predict future achievement on the basis of present performance. Coaches and parents of little leaguers often indulge in such predictions, especially if the program serves as a "feeder" to more advanced programs. It is common practice for coaches to spend more time with the outstanding performers than with the less skilled athletes. At the time they enter the program, the less skilled athletes may not be psychologically or physiologically ready to perform at the required levels, but they might prove to be fine athletes once they are ready. Those who were initially more skilled might not progress at the expected rate. Less skilled athletes can be discouraged by early failure and lose interest. When they are ready to achieve, they may no longer be motivated to perform.

6. Last, and perhaps most important, is the concern voiced by educators and psychologists about early specialization in a sport. Those who work with young athletes must be aware that children need a variety of experiences during their growing years. If specialization in a sport comes too early, the child may be prevented from developing a range of motor skills. If personality is in fact influenced by sport, a highly specialized sport experience could limit the development of certain personality traits. A child who may someday be an athlete must have the opportunity to use a variety of skills.

Athletes of all ages can be better understood by the coach who is familiar with the development of motor ability, perception, and self-concept. The following sections of this chapter have been designed to acquaint the coach with these subjects.

DEVELOPMENT OF MOTOR ABILITY

The ability to move, to explore our environment, is fundamental to learning. We have to move to perceive our relationship to our surroundings. Movement begins in the womb; the fetus usually moves in an arrythmic and involuntary manner. The newborn infant is almost immediately capable of reflex actions. These actions, many of which are innate, rather than conditioned or learned, include the *startle reflex* (extending the arms and legs at sudden fright), the *crawling reflex,* the *grasping reflex,* and the much-discussed *swimming reflex.* A detailed discussion of these and other reflex actions is presented by Cratty, and by Arnheim and Pestalosi [1, 2].

The reflex phenomenon in infants initiates the development of movement skills that lead to interaction with parents and peers. A parent responds to an infant, even when the infant's movements are reflexive. This parental response begins to mold the psychological makeup of the child. For example, when an infant executes the grasping reflex—the uncontrolled grasping of an object—the object that is usually grasped is the finger of the father or the mother. This nonvolitional movement by the child initiates an interaction with the parent. Anything that is grasped becomes important to the infant, who thus unintentionally begins to explore his or her environment. After a few months, the infant not only grasps objects, but is also able to release them voluntarily, an action requiring greater control. During this time, the infant should be exposed to various objects that can be held and examined. Parents become involved in the child's exploration by providing such objects. It is by exploring, at first reflexively, and later purposefully, that children begin to interact with those around them.

At about six months of age the infant begins to move and explore without the direct aid of a parent. The child initiates locomotor actions. With her abdomen resting on the floor, the child crawls by pulling with both arms and pushing with both legs. Homolateral crawling is the next stage. The child moves first the arm and leg on one side of the body, then the arm and leg on the other. The final stage in the crawling process comes when the child is able to raise her body from the floor and support it on her hands and knees. The child eventually develops the ability to make crosslateral movements—moving the left arm gradually forward at the same time as the right leg. These are the stages through which children usually progress before walking. Some psychologists believe that a child who does not crawl before beginning to walk is more likely to have readiness problems in school than the child who passes through the complete developmental sequence.

As the child learns to execute locomotor skills, several important physiological and psychological characteristics are growing and developing. Physiologically, the child is developing strength, body control, and the ability to execute voluntary movements. The child's interaction with her environment also facilitates psychological development. She is able to perceive objects and to recognize the objects when she sees them again. The child responds to her parents and interacts with them, perhaps not verbally but through facial expressions or other body movement. The child begins to develop and use perceptual mechanisms, a necessary step in acquiring skills that might later be necessary for athletic participation. Self-concept, a topic to be discussed later, is significantly affected by the development of motor skills.

PERCEPTUAL DEVELOPMENT

The four aspects of perception most often discussed are visual perception, auditory perception, tactile perception, and kinesthetic awareness.

VISUAL PERCEPTION

We mention visual perception first, because the infant probably begins to perceive objects visually before doing anything else with them. By two weeks of age, the infant has already begun to track objects—to follow them with her eyes. Visual perception includes tracking, figure-ground differentiation, convergence, visual-spatial awareness, visual acuity, and visual memory. These are the perceptual abilities most often used in athletics. Figure-ground differentiation is the ability to distinguish an object from its background. We buy brightly colored toys for infants to help them practice this skill.

Convergence, an aspect of tracking, is the ability to exert enough control over ocular muscles to follow an object as it moves toward or away from the body. Visual-spatial awareness, which may be described as more advanced figure-ground differentiation, is the ability to pick out an object in space. What does this have to do with athletics and coaching? The coach must engage children in activities that will help them develop these abilities. This is especially important for young participants, such as those in little league baseball.

For a participant in sport, vision is the primary mode of perception. In baseball the background must be such that the batter can see the pitched ball as it approaches the plate. Both the centerfield background and the pitcher's uniform, which can be manipulated by adults in charge of the program, can affect the batter's ability to track the ball. Defensive players in the field must be able to track and intercept the ball once it has been hit. They need to ascertain their own location in relation to that of the moving ball. Infants and young children, like sport participants, enjoy using their perceptual skills. Adults can provide safe and interesting objects for the child to examine, and can engage the child in simple games of catch.

AUDITORY PERCEPTION

Auditory perception includes several of the same subtopics as visual perception: figure-ground differentiation and auditory spatial awareness are examples. Auditory perception also includes auditory localization, the ability to locate a sound. Figure-ground differentiation is the ability to pick out a meaningful sound from a background of noise. Children develop this skill by hearing various sounds, by seeing that movement can create sound, and by observing others create noise through movement. Children in a classroom or on an athletic field are often described as inattentive. A coach or teacher may say, "He just doesn't listen," or "I explain the task and he does just the opposite." The child may be distracted by something, or may be unable to distinguish the directions from the background noise. A child who is not receiving the directions cannot translate them into physical action. Before giving up on an apparently inattentive young athlete, a coach should be sure the child can hear what he or she is meant to.

TACTILE PERCEPTION

One of the most important aspects of perception is tactile perception, the ability to use the sensation of touch to differentiate between objects of various shapes, sizes, weights, and textures. The ability to gauge pressure or to distinguish a light grip from a heavy grip on an object is important in sport: the child must feel an object to manipulate the object. Only through exposure to objects of various sizes, shapes, weights, and textures will a child develop the ability to differentiate during sport performance and make appropriate decisions. In baseball, for example, pitchers from the little leagues to the pros will often ask for a different ball because theirs is too smooth, has a rough mark, or has seams too high or two low.

KINESTHETIC AWARENESS

To perform competently in any motor skill children must have good kinesthetic sense, or body awareness. A child must be able to control the position of the body, and to know where each body part is at all times. Kinesthetic awareness enables the child to jump, to run quickly or slowly, to change directions suddenly, and to perform any other movement necessary for the smooth execution of an athletic skill. Every child should be given the opportunity to move freely and to explore the consequences of various movements.

Seldom will an activity involve only one kind of perception. The integration of all four aspects of perception is required for complete perceptual development—development that is necessary for participation in any skill, whether it be cognitive (mental) or psychomotor (physical). Coaches should be aware that perceptual development is continuous. Athletes perceive and process new information even during athletic contests. Perception is an essential part of performance at all levels of skill. Good perceptual skills will often lead to better performance than will physical talent alone. Adequate perceptual development allows the athlete to use his or her physical abilities at the optimal level.

PHYSICAL ATTRIBUTES

The importance of perceptual development in motor performance cannot be over-emphasized. Perception is a prerequisite to information processing and subsequent performance. But perceptual competence cannot be used unless there is adequate development of physical ability. The description of physical skills that follows is presented to help coaches understand the relationship between physical and perceptual development.

STRENGTH

Strength is the ability to exert force in one of three ways against a movable or immovable object. The three types of strength are explosive, static, and dynamic. Strength develops simultaneously with musculature in the fetus. Although movement at this stage of life is arrythmic and reflexive in nature, strength is what makes fetal movement possible. Once myelinization has occurred, strength begins to take on a definite nature. Strength is necessary as the child moves to grasp, to push and pull, and to support the body. As the child acquires motor skills, present perception and past experience determine the type of strength that will be used in a given situation: explosive, static, or dynamic. Depending on the perception and past experience of the participant, one of these types of strength will be employed.

Explosive strength is used when the task requires a sudden expenditure of energy. Many sports require such sudden bursts of strength. Explosive strength is necessary for success in sprinting or putting the shot. In football, linemen rely on explosive strength; in basketball, jumping requires explosive strength. These are only a few examples of sports or positions in which this kind of strength is an important factor in performance. Any activity that requires sudden expenditure of energy could be included in the list.

Dynamic strength may be described as the expenditure of energy against a movable object, or expenditure in which muscular movement occurs. Dynamic strength is used in weight lifting, when there is actual limb or trunk movement. This type of exercise requires isotonic strength. The ability to press against and move an opponent requires dynamic strength. In wrestling, a participant needs dynamic strength to be able to manipulate an opponent.

When muscular energy is directed against an immovable force and there is little or no movement of the limbs or trunk, *static strength* is employed. Isometric exercises develop static strength. To be able to exert all three types of strength, many athletes follow both isotonic and isometric exercise programs. Because most skills require a range of motion, isotonic exercises are usually preferable. Once the athlete has analyzed an activity, the amount of strength and endurance required to complete the activity depends on the athlete's perception of the situation.

ENDURANCE

Endurance may be described as the ability to withstand stress, to sustain muscular pressure, or to sustain movement for an extended period. Like strength, endurance begins to develop in early childhood. There are two types of endurance: *muscular endurance* and *cardiovascular endurance.* The extent to which we can develop endurance depends on many physiological factors, including height, weight, and build.

Understanding the development of endurance is important for coaches, especially those who work with young children. Children grow, develop, and mature at different rates. Muscular endurance and cardiovascular endurance may be thought of as the maturing of the physiological system of the body. A coach should try to find out about a child's past physical activities. If a child has been encouraged to run, jump, and hop, his or her endurance will be greater than that of a child whose physical activities were more restricted. Given time, opportunity, and encouragement, the less active child can develop endurance. Unfortunately, coaches too often pay more attention to the children who can already "do everything." It is unfair to assume that the less skilled children will always be on a level below that of their more skilled peers. Coaches who work with younger athletes should make maximum participation for all children their objective.

BALANCE

Balance is necessary for the performance of almost every skill. An infant who tries to right herself or to hold her head upright is demonstrating the "righting reflex." When working with handicapped children, clinicians often refer to trunk equilibrium, the ability to sustain the posture position. Muscular development is a prerequisite to balancing ability.

Posture is the only common balance trait. Research has demonstrated that the balance traits used in performing a particular skill are specific to the activity: the combination of balance traits employed in tennis differ from that used in basketball or baseball [3]. There are two types of balance: dynamic and static. *Dynamic balance* is the ability to sustain equilibrium while the body is moving; a child on a teeter-totter relies on dynamic blance. *Static balance* is the ability to sustain equilibrium while stationary—standing on one foot, for example. Dynamic balance is dominant in most athletic activities.

Several researchers have attempted to define balance. Heeschen found that when the results of four different balance tests were compared, the correlations were very low [4]. The tests used were the balanciometer, the Illinois progressive balance beam test, the Bass stick test, and the Springfield beam walking test. The results of Heeschen's study support the hypothesis of balance specificity. Melnick and Chasey, in separate studies, employed a stabilometer and a hopping skill respectively [5, 6]. Many researchers have defined ability on the balance board, or stabilometer, as a gross motor skill. This remedies in part the difficulty of defining balance. (Traits other than balance may be involved in performance on the stabilometer.)

Because balance is task-specific, a variety of experiences is necessary for balance development. Specializing in one sport at an early age denies the child the opportunity to acquire a range of skills. The child who later decides to change sports will be at a disadvantage. Coaches should be aware, however, that a child who has not had varied experiences may catch up to the other athletes, if offered the chance to develop new skills.

FLEXIBILITY

Although flexibility is a desirable quality for any athlete, the training and practice procedures of some sports actually limit the athlete's flexibility. Everyone who is concerned with physical well-being would like to be able to execute the most common flexibility exercise—touching the toes. But few sedentary people of middle age can execute this simple exercise. The fact is that from birth, our flexibility begins to diminish. Although infants demonstrate extraordinary trunk and joint flexibility, they gradually lose the ability, for example, to chew on their toes.

Flexibility diminishes in part as a result of physiological development and bone and muscle growth. But flexibility can also suffer from disuse. Children are not required to move to a great extent to fulfill many basic needs. Since children have begun to enter school at an earlier age, greater emphasis has been placed on cognitive achievement, and motor development has come to occupy a secondary role in children's experiences. A child whose motor development continues to be neglected will be deficient in motor skills, including flexibility.

Sports that limit flexibility limit children's alternatives in sport selection. For example, if a boy is a football lineman throughout elementary and junior high school, his narrow range of movement skills will often dictate that he continue to play lineman in high school. Athletes can also be limited in their choice of sports. Suppose a child wants to drop football and try basketball: chances are that his lack of flexibility and other skills will limit his chance of success. Wrestling is another sport that is moving to the elementary grades. Children begin to compete in wrestling as early as the fourth grade. A child who has done nothing but wrestle will be limited in his choice of sport when he gets older.

Coaches should do all they can to give children the opportunity to develop all their abilities fully. Children who have participated exclusively in one sport during their formative years cannot be expected to have a repertoire of skills that will allow them to participate in several sports as teenagers or adults.

AGILITY

Agility is the ability to move quickly and efficiently. An obstacle course in which the participant is required to change directions quickly is commonly used to measure agility. Children can exercise their agility either in everyday play activities or in structured motor programs. Sports such as basketball and soccer require their players to change directions constantly—forward, backward, and laterally. Many drills in basketball and football are labelled agility drills. Coaches of these and other sports devote a great deal of time to agility drills.

COORDINATION

Coordination is defined as the ability to integrate perceptual and motor skills in the efficient execution of specific movements. The kind of coordination that is used seems to be specific to the task. Catching, for example, requires hand-eye coordination. In football, punting requires hand-eye-foot coordination. Researchers have tested hand-eye coordination by requiring a subject to react—usually by repositioning the hand—to a visual stimulus such as a light source. Although a fine motor skill like hand-eye coordination can be improved through practice, coordination itself is a neurologically based process. The participant receives information through various receptors, processes the information, and executes a coordinated response. An athlete who seems uncoordinated may not have developed the perceptual and motor abilities the task requires. Researchers in the field of motor development believe that there is a critical learning period during which the child is ready to learn skills [7].

CRITICAL LEARNING PERIODS

The most interesting aspect of the growth, development, and maturation of children is the concept of critical learning periods or stage development. Thanks to extensive research, much of it with animals, the concept of stage development is generally accepted by those studying the learning process in children. When we refer to the critical learning period for motor skills, we assume that the child has progressed through the perceptual and physiological processes necessary for skill execution.

A critical learning period is the time in a child's life when physiological, psychological, and motivational development are at the optimal stage for learning certain skills. Since most skills are specific to certain activities, the critical learning period for the acquisition of a given skill differs from activity to activity and from child to child. Piaget is a strong supporter of the concept of stage development. Both Kephart and Delacato have created programs designed to guide children through such stages of development.

Kephart's Purdue Perceptual Motor Survey is one of the most popular surveys of perceptual development in use today. The twenty-two–item survey covers all major areas of perceptual development, including laterality, directionality, balance, and manipulation. Kephart believes that locomotor skills acquired in a logical sequence are necessary to proper development [8]. Delacato's work covers topics similar to those covered by Kephart. Delacato, however, approaches his program from a neurological perspective. Although a detailed description of their work is beyond the scope of this text, Getman, Frostig, and Barsch have also designed programs to facilitate the proper development of perceptual ability [9, 10, 11].

The coach or prospective coach must be aware that critical learning periods occur not only during early childhood, but extend through the years when children are introduced to competitive athletics. We cannot ignore the children who are not ready to learn the skills involved in a particular sport. An advocate of critical learning periods has said that it is not the earliness at which we teach activities but the timeliness that is important [12].

This brings up a point important for coaches and perhaps more important for parents. Parents often think that they should give their children a head start in athletics by demanding that they participate in sport at a very early age. It seems that every year, coaches encourage younger and younger children to join organized leagues that may act as "feeder" programs for the more advanced levels. Neither the parents' nor the coaches' attitudes can be substantiated by the literature. There are too many variables, both in athletics and in the child's environment, to allow us to predict future achievement on the basis of present performance.

Although many prospective athletes seem physically ready for participation in sport, they are not allowed in competition because they are "awkward." The seventh- or eighth-grade athlete who seems awkward may not have attained the level of psychological and physiological maturity necessary for performance. Other athletes of the same age may already have reached the optimal time for acquiring athletic skills. By the time the athletes are in senior high, an observer might not be able to distinguish between those who had been "awkward" and those who had not. If properly coached both from a psychological and physiological point of view, the athlete who was less skilled in junior high can become as successful as those who had demonstrated their proficiency at an earlier age. Particularly in this instance, the coach must be sensitive to motivational processes in athletics—both psychological and physiological.

DEVELOPMENT IN BOYS AND GIRLS

Because of the sudden growth of women's athletics and recent court rulings allowing girls and women to compete on male athletic teams, *all* athletic coaches should become familiar with patterns of growth and development in both sexes. In the past, women have often been deprived of the opportunity to compete in sport. This situation is changing and we hope it will continue to change until women have athletic programs equal to those of men.

Coaches have traditionally assumed that girls and women of all ages were physiologically inferior to their male counterparts. There is actually no reason to prevent girls from participating on boys' teams at the beginning levels of competition, such as in little league. In reviewing the research, we find that up to the age of five years the sexes are nearly equal in their potential for performance in motor skills, although girls are slightly ahead of boys in some skills. The girls may have an edge because many of the skills tested, such as hopping and skipping, are more familiar to girls than to boys. Recent literature using sport-related skills shows that girls may not be slightly ahead of boys at this age [13].

By the age of twelve, boys have reached the same skill levels as girls. Some studies have found that girls score higher than boys in grip strength as late as age thirteen. But motor ability in girls generally begins to diminish after the age of twelve—or rises only slightly. Motor ability in boys rises rapidly after the age of twelve, and continues to do so at least to the late teens. Assuming conditions are conducive to continued development, men reach their peak years of athletic performance in their middle to late twenties. With improved training and opportunities, this could also be true of women in the near future. Young athletes of both sexes are adept at activities requiring explosive strength. Distance running, a sport requiring tremendous cardiovascular endurance, is more suited to athletes in their thirties.

Why does athletic ability decrease in adolescent girls, while it increases in boys of the same age? The answer seems to lie in the structure and expectations of society. Girls are expected to be feminine, socially oriented, and to avoid strenuous activities. Boys are expected to be competitive, aggressive, and adept at motor skills. Success in physical endeavors is an important aspect of the self-image of men in our society.

Because of increased opportunities for participation, girls and women are competing in a variety of sports—not just golf, tennis, and swimming. Given the physiological differences between men and women of senior high and college age, women will probably not be participating in combative sports or sports in which height and weight are primary factors of success. Male coaches must nevertheless be prepared to coach female athletes and to understand them—both psychologically and physiologically.

SELF-CONCEPT

As we mentioned earlier in this chapter, one of the primary goals of athletic programs is the development of the athlete's self-concept. This is especially true in those programs serving children from five to thirteen years of age. Children in this age group are especially vulnerable to the influence of both peers and adults.

Research shows that the development of self-concept is based primarily on physical competence. Sociograms consistently indicate that the most popular students are those who are able to demonstrate physical skills to their peers. Coleman, in his classic study of adolescent society, concluded that high school students valued the "star athletes" significantly more than they did the "brilliant students" [14]. In 1975, sixteen years after the original study, Eitzen replicated Coleman's work and found almost identical results [15]. The popularity of high school athletes could be due to the social status our society accords professional athletes. Or perhaps the high visibility of athletes accounts for their value to their peers. Talented athletes naturally enjoy demonstrating their abilities.

Research has also shown that students who are skilled in athletics are often academically skilled as well [16]. Researchers have speculated on the relationship of physical competence to academic skill. Many students with academic difficulties have been placed in perceptual-motor programs designed to improve their academic performance. The relationship between mental and physical competence may be indirect. Improving his or her physical skills may improve the student's self-concept. When we feel good about ourselves, we are perhaps apt to study more efficiently and to learn more thoroughly. In other words, the physical program contributes to the development of a favorable self-concept.

Those in charge of administering athletic and physical education programs should try to make the sport experience a positive one. Athletic programs can and should make beneficial contributions to the self-concepts of the participants. As we noted earlier, students should not be placed in an environment that is either psychologically or physiologically inappropriate. A student who is not psychologically prepared for the success and the failure that are both a part of sport will not benefit from the athletic experience. Competition can only be harmful to the self-concepts of students who fail because they are not physically ready to participate in sport.

Coaches can avoid such problems by remembering that each child follows his or her own pattern of mental and physical development; this must be taken into account when sport programs are designed.

SUMMARY

In this chapter, we related the processes of growth and development to sport psychology. With sport becoming a way of life for nearly twenty million youngsters, the effect of sport on the psychological development of children is extensive. The importance of a knowledge of growth and development for prospective coaches and teachers is emphasized by the following points:

1. Psychological makeup is influenced tremendously by physical ability.
2. All children do not grow and mature at the same rate.
3. Coaches are now working with such young children that an understanding of developmental processes is necessary.
4. Boys and girls are now competing on the same teams, at least at the little league level.
5. It is almost impossible to predict future achievement on the basis of present performance.
6. Educators and parents are concerned about early specialization in a sport.

The primary objective of youth programs should be the teaching of basic physical skills and the facilitation of social development. It is not early specialization and achievement that are important in athletics, but the acquisition of physical and social skills. Aspects of physical development that should be of concern to coaches include reflex development, perceptual development, and the development of physical characteristics such as strength, endurance, balance, flexibility, agility, and coordination.

Critical learning periods refer to the times in a child's life when he or she is "ready"—psychologically, physiologically, socially, and emotionally—to pursue certain skills and activities. These periods vary from youngster to youngster, and from sport to sport for the same youngster.

The most important objective in sport, especially for young performers, is the development of a good self-concept. Youngsters should be encouraged to view sport as a rewarding experience. They may not always win, but they should be given every opportunity to enjoy athletics.

STUDENT LEARNING ACTIVITIES

1. Observe a variety of youth sport leagues in the community; note such things as:
    a. range of heights and weights in the same age group
    b. relationship of successful performance to height or weight
    c. sizes of girls and boys in same age group.
2. Research the historical background of selected famous athletes to discover at what age they began their athletic competition.
3. Administer a perceptual-motor test to six- and seven-year-olds participating in youth sport and compare the results to those for nonparticipants of the same age. Consult an evaluation or elementary physical education textbook for text source.
4. Compare the physical abilities of athletes and nonathletes, or male athletes and female athletes of the same age. Use strength, speed, balance, and other abilities as criteria. Consult an evaluation text for test sources.
5. Administer a published kinesthetic awareness test to athletes and nonathletes in several age groups, youth to college age.
6. Research the historical background of Olympic records. Compare with modern achievement records by charting examples of times and/or distances.

NOTES

1. Bryant J. Cratty, *Movement Behavior and Motor Learning*, 3rd ed. (Philadelphia: Lea & Febiger, 1973).
2. Daniel Arnheim and Robert Pestalosi, *Elementary Physical Education: A Developmental Approach*, 2nd ed. (St. Louis, Mo.: C. V. Mosby Co., 1978).
3. Richard Heeschen, "A Comparison of the Balanciometer to the Illinois Progressive Balance Beam Test, the Bass Stick Test, and the Springfield Beam-Walking Test" (Master's thesis, Florida State University, 1962).
4. Ibid.
5. Merrill J. Melnick, "Effects of Overlearning on the Retention of a Gross Motor Skill" (microcarded doctoral diss., Ohio State University, 1968).
6. William C. Chasey, "Overlearning as a Variable in the Retention of Gross Motor Skills by the Mentally Retarded," *Research Quarterly* 42 (1971): 145-150.
7. Robert N. Singer, *Coaching, Athletics and Psychology* (New York: McGraw-Hill, 1972), p. 62.

8. Newell Kephart, *The Slow Learner in the Classroom* (Columbus, Ohio: Charles E. Merrill, 1960).

9. G. Getman, *How to Develop Your Child's Intelligence: A Research Publication* (Luverne, Minn.: G. N. Getman, 1962).

10. Marianne Frostig, *Developmental Test of Visual Perception: Administration and Scoring Manual* (Palo Alto, Calif.: Consulting Psychologists Press, 1966).

11. R. Barsch, *Achieving Perceptual Motor Efficiency* (Seattle: Special Child Publications, 1967).

12. Singer, *Coaching, Athletics and Psychology,* p. 62.

13. Jacqueline Herkowitz, "Sex Role Expectations and Motor Behavior of the Young Child," in Marcella V. Ridenour, ed., *Motor Development: Issues and Applications* (Princeton: Princeton Book Co., 1978). p. 83.

14. James S. Coleman, "Athletics in High School," *Annals of the American Academy of Political and Social Science* 338 (1961): 33-43.

15. D. Stanley Eitzen, "Athletics in the Status System of Male Adolescents: A Replication of Coleman's 'The Adolescent Society,'" *Adolescence* 10 (1975): 268-276.

16. Hans C. Buhrmann, "Scholarship and Athletics in Junior High School," *International Review of Sport Sociology* 7 (1972): 119-128.

Chapter 3

Personality Defined

Psychology of sport encompasses many topics. National and international sport psychology conferences usually focus on subjects such as motivation, aggression, anxiety, and personality. Of these, personality has received the most attention in recent research.

"Personality" is a term commonly used by people concerned with almost every aspect of human interaction. When interviewing applicants for positions in education, administrators place great emphasis on the personality of the prospective employee. A coach evaluating an athlete will often refer to his or her personality. Sport commentators often use "personality conflicts" to account for a team's poor performance. Parents sometimes compare their children on the basis of personality traits. Numerous other examples of the importance of personality in our society could be cited. In keeping with the focus of this text, we will discuss and define personality as it relates to sport psychology.

Although he admits to having reservations "as to the importance of personality in athletic performance," Rushall also feels that "knowledge of the personality of an individual is important for maximizing individual responses" [1]. He has made the following suggestions for the use of personality information:

1. A provision of a better understanding of an individual's behavior tendencies. This information can be used to predict behaviors and to eliminate situations that will produce undesirable behaviors.
2. Coach-player interactions can be better effected by producing situations which will eliminate undesirable consequences.
3. From the above two statements, it can be asserted that player manipulation may be improved to the extent of trying to maximize training and competitive performance and participation. This would lead to a rise in the efficiency of the training system or program.

4. If a relationship between personality and physical performance exists, one could differentiate, for selective purposes, between players of equal skill.
5. Repeated testing of players gives an indication of change in athletes. The coach can then readjust his player control procedures to these changes. [2]

Although these suggestions seem feasible, the application of personality information to athletics remains difficult, principally because the traits identified by psychologists seem to defy specific definition—particularly when the same trait is defined differently by different researchers. What coaches must understand is that by the time childrn enter organized athletics, their personality traits are developed. These traits may be affected by experience, but the foundation has been laid. Each child has certain behavioral tendencies—tendencies that are partly inherited, partly determined by environment. Before we discuss the relation of personality to performance, we must select a definition of personality.

DEFINITION OF PERSONALITY

Definition of personality vary as much as designations of trait. Cattell, author of a psychological inventory frequently used by sport psychologists, has defined personality as "that which tells what a man will do when placed in a given situation" [3]. Alderman defines personality as "an integration or merging of all the parts of one's psychological life—the way one thinks, feels, acts, and behaves" [4].

Alderman's definition suggests that personality is twofold: one side thinks and feels; the other acts and behaves. Singer has suggested that an individual has both basic personality traits and an external personality. Together these make up the "real person" [5]. The examples used in the initial section of this chapter refer for the most part to the external personality. It is our external personality that determines how we are seen by others. We are all concerned about how others perceive us, and this may be particularly true of athletes, who are so constantly in the public eye. Although many authors would say that external traits are not necessarily indicative of deeper traits, it is external traits that coaches are most likely to perceive—and most likely to affect. Singer has suggested that there are personality traits inherited and nurtured by society [6]. These traits as a group make up the individual or the "real person." Because of the various methods used in evaluating a personality, it is difficult to specifically define the various traits.

DEVELOPMENT OF PERSONALITY

Alderman, in discussing the development of personality, has said that individuals are born with a "blueprint" of basic traits [7]. For example, the child of athletic parents might inherit certain basic traits which, if nurtured, could lead him or her to select sports the same as or similar to those of the parents. This blueprint underlies behavior. Some personality traits may be encouraged by the child's experiences; others will diminish or remain latent. The blueprint may also fix boundaries to the development of certain traits—whatever the nature of the child's experiences. Alderman has summarized the relation of personality to heredity.

> A case . . . can be made for connecting the development of an individual's personality to heredity. To what extent environment rather than heredity influences personality is, however, a more difficult question. Generally, the position taken is that genetic factors provide the limits within which development takes place, but that particular environmental conditions are the primary causes of certain kinds of personality traits emerging within these limits. When athletes come from athletic families, it is probably due to a combination of the traits which they do inherit from their parents and the particular family environment . . . [8]

Other psychogolists have supported Alderman in his effort to explain the origin of personality and to examine sequence in personality development. Personality begins to develop at birth, when infants interact with those around them. As the child grows older, he or she begins to display behaviors that can be traced to specific personality traits. Although the potential for a given behavior must first be present, a trait—aggression, for example— will either be nurtured or not, depending on the environment. Parents often say, "He is so aggressive, I don't know where he got that!" Parents are rarely aware of how they may be influencing the child's behavior. A child raised in an environment where there is constant confusion and arguing will often reflect the anxiety, tension, and aggression present in the home.

Now we return to the basic question: what are personality traits? How have these traits been defined?

GENERALLY RECOGNIZED TRAITS

Several researchers have undertaken the task of labeling personality traits and explaining their origin. Semeonoff has suggested that personality traits are divided into the three following areas:

1. *Dynamic Traits*—motivation, action, purpose, attitudes, sentiments, desire, need, habit, prejudice, and will;
2. *Temperament Traits*—pervasive, unchanging qualities and tempos in our actions;
3. *Ability or Cognitive Traits*—intelligence, verbal, spatial and musical. [9]

Dynamic traits such as motivation, action, and attitudes are likely to change in response to outside influences. Temperament traits are either static or slow to change. The qualities characterized by Semeonoff as dynamic traits determine to what extent an athlete is willing to be committed to sport. The prominence of a given trait will vary with the circumstances and the athlete's perspective. The same stimulus may motivate an athlete one day and be a deterrent to the same athlete the next (see Chapter 6). Needs can also vary. We share certain basic needs: the need to compete, to achieve, and to belong. But to some people, competition may be more important than belonging, or achievement more important than competition. Nor does an individual always feel the drive to belong at the same level of intensity.

Semeonoff's list of dynamic traits suggests that the coach is in a position to influence the personality development of children and young adults. Because the coach is important to an athlete, the coach can influence the fulfillment of the athlete's needs.

Guilford has also proposed a model for the development of personality traits [10]. He suggests that certain modalities interact to form an individual's personality. These modalities are attitudes, temperament, interests, aptitudes, needs, physiology, and morphology. Guilford's structure is similar to that presented by Semeonoff.

Cattell classifies traits as either *source* traits or *surface* traits [11]. The changes we observe in athletes are changes in surface traits. Although surface traits are susceptible to change, such changes do not occur quickly. We could not expect an athlete to change his or her personality in the span of a few weeks. Alderman, in summarizing theoretical positions dealing with trait changes, proposes the following explanation:

> Certain personality traits can be learned while participating in any endeavor, including sport, but this acquisition is dependent on a highly complex interaction between each individual's genetic endowment, his previous and current environments, and his own particular behavior patterns. In addition, it would appear that personality changes occur only over a fairly significant length of time, and that these changes are probably just modifications of surface traits, not the actual changing of deeper source traits . . . [12]

Although coaches need to attend to source traits, the surface traits should be their primary concern. Surface traits are those that the coach can more easily perceive, and more easily affect. The younger the athlete, the easier it is to change his or her surface traits. The more established traits of older athletes are more difficult to alter, especially if they have taken part in only one or two sports since the beginning of their participation in athletics. This point will be discussed in detail later in this chapter.

EVALUATING PERSONALITY

Research in personality offers several methods of evaluating personality. It is appropriate to discuss these methods of evaluation before delving into the research and trying to interpret the conflicting results. Methods of measurement include (1) psychological inventories, (2) observation, (3) ratings, (4) projective tasks, and (5) interviews.

The most frequently used method is that of psychological inventories. There are several inventories available today and others are being developed. Many inventories seem, at least superficially, to measure the same traits. But in reviewing the test manuals closely, we often find that the same traits are given different names on different tests. A complete explanation of the design, administration, and evaluative techniques of each inventory is beyond the scope of this text. We will briefly discuss the most commonly used inventories and the traits each test is designed to measure.

CATTELL SIXTEEN PERSONALITY FACTOR QUESTIONNAIRE (CATTELL 16PF)

The 16PF, the result of over twenty years of research, is probably the test most frequently used to assess the personality traits of athletes [13]. The test is easy to understand and can be administered in approximately forty-five minutes. It consists of 187 questions, each of which is answered "yes," "occasionally," or "no." There are six forms, lettered *A* through *F*. *A* and *B* are the most appropriate forms for fully literate individuals ranging in age from seventeen through adulthood. A scoring system enables the examiner to work with four broad traits instead of the original sixteen. These four are *anxiety, extraversion, tough poise,* and *independence.* The following traits represent sixteen functionally independent dimensions of personality:

A
Reserved—Detached, critical, cool
Outgoing—Warmhearted, easy-going, participating
B
Less intelligent—Concrete-thinking
More intelligent—Abstract-thinking
C
Affected by feelings—Emotionally less stable, easily upset
Emotionally stable—Faces reality, calm, mature
E
Humble—Mild, accommodating, conforming
Assertive—Independent, aggressive, stubborn (dominance)
F
Sober—Prudent, serious, taciturn
Happy-go-lucky—Impulsively lively, gay, enthusiastic
G
Expedient—Evades rules, feels few obligations
Conscientious—Persevering, staid, rulebound
H
Shy—Restrained, diffident, timid
Venturesome—Society-bold, uninhibited, spontaneous
I
Tough-minded—Self-reliant, realistic, no-nonsense
Tender-minded—Dependent, overprotected, sensitive
L
Trusting—Adaptable, free of jealousy, easy to get along with
Suspicious—Self-opinionated, hard to fool

M
Practical—Careful, conventional, proper
Imaginative—Careless of practical matters
N
Forthright—Natural, artless, sentimental
Shrewd—Calculating, worldly, penetrating
O
Placid—Self-assured, confident, serene
Apprehensive—Worrying, depressive, troubled
Q_1
Conservative—Respecting established ideas
Experimenting—Critical, liberal, analytical, free-thinking
Q_2
Group-dependent—A "joiner" and sound follower
Self-sufficient—Prefers own decisions, resourceful
Q_3
Undisciplined self-conflict—Careless of protocol, follows own urges
Controlled—Socially precise, following self-image
Q_4
Relaxed—Tranquil, torpid, unfrustrated
Tense—Frustrated, driven, overwrought

The raw scores can be converted to sten scores (standard scores). The sten scores for each trait are recorded on a score sheet. A score of 1 to 3 is low; 8 to 10 is high. Scores of 4 to 7 are within the average range. High scores would be desirable on some traits, whereas low scores would be desirable on others.

Another form of the Cattell questionnaire has been designed for use with students of junior and senior high school age. This questionnaire, called HSPQ, contains 142 items and measures fourteen traits.

THE MINNESOTA MULTIPHASIC PERSONALITY INVENTORY (MMPI)

Another popular instrument, the MMPI, is much more time-consuming that the Cattell 16PF [14]. The MMPI contains 550 items that must be answered either true or false. Because of the difficulty of interpreting the scores and the nature of the traits measured, the MMPI should be administered by a psychiatrist. The following traits are measured:

Hypochondriasis
Depression   Masculinity-Femininity
Hysteria   Schizophrenia
Psychopathic Deviation   Hypomania

THE EDWARDS PERSONAL PREFERENCE SCHEDULE (EPPS)

The EPPS consists of 210 items designed to measure fifteen traits representing manifest needs [15]. The test takes approximately forty minutes and is designed for subjects at least fifteen years old. The EPPS is gaining popularity among researchers interested in the psychological assessment of athletes.

Achievement	Succorance
Deference	Dominance
Order	Abasement
Exhibition	Change
Autonomy	Endurance
Affiliation	Heterosexuality
Intraception	Aggression
Nurturance	

THE CALIFORNIA PSYCHOLOGICAL INVENTORY (CPI)

The CPI is a frequently used inventory that contains 480 items to be answered either true or false. Although the test is divided into four major categories, several traits are assessed within each category.

1. Measures of poise, ascendancy, and self-awareness:
   Dominance
   Capacity to status
   Sociability
   Social presence
   Self-acceptance
   Sense of well-being
2. Measures of socialization, maturity, and social responsibility:
   Responsibility
   Socialization
   Self-control
   Tolerance
   Good impression
   Communality
3. Measures of achievement potential and intellectual efficiency:
   Achievement via conformance
   Achievement via independence
   Intellectual efficiency
4. Measures of personal orientation and attitudes toward life:
   Psychological mindedness
   Flexibility
   Femininity [16]

ATHLETIC MOTIVATION INVENTORY (AMI)

The AMI was developed by Tutko, Ogilvie, and Lyon at the Institute for the Study of Athletic Motivation. Through extensive research dealing with athletes, certain personality traits related to high athletic achievement were determined. The traits are divided into two general areas: desire factors and emotional factors. The traits are scored 1 to 9 (1 to 3 is low; 4 to 6 is average; and 7 to 9 is high).

I. Desire Factors
   1. Drive—desire to be successful
   2. Determination—does not give up easily
   3. Intelligence—ability to grasp things quickly
   4. Aggression—thinks it is necessary to be aggressive to win
   5. Leadership—likes to influence teammates
   6. Organization—places things in perspective
II. Emotional Factors
   1. Coachability—respects coach and accepts his advice; good team player
   2. Emotionality—can control emotions and is mature and stable; not easily depressed
   3. Self-confidence—sure of himself and his ability; not prone to worry
   4. Mental Toughness—insensitive to feelings and problems of others; able to accept strong criticism
   5. Responsibility—accepts responsibility for actions and works to improve his mistakes; some will punish themselves for their mistakes
   6. Trust—accepts people at face value; does not look for ulterior motives
   7. Conscience Development—likes to do things as correctly as possible; places good of team above his own well-being [17]

This review has included only the most commonly used inventories. Most can be administered by those with a minimum of training; the MMPI should be administered by a professional psychologist. Several precautions should be kept in mind when using the results of these tests.

   1. Make only constructive use of the results. Never use information to punish or embarrass athletes.
   2. Before using test results, be familiar with the sport in which an athlete participates. It would be unfair to evaluate an athlete without observing his participation or without any knowledge of the sport in which he competes.
   3. Do not rely on test results for predicting performance. Many variables can influence performance from day to day.
   4. Traits are defined differently in each test. When interpreting test results, the evaluator should be familiar with the definitions of each trait as it is used in that particular test.
   5. Most of the tests have a minimum age level at which the test is applicable. Because the norms are established for specific age groups, the tests should be used only for the appropriate age group.

If such precautions are kept in mind, the administration of psychological inventories can yield useful results.

There seems to be a trend today toward the evaluation of specific traits; several scales are being developed to be used in particular sports. Coaches and other evaluators of athletes must use the best resources available to assess talent. The chapter that follows has taken into account both the use of inventories and of other assessment techniques.

SUMMARY

Research in personality and athletics has received a great deal of attention in recent years. Although many physical educators and sport psychologists have published studies dealing specifically with the personality traits of athletes, in the United States the discipline of sport psychology is still in its infancy.

There is evidence that everyone is born with a "blueprint" of personality traits. These traits can be described as *source* traits or what Semeonoff calls *temperament* traits. Similar traits have been identified by Guilford. Such traits are permanent or slow to change.

Personality traits that are important in athletics are those traits subject to influence by the athletic environment. Such traits are described by Cattell as *surface* traits and by Semeonoff as *dynamic* traits. Singer calls the manifestation of such traits the *external personality.*

Several methods of assessing personality were mentioned: (1) psychological inventories, (2) observation, (3) ratings, (4) projective tasks, and (5) interviews. Psychological inventories are the method employed most often in the literature and the method examined in the chapter. Five psychological inventories were described:

1. Cattell Sixteen Personality Factor Questionnaire (Cattell 16PF)
2. Minnesota Multiphasic Personality Inventory (MMPI)
3. Edwards Personal Preference Schedule (EPPS)
4. California Psychological Inventory (CPI)
5. Athletic Motivation Inventory (AMI)

STUDENT LEARNING ACTIVITIES

1. Discuss in class the personality traits of athletes as the students see them. Contrast the personality traits of successful and not-so-successful athletes. Bjorn Borg could be compared to Ille Natase.
2. Contrast the types and categories of personality traits presented by Semeonoff and Cattell.
3. Administer a personality inventory to the class and discuss its results.

NOTES

1. Brent S. Rushall, "Some Practical Applications of Personality Information to Athletics," in Gerald S. Kenyon, ed., *Contemporary Psychology of Sport: Second International Congress of Sports Psychology* (Chicago: Athletic Institute, 1970), pp. 167-174.
2. Ibid.

3. Raymond B. Cattell, *The Scientific Analysis of Personality* (Baltimore: Penguin, 1965).

4. R. B. Alderman, *Psychological Behavior in Sport* (Philadelphia: W. B. Saunders Co., 1974), p. 136.

5. Robert N. Singer, *Coaching, Athletics and Psychology* (New York: McGraw-Hill, 1972).

6. Ibid., p. 116.

7. Alderman, *Psychological Behavior in Sport*.

8. Ibid.

9. Boris Semeonoff, *Personality Assessment* (Baltimore: Penguin, 1966), p. 51.

10. J. P. Guilford, *Personality* (New York: McGraw-Hill, 1959).

11. Cattell, *The Scientific Analysis of Personality*.

12. Alderman, *Psychological Behavior in Sport, p. 122.*

13. Raymond B. Cattell and Herbert Eber, *Sixteen Personality Factor Questionnaire* (Champaign, Ill.: Institute for Personality and Ability Testing, 1962).

14. W. G. Dahlstrom and G. W. Walsh, *A Minnesota Multiphasic Personality Inventory* (Minneapolis: University of Minnesota Press, 1960).

15. Dale G. Lake, Matthew B. Miles, and Ralph B. Earle, eds., *Measuring Human Behavior* (New York: Columbia University Press, 1973), pp. 69-72.

16. Ibid., pp. 37-38.

17. Thomas A. Tutko and Jack W. Richards, *Coach's Practical Guide to Athletic Motivation* (Boston: Allyn & Bacon, 1972), pp. 148-149.

Chapter 4

Personality and Performance

Personality assessment has always been an area of interest to psychologists. In recent years, the study of the personalities of athletes, coaches, and spectators has become a popular topic of sport research. One of the goals of this research has been to ascertain the role of the athlete's personality in successful competition. Although the athlete's personality is important in athletic success, it is a mistake to ignore other factors that can affect the outcome of athletic competition. One such factor is the personality of the coach.

PERSONALITY AND THE COACH

Most coaches, asked whether they are familiar with the personality traits of their athletes, would answer in the affirmative. What many coaches do not realize is that they only see the surface or external traits of the athletes. Deep-seated personality traits, those traits referred to by Cattell as source traits, are less evident [1]. It is by observing these surface traits that coaches form an image of the traits an athlete must have in order to succeed. But coaches rarely reflect on their own personality traits. What traits must the coach possess to be successful? Should the coach have the same traits as his or her athletes? Does the coach develop certain traits through coaching?

Although the research is sparse, there have been attempts to assess the personality traits of coaches. In a large sense, all coaches are teachers. Several studies have examined those qualities that contribute to the hiring of teachers and to their teaching success. Cubberly, in establishing a list of criteria for the selection of physical education teachers, listed personality first out of seven essential criteria [2]. Archer, and Davis and Lawther, in separate publications, also stressed the importance of personality in the selection of teachers [3].

John Wooden, the highly successful basketball coach formerly of UCLA, has said that the personality of a basketball coach is an important determinant of his success [4]. According to the theory of occupational socialization, we would expect coaches to possess the same or similar personality traits. We can even speculate that coaches within each sport might also possess similar traits. George Sage conducted an occupational socialization study using head coaches in college football, track, and basketball [5]. The purpose of his investigation was to "(a) assess and compare the value orientations of college athletic coaches from three sports; (b) to compare the value orientations of the younger age group of coaches with the older age group of coaches." The results of the Polyphasic Values Inventory (PVI) showed that there were no significant differences among the three groups. The findings did, however, support the hypothesis that athletic coaches have similar values.

Hendry conducted two personality studies dealing with swimmers and swimming coaches. In one study, Hendry administered the Cattell 16PF Questionnaire to 126 swimmers and 56 coaches [6]. As in Sage's study, the coaches were divided into two groups, those under forty years of age and those over forty years of age. The swimmers and coaches rated each other on several personality traits; the coaches also rated themselves. The coaches over forty years of age were shown to be insecure, tense, emotionally unstable, and more anxious than the younger coaches. Coaches who have been involved in athletics for a number of years can probably understand the traits demonstrated by the coaches over age forty. As a coach experiences the consequences of success and failure over several years, he or she may develop certain characteristic attitudes. Younger coaches have not been in the profession long enough to demonstrate the apparent paranoia of older coaches. The younger coaches are confident, self-assured, and not highly anxious.

In his second study, Hendry investigated the personality traits of highly successful swimming coaches [7]. Again, both swimmers and coaches were used in the study. Using the Cattell 16PF, the forty-eight swimming coaches and thirty swimmers constructed a personality profile for the "ideal" coach. Both groups agreed that the ideal coach should be an "outgoing, dominating, stable individual, highly intelligent, conscientious, realistic, practical, confidently secure; a man willing to break with tradition, make his own decisions, and very self-sufficient." When compared to these ideal traits, the successful swimming coaches varied from the ideal on fourteen of the sixteen traits on the Cattell 16PF: dominance and willingness were the only two traits on which the ideal and the real lists coincided. According to Hendry, the results showed "that appropriate role playing and the *possession* of materially useful abilities by the coach may be of more use to their swimmers than a particular personality pattern."

Using the *Edwards Personal Preference Schedule,* Femrite compared more successful and less successful basketball coaches. He found no significant difference between the two groups on any of the fifteen items of the test [8]. When the two groups of coaches were compared to the norms established for the EPPS, the coaches were higher than the norms in dominance, achievement, heterosexuality, intraception, and exhibition.

Hartman also used basketball coaches to determine whether coaching experience influenced personality traits [9]. He administered the Cattell 16PF questionnaire to fifty-seven coaches. The coaches were divided into groups according to years of experience as head coaches: less than one year's experience; one to three years' experience, and five or more years' experience. The analysis of variance showed that the only significant difference among the groups was on Factor M (Practical) of the 16PF. A follow-up test demonstrated that those with one to three years' experience and those with more than five years' experience were more likely to suffer from inner anxiety and to disregard practical matters than were those with less than one year's experience. Perhaps as a coaching career progresses, the pressure for success creates anxiety. When compared to the Cattell 16PF norms, the coaches who had coached for five years or more were significantly higher in intelligence, persistence, conscientiousness, conservatism, control, willpower, tenseness, and excitability. This same group was lower than the norm in sophistication and polish.

Ogilvie and Tutko conducted a study that did not differentiate coaches according to their sport, but that nevertheless provided some interesting results. One hundred coaches were administered the EPPS and were later asked to rate themselves from 1 to 100 on each of the traits being measured. Their self-ratings and their actual scores were quite different. Their actual scores in areas such as intraception and affiliation were much lower than their self-ratings. On the basis of this study, Ogilvie and Tutko reached the following conclusion:

> The men measure high in achievement need, deference, order, dominance, endurance, abasement, and aggression. They are low in needs, intraception, exhibition, nurturance, and change. This study supports the generalization that, for those traits which determine getting ahead and succeeding that do not necessitate personal involvement, coaches score high. In those traits of personality which contribute most to being sensitive and also support close interpersonal relationships, they score low. [10]

Tutko and Ogilvie have continued to investigate the personality traits of coaches, and have proposed several interesting hypotheses based on their research. They have suggested that aggressive coaches on the college level try to choose aggressive players; conservative coaches tend to recruit conservative athletes. Tutko and Ogilvie have concluded that coaches work best with players who have personalities similar to their own [11]. Typical coaching situations may or may not support such findings. On the basis of years of personal participation in athletics, it seems to us that many coaches can work successfully with athletes who possess personality traits very different from their own. An aggressive, "hard-nosed" coach often works best with athletes who prefer to be dominated. Of course, a coach may have such a significant influence on the athletes that the personality traits of the athletes may in fact be molded to conform to those of the coach. Such changes would be gradual, and are not unique to relationships between coaches and athletes. Recent data collected at a university show that those students who were majoring in a particular discipline had personality traits very similar to those of their advisors, with whom they had worked very closely for several hours per week [12]. The question is whether the students possessed these traits before they entered the program, or developed the traits as a result of working closely with their advisors.

In professional athletics, there is little or no psychological assessment of athletes prior to their signing contracts. Contracts are offered on the basis of demonstrated physical talent. It is virtually impossible in professional sport to match players to managers or to coaches on the basis of their psychological makeup. This is not to say that personality traits are not important once the athletes are involved in professional sport. Even though psychological makeup may not be taken into account at first, teams are now hiring sport psychologists to help management and players communicate. There have also been isolated instances in which psychologists have helped in the initial selection of players.

As an athlete progresses from junior high to senior high to college sport, he or she will encounter coaches of various types. Because there is always a line of athletes waiting for a chance to play, many coaches see no need to adjust to the personality of a particular athlete. If the coach can't communicate with one player, there are a hundred other players with whom he or she may be able to communicate. Only in the rare instances when the athlete is a "super-star" will the coach make any special effort to ensure good communication with the athlete: if the coach can keep the "super-star" happy and productive, the coach's own position is that much more secure.

Tutko and Richards have made a worthy attempt to classify coaches according to their psychological makeup and their mode of operation [13]. Coaches were classified as *hard-nosed authoritarians, nice guys, intense* or *driven, easygoing,* or *businesslike.* There are undoubtedly basic personality structures that distinguish these coaches from one another. An extensive discussion of these personality types is presented by Tutko and Richards in their book *Psychology of Coaching* [14]. They have observed that although few coaches would fit into only one category, overriding characteristics usually place coaches in one category or another.

Which personality type produces the most successful coach? When a team is winning and everything is on an even keel, no one seems to bother with psychological classifications either of coaches or players. If the businesslike coach is winning, then the best method seems to be the businesslike method. If the team begins to lose, the coach is usually accused of being impersonal and unable to communicate with the players. In many cases the coach's personality gets the credit for wins or losses, whatever the state of available athletic talent.

Prospective coaches should not misunderstand these observations. Personality *is* an important factor in communication between coaches and players. Coaches must be adept at dealing with many kinds of players; this is especially important for coaches who work with athletes below the college or professional levels. From youth programs through the high school level, coaches must work with the available athletes, regardless of the psychological makeup of the players. It is only at the college level that coaches can consciously recruit athletes whose personalities are compatible with their own. The college coach can thus be less flexible and remain effective as a coach.

Consistently great athletic teams, such as UCLA and Marquette in basketball, offer examples of psychological similarities between coaches and athletes. The importance of the relationship between players and their coach has been accented by the transfer of athletes from one school to another. For example, a "blue-chip" athlete may not work well with a particular coach; transferring to a different school and coach may improve the athlete's performance.

In professional sport, the personality traits of coaches or managers have not seemed as important as technical skills. This seems to be changing, at least in baseball. During the past two years, three major league baseball managers have been fired for being unable to communicate with their players. Two teams are now dealing with this issue by hiring professionals to help players and managers communicate.

As we observed earlier, there is little research available on the ideal personality traits of coaches; the few studies there are indicate contradictions in predicted athletic success. Coaches who have an idea of the most appropriate personality traits for their particular sport do not necessarily demonstrate these traits themselves. There are far too many variables in coaching for one to prescribe an *ideal* coaching personality for each sport. There are societal and environmental influences too many to mention, as well as personal events that can affect a coach's behavior from one year to the next. In addition, the coach is faced with different kinds of athletes each year, especially at the high school level.

The successful coach would seem to be one who is flexible, sincere, and pragmatic in his or her approach to athletics. The coach must be able to put each situation in perspective and to place the welfare of the athlete above all other concerns.

Although there is sparse research on the personalities of coaches, there have been several studies aimed at distinguishing between athletes and nonathletes, among athletes in different sports, between male and female athletes, and between athletes in team sports and athletes in individual or dual sports.

PERSONALITY AND THE ATHLETE

"Athletics builds personality!" This statement is made more often by the diehard supporters of the social-development benefits of athletics than any other statement. Since the beginning of sport, we have clung to the belief that a participant in athletics is building character strengths necessary in the real world. Outstanding athletes have been made national heroes. Because they are constantly in the public eye, athletes have had to learn to live up to our expectations. They are required to be cooperative and competitive, to accept victory and defeat in a sporting manner, to demonstrate a sense of fair play, and to be socially outgoing.

The problem with these descriptions of the modern athlete is that they are not always appropriate. This is not necessarily the fault of the athlete. In the past, the sport arena was a place to compete, to participate in physical activity, and to enjoy the participation. But American society no longer looks at athletics as a simple opportunity to compete, to participate, and enjoy. Coaches often say, "We played well but we lost," or "The way we played, we deserved to win." These are very sincere comments: American society is not in the business of losing. Defeat has become a terrible reality in American sport. One coach with whom the author is familiar does not allow any of his athletes to say the word "defeat." He believes that if they do not say the word they will not think about defeat. This may not be an uncommon practice among coaches.

The pressure to win has become so intense that some people have begun to question the value of athletics. If athletics builds character and molds personality, and only winning is acceptable, what kind of character or personality is being shaped by sport? Are athletes "good sports"? A more complex question is: does an athlete select a sport because it suits his or her personality, or does participation in particular sports develop certain personality traits?

The next section presents a review of several studies that have attempted to answer such questions. Although the literature does include some conflicting results, most studies show that athletes are different in personality from nonathletes.

ATHLETES VERSUS NONATHLETES

Several attempts have been made to identify the differences, if any, between the personality of the athlete and the nonathlete. Rushall, in an evaluation of physical performance and personality, concluded that "personality is not a significant factor in sport performance" [15]. This conclusion was supported by Ellison and Freischlag, who found that the pain tolerance, arousal, and personality of male college athletes and nonathletes are substantially similar [16].

Cooper, however, found differences between athletes and nonathletes. In a review of the literature dealing with both personality types, he described the athlete as:

1. more outgoing and socially confident;
2. more socially aggressive, dominant, and leading;
3. having higher social adjustment, prestige, social status and self-confidence;
4. stronger competitors;
5. less compulsive;
6. less impulsive;
7. having greater tolerance to pain;
8. having lower feminine and higher masculine interests . . . [17]

Sperling, who used six assessment instruments to study college athletes and nonathletes, found results similar to those of Cooper [18].

Using the Minnesota Multiphasic Personality Inventory (MMPI), Booth compared the personality traits of 141 athletes to those of 145 nonathletes [19]. The nonathletes scored higher than the athletes only on anxiety and depression.

Malumphy used the Cattell 16PF to compare the personality traits of 120 women: 77 athletes and 43 nonathletes [20]. In a further study, Malumphy found that athletes who played individual sports were more extroverted than those who played team sports.

With the exception of Rushall and Ellison and Freischlag, researchers have found that athletes differ from nonathletes. Whether athletes are "better" or "worse" than nonathletes depends on the values of the observer. It does seem that athletes' traits are usually positive. For example, athletes have been described as extroverted, outgoing, and socially aggressive. These are positive attributes that would probably benefit athletes in any social situation. That athletes are highly competitive is generally accepted as fact. We assumed that an individual has to have a strong competitive drive to participate in sport. After all, competition is the name of the game. When athletes compete successfully, the competitive trait seems to be strengthened. Intermittent failure can also increase competitive drive. Coaches working with highly competitive athletes will have an easier task in preparing the team for an opponent: more time can be devoted to technical preparation than to motivation. On the other hand, the coach must always be aware that a negative experience can blunt the athlete's urge to win and damage his or her performance. To the coach, psychological preparation must be as important as technical preparation.

Coaches and laymen often comment that athletics and competition help young people become good sports. This was perhaps true in the years when little or no financial aid was awarded to athletes, where there was little societal pressure to win, and when the bleachers were filled with spectators—not fanatics. Recent research efforts have confirmed the diminishing role of sportsmanship in athletic competition.

Kistler compared 116 college varsity male athletes with 116 nonvarsity athletes. He found that the varsity players demonstrated poorer sportsmanship than the nonvarsity players [21]. His findings are supported by those of Richardson in a study comparing athletes who had won letters with athletes who had not [22]. Using 233 students, Richardson discovered not only that the letter-winners scored lower in sportsmanship than those who had not won letters, but that subsidized athletes scored lower in sportsmanship than athletes who were not subsidized.

These studies raise some interesting points. The coach must decide whether or not his or her sport causes these psychological traits to appear in athletes. The ideal method for determining the value of sport would be a longitudinal study, extending from some prescribed pre-sport experience in a child's life to the end of the sport experience. The problems inherent in such a research project are clear; but until such a study is undertaken, the actual psychological effects of athletic participation will remain a mystery.

Seymour made an attempt in 1956 to evaluate the effects of a single baseball season on the personality traits of little league participants [23]. Various traits of 114 little league baseball players were compared with those of 114 nonparticipants before and after the baseball season. The subjects were rated by teachers, by classmates, and by themselves. According to their teacher's ratings, the participants had higher leadership qualities and were more accepted by their peers. But there were no significant differences between the participants and nonparticipants. Similar and more recent research is now being conducted with youth sport groups, the results of which should be interesting.

Does an athlete choose a particular sport because he or she possesses traits conducive to performance in that sport? Does participation in sport mold the athlete's personality? Such questions are difficult if not impossible to answer. We do know that those who participate in sport demonstrate different levels of certain traits than those who do not participate. To coaches, the personality traits associated with athletes are desirable—and to be nurtured and encouraged.

ATHLETES IN VARIOUS SPORTS

The next question has received national and international attention: do the personality traits of an athlete in one sport differ from those of an athlete in another sport? Although there are problems associated with personality testing, several studies have compared athletes in different sports.

A disproportionate number of personality studies have used football players as subjects, perhaps because there are so many football players and because they are readily accessible to investigators. Other sports, however, such as baseball, karate, and judo, have come under study in recent years. Because there were few women's athletic teams, and because women who did compete often participated in more than one sport, researchers have only recently begun to use women as subjects. Those personality studies that were conducted usually compared women athletes in team sport to those in individual sport, or women athletes to nonathletes. Most studies have used college students; a few have employed high school students. Few studies have attempted to assess the personality traits of young performers—those who are perhaps most in need of attention and understanding.

The available research has relied on many instruments for personality assessment. This may in part explain the conflicting results.

Ikegami, in studying personality changes in athletes, suggested that both men and women athletes were extroverts [24]. He uses "+ points" and "– points" to label athletes.

+ Points	*– Points*
Sociable	Emotionally unstable
Rathymia (Carefree)	Short of linguistical expression
Sympathetic	Careless
Cheerful	Easily Frustrated

Ikegami also discusses the length of sport experience and personality changes [25]. He compared groups that had had nine to ten years' experience with groups with one to two years' experience. Ikegami found that the more experienced group was significantly higher than the less experienced group in social extroversion, rathymia, general sociability, and social leadership. Because personality traits change gradually, Ikegami cautions against reading the results as a demonstration of cause and effect. That changes occur with experience is clear. The problem occurs when we try to analyze all the elements that make up the "experience."

Kroll and Crenshaw used the Cattell 16PF to study 387 athletes. The group under study consisted of 81 football players, 141 gymnasts, 94 wrestlers, and 71 karate participants. On the basis of certain traits, the four groups seemed to fall into two groups: the football players and wrestlers were similar in their psychological profiles; both groups were significantly different from gymnasts and karate participants. The results are surprising because football is a team sport and wrestling is an individual sport. Past research has generally indicated that team sport participants differ from individual or dual sport participants. The findings of Kroll and Crenshaw are perhaps explained by the fact that both football and wrestling are combative activities requiring strength, endurance, and agility. It is common in junior high schools and high schools to find football players who are on the wrestling squad and vice versa. On the other hand, few gymnasts are also football players or wrestlers. In summary, the results showed:

> gymnasts to be rather intelligent and relaxed, possessing weaker super-ego strength, and with a serious outlook toward life. Karate participants reflected an opposite set of characteristics being tense, conscientious, and rule-bound and independent. Both groups were more self-sufficient, more reserved and detached than wrestlers and football players. [26]

Singer administered the Edwards Personal Preference Schedule (EPPS) to baseball and tennis players, and to a group of nonathletes [27]. He found that the nonathletes scored higher than the baseball group in autonomy; the tennis group was higher than the baseball group on intraception. The results also showed that tennis players were higher in dominance than baseball players. Baseball players scored higher than tennis players in abasement.

Other studies have also shown that athletes are high in those traits associated with leadership, power, prestige, esteem, and sociability. The hypothesis that athletes in a given sport possess traits specific to that sport is supported by the evidence. As Kroll's study indicated, certain sports attract certain types of athletes [28]. For example, it is the performance of the individual tennis player that determines whether the match is won or lost. Because tennis is not a sport requiring group cooperation or effort, tennis players might not score high on sociability or extroversion. On the other hand, they might be expected to score high in dominance. Individual sport might attract participants who fit Alderman's definition of dominance: "self-confidence, extreme assertiveness, boasting, conceit, aggressiveness, vigor, force, egotism, unhappiness, an insensitivity to social disapproval, unconventionality, and a tendency to extra-punitiveness" [29]. Personal observation confirms that many successful participants in individual sport exhibit such qualities: examples from professional tennis would be Jimmy Connors, Ille Nastase, and John McEnroe. Other successful tennis players such as Chris Evert and Bjorn Borg do not exhibit such traits—at least in public.

In summary, the literature shows that athletes in one sport differ in personality type from athletes in other sports. The differences do not favor one group over another. Football players probably need to be more aggressive or more anxious than tennis players or golfers. Perhaps within a sport such as football, various positions require that successful participants be of a particular personality type. The task of evaluating the role of personality in sport is easier at the college level, where athletes usually participate in a single sport. This is probably why college athletes are used as research subjects. It is more difficult to define a sport personality type in high school, where many athletes compete in three or four sports.

PERSONALITY AND LEVEL OF SKILL

Coaches have always been puzzled by athletes who have similar physical abilities, yet perform at different levels in competition. Assuming that the physical talents are in fact similar, the logical explanation seems to be that the athletes differ in psychological makeup. Coaches often describe the more successful athletes as highly competitive, and capable of leadership. Less successful participants are said to have poor competitive spirit.

Researchers have attempted to differentiate between superior and inferior performers in various sports. Others have investigated the psychological qualities of champion athletes. Johnson, Hutton, and Johnson used the Rorschach Ink Blot Test and the House-Tree-Person (H-T-P) test to evaluate personality traits of twelve national champion or All-American athletes [30]. These athletes were able to achieve an exceptional level of concentration on desired goals. The champions were aggressive, highly anxious, and demonstrated high levels of intellectual aspiration and exceptional feelings of self-assurance. Biddulph also found differences between superior athletic groups and less skilled groups: The superior athletes showed higher levels of personal and social adjustments [31].

In our effort to present an unbiased review of the literature, we now cite several studies that have indicated little or no difference between highly skilled and less skilled athletes. Kroll and Carlson reported no differences between participants of various levels of ability in wrestling and karate [32]. The wrestlers were Olympians, excellent college wrestlers, and average or below-average wrestlers. The karate participants were drawn from advanced, intermediate, and novice groups. Singer, in a previously mentioned study comparing baseball and tennis players, also found no differences between highly successful and less successful tennis players [33].

The conflicting results of research comparing advanced performers and average performers leave the psychological distinction between the two groups relatively unclear. There are, however, possible explanations for some of the conflicting findings. Many studies have relied on ratings by coaches or win-loss records to distinguish champion athletes from average performers. This is the logical procedure to follow. But we must remember that an excellent athlete in one part of the country may be considered an average performer in another. We know of one athlete who was an average or slightly above-average performer in one town; he transferred to another, where he was regarded as the top performer in the conference. Other athletes have experienced just the opposite. This difficulty in assessing athletes will always exist. Only in studies that use athletes selected nationally, such as Olympians, can researchers hope to control geographical variations in the definition of a champion.

Keeping the limitations of the research in mind, we can make some generalizations about above-average performers. Perhaps the best description of the outstanding athlete is that he or she is a participant who, in a given situation, has the physical and psychological readiness to direct complete attention to the task being performed. The ideal combination of psychological traits that make for readiness to perform is still a mystery to researchers and coaches.

It is possible that outstanding athletes in various sports have certain personality traits in common. It is also possible that an athlete's physical characteristics dictate his or her choice of sport. It is not uncommon, however, for professional football receivers to have been either outstanding basketball players or track performers. Such performers may not have participated in football until their professional experience. Although their success in football may be primarily due to their physical abilities, the personalities of outstanding sprinters, basketball players, and wide receivers may be similar. Research has offered no conclusive results to prove otherwise. Outstanding participants in all three sports would probably possess drive, competitiveness, and aggression.

SUMMARY

A review of the literature on the personality characteristics of coaches yields interesting results. Groups of coaches were classified according to success, years of experience, and the sport they coached. When successful coaches were compared to unsuccessful coaches, no significant differences appeared. Both groups were, however, higher than the norms in dominance, achievement, heterosexuality, and intraception. Coaches also scored low as a group in traits that affected interpersonal relationships. Coaches with five years or more of experience scored higher in anxiety than less experienced coaches. They also scored higher than the norm on eight personality traits. Tutko and Richards have suggested five personality types for coaches: hard-nosed authoritarians, nice guys, intense or driven, easygoing, and businesslike.

Although the results of the research are contradictory, it does seem that coaches must be flexible, sincere, and pragmatic in their approach to athletes. Coaches must be able to offer an external personality that suits the personalities of their athletes.

Efforts have also been made to research the psychological characteristics of athletes. The investigations have followed several avenues: athletes in select sports have been compared either to nonathletes or to athletes in other sports. Most of the literature dealing with women athletes has compared women athletes and nonathletes or team sport athletes and individual sport athletes. Women in one sport have not been compared to women in another because college women have only recently begun to specialize in one sport. As more college athletic scholarships become available to women, more women will begin to specialize.

Although the results of the literature may be inconclusive, they have been interesting. Athletes are generally perceived as more outgoing, socially confident, competitive, and less anxious than nonathletes. One study showed that the more experienced athletes were significantly higher than less experienced athletes in traits such as extroversion, general sociability, and social leadership. Other studies found differences in personality traits between athletes in one sport and those in another.

Research has been conducted on sportsmanship among athletes. The results of the studies have not been pleasing to the supporters of the notion that athletics builds sportsmanship. There is, however, no universally accepted definition of sportsmanship, and the research must be read with this in mind.

Interest in predicting successful performance has spurred investigations of the psychological makeup of athletes. Specific athletic groups do seem to possess certain traits. But the available literature is not conclusive enough to allow predictions of athletic success or failure.

STUDENT LEARNING ACTIVITIES

1. Using Tutko and Richard's classification for men coaches (p. 280) and Voelz's classification for women coaches (p. 281), observe and classify the personalities of a number of coaches in the community. Justify or explain your classification.
2. Report on current articles that reveal the personality types of well-known athletes and/or coaches.
3. Arrange a formal class debate on the topic: "Athletics builds character."
4. Research examples of former athletes who were strong leaders in their sport personalities and whose lives are still affected by this strong personality trait. Jack Kemp, former NFL quarterback, now a congressman, is an example.

NOTES

1. Raymond B. Cattell, *The Scientific Analysis of Personality* (Baltimore: Penquin, 1965).
2. Hazel Cubberly, "The Selection and Guidance of Prospective Teachers of Physical Education: a Symposium," *Journal of Health and Physical Education* 12 (December 1941): 551-552.
3. Clifford Archer, "Recruitment, Institutional Selection and Guidance of Teachers," *Review of Educational Research* 16 (June 1946): 209-216; E. C. Davis and D. L. Lawther, *Successful Teaching in Physical Education* (Englewood Cliffs, N.J.: Prentice-Hall, 1941).
4. John R. Wooden, *Practical Modern Basketball* (New York: Ronald Press, 1966), p. 5.
5. George Sage, "Occupational Socialization and Value Orientation of Athletic Coaches," *Research Quarterly* 44 (October 1973): 269-277.
6. L. B. Hendry, "Assessment of Personality Traits in Coach-Swimmer Relationship, and a Preliminary Examination of the Father-figure Stereotype," *Research Quarterly* 39 (October 1968): 548.
7. L. B. Hendry, "A Personality Study of Highly Successful and Ideal Swimming Coaches," *Research Quarterly* 40 (May 1969): 299.
8. Arnold Femrite, "Relationship of the Personality of Selected Basketball Coaches to Their Coaching Success" (Master's thesis, Mankato State Teachers College, 1967).
9. David Hartman, "Personality Characteristics of Selected Basketball Coaches" (Master's thesis, Mankato State College, 1972).
10. Bruce C. Ogilvie and Thomas A. Tutko, "Self-Perception as Compared with Measured Personality of Selected Male Physical Educators," in Gerald S. Kenyon, ed., *Contemporary Psychology of Sport: Second International Congress of Sports Psychology* (Chicago: Athletic Institute, 1970), p. 76.
11. Thomas A. Tutko and Jack W. Richards, *Psychology of Coaching* (Boston: Allyn & Bacon, 1971).
12. James Lovett, "Personality Assessment of Undergraduate Athletic Training Majors" (Paper, Mankato State University, 1977).
13. Tutko and Richards, *Psychology of Coaching.*
14. Ibid.
15. Brent S. Rushall, "An Evaluation of the Relationship Between Personality and Physical Performance Categories," in Gerald S. Kenyon, ed., *Contemporary Psychology of Sport: Second International Congress of Sports Psychology* (Chicago: Athletic Institute, 1970), p. 173.
16. Kerry Ellison and Jerry Freischlag, "Pain Tolerance, Arousal, and Personality Relationships of Athletes and Nonathletes," *Research Quarterly* 46 (May 1975): 250-255.
17. Lowell Cooper, "Athletics, Activity, and Personality: A Review of Literature," *Research Quarterly* 40 (March 1969): 17-22.
18. Abraham Sperling, "The Relationship Between Personality Adjustment and Achievement in Physical Education Activities," *Research Quarterly* 13 (1942): 351-363.
19. E. Booth, "Personality Traits of Athletes as Measured by the MMPI," *Research Quarterly* 29 (May 1958): 127-138.
20. T. M. Malumphy, "Personality of Women Athletes," *Research Quarterly* 41 (1970): 446-453.
21. J. Kistler, "Attitude Expressed about Behavior Demonstrated in Certain Specific Situations Occurring in Sports," *Proceedings of the National College Physical Education Association for Men* 50 (1957): 55-58.
22. Deane Richardson, "Ethical Conduct in Sports Situations," *Proceedings of the National College Physical Education Association for Men* 66 (1962): 98-103.
23. Emery W. Seymour, "Comparative Study of Certain Behavior Characteristics of Participant and Non-participant Boys in Little League Baseball," *Research Quarterly* 27 (1956): 339-346.
24. Kinji Ikegami, "Character and Personality Changes in the Athlete," in Gerald S. Kenyon, ed., *Contemporary Psychology of Sport: Second International Congress of Sports Psychology* (Chicago: Athletic Institute, 1970), pp. 51-60.
25. Ibid.
26. Walter Kroll and William Crenshaw, "Multivariate Personality Profile Analysis of Four Athletic Groups," in Gerald S. Kenyon, ed., *Contemporary Psychology of Sport: Second International Congress of Sports Psychology* (Chicago: Athletic Institute, 1970), pp. 97-106.

27. Robert N. Singer, "Personality Differences between and within Baseball and Tennis Players," *Research Quarterly* 40 (October 1969): 582-587.
28. Walter Kroll, "Sixteen Personality Factor Profiles of Collegiate Wrestlers," *Research Quarterly* 38 (March 1967): 49-56.
29. R. B. Alderman, *Psychological Behavior in Sport* (Philadelphia: W. B. Saunders Co., 1974), p. 123.
30. Warren Johnson, Daniel Hutton, and Granville Johnson, "Personality Traits of Some Champion Athletes as Measured by Two Projective Tests: The Rorschach and H-T-P," *Research Quarterly* 25 (1954): 484-485.
31. Lowell Biddulph, "Athletic Achievement and the Personal and Social Adjustment of High School Boys," *Research Quarterly* 25 (1954): 1-7.
32. Walter Kroll and Robert B. Carlson, "Discriminant Function and Hierarchial Grouping Analysis of Karate Participants' Personality Profiles," *Research Quarterly* 38 (1967): 405-411.
33. Singer, "Personality Differences between and within Baseball and Tennis Players," pp. 582-587.

Chapter 5

Motivation

Motivation occupies a central place in American society. Motivation is used in industry to increase worker productivity. Parents use motivation to persuade their children to eat their vegetables or clean their rooms. Businesses use motivational techniques to convince consumers to buy their products. The role of motivation in the educational process is also widely recognized. Motivation is essential to the learning process. The old adage "You can lead a horse to water but you can't make him drink" is an excellent way to describe the function of motivation in learning. People can be placed in learning situations, but if they are not motivated, they will not learn.

Motivation plays an equally important role in coaching. Coaches know that the success of a sport program depends on their ability to motivate the athletes. But what motivates the coaches? The businessperson, for example, may strive to motivate others because of his or her need to achieve recognition or a promotion. The achievement records of students are sometimes considered a measure of a teacher's success. Teachers can be motivated by the self-satisfaction they feel when the achievement records of a class improve. For the coach, motivation may be based on a need for recognition and achievement, as measured by win-loss records. The satisfaction of seeing the continued success of their former students can also motivate coaches, as can the need for job security.

Where performance is a gauge of success, motivation is a term used as commonly as competition, aggression, and cooperation. Motivation is necessary for successful performance, whether the task requires primarily cognitive skills or psychomotor skills. Although motivation is recognized as essential to athletic performance, its precise role in a given situation is still unclear to sport psychologists. For example, what motivates one performer may very well discourage another; what motivates an athlete one day may have no effect the next. When the use of motivation by the coach outweighs the performer's need for external motivation, performance can actually suffer. The phenomenon of "over-motivation" will be discussed later in the chapter.

In the discipline of psychology, approximately one-third of the research literature is concerned in some way with motivation. But even with all this attention, the issue of optimal levels and techniques of motivation is still undecided. Most of the research has tested either fine motor skills using the pursuit rotor and pegboard manipulation, or cognitive skills such as the learning of phrases, nonsense syllables, or other verbal matter. In these studies, external incentives—such as candy or money—were offered as motivation for success.

Only recently has motivation research begun to deal specifically with athletes. The laboratory and nonathletic research must therefore be perceived as a base from which we can extrapolate principles applicable to coaching. This chapter examines the foundational material, as well as its implications for coaches and for men and women athletes of all ages.

DEFINITION OF MOTIVATION

The definitions of motivation are as various as the definitions of personality. Many writers in the discipline of sport psychology have offered definitions. Cratty defines motivation as "a personality characteristic related to the general state of arousal and subsequent level of attention paid to a problem or task facing an individual" [1]. Alderman defines motivation as the "general level of *arousal* to action in an individual" [2]. Singer regards motivation as the "urge to push toward a specific goal" [3]. He also proposes the following formula to define the relation of motivation to learning and performance:

Performance	=	Learning	+	Motivation
(behavior in		(past experience)		
a situation)				

Rushall and Siedentop, in relating motivation to the study of operant conditioning, define it as "the act of working for reinforcement. More specifically, the nature of motivated behavior lies in the functional relationship between an operant and its reinforcing consequences" [4].

Although the definition of motivation varies from researcher to researcher, most psychologists agree that motivation is necessary for performance—either cognitive or physical. We can extrapolate from the definitions that motivation is not a superficial trait, but a source trait. Like other deep-seated characteristics, it is present in each individual to a different degree.

MOTIVATION RESEARCH

The importance of motivation is almost invariably supported by the research. Hansen, in a study of the influence of select motive-incentive conditions on the effectiveness of an isometric training program, found that all motivated groups improved significantly more than the nonmotivated group. There was, however, no one motivational technique that was superior to the others [5].

In a similar study, Johnson and Nelson tested the effect of applying different motivational techniques to the training and testing of strength performance. One hundred and twenty subjects, who were tested on an isometric press exercise, showed that motivated training promoted significant strength gains. No deliberate or conscious motivational. techniques were applied to the control group. The nonmotivated training had little effect on strength performance [6].

In another study of physical performance, Ryan tested the effect of select motivational techniques on grip strength. In the four matched subgroups, there was no correlation between the technique of motivation and the level of performance. Improvement of performance in all motivated groups was, however, significantly greater than that of the nonmotivated group [7].

Using an elbow flexion ergograph, Nelson compared the effect of various motivational situations on endurance. The improvement in performance of all motivated groups was significantly greater than that of the control group, which was not motivated. No one motivational technique was statistically superior to the others [8].

To continue our examination of the literature would only offer further support for the hypothesis that almost any external motivation will have a positive influence on performance. It is the consensus of researchers that the presence of motivation, not the kind of motivation, is the important variable. We all seem to need some type of incentive to perform.

DRIVES AND NEEDS

The origin of motivation lies in the drives and needs of each individual. As defined by Alderman, a *drive* is a "construct concerned with the impetus to action or as the activator of a behavior" [9]. Drives can be either primary or secondary. *Primary drives* are those initiated by receptors that receive information and transmit it to the central nervous system. Primary receptors notify us of hunger, thirst, or pain. *Secondary drives* are usually conditioned or learned drives: fear and anxiety are examples. Coaches often say that an athlete is successful because he or she "has drive." That "drive" is necessary for success is also a common idea in the business world.

Needs have been classified by Maslow as either sociological, physiological, or psychological in origin [10]. Needs make themselves felt in response to deprivation. Physiological needs include food, rest, self-protection, and activity. An examination of any athletic program can help document the need for activity. Athletes thrive on activity, particularly when it is directed toward a goal. The game itself fulfills physiological needs. But this discussion will focus more on the fulfillment of sociological and psychological needs than on the physiological aspects of physical activity.

Psychological needs include love, acceptance, belonging, self-esteem, and self-actualization. Our psychological development can be damaged if we are deprived of such things as love, acceptance, or self-esteem. We are all motivated to fulfill psychological needs; participation in athletics can contribute to this fulfillment. To youngsters, being part of a group is important. Participation in sport gives young people an opportunity to demonstrate physical skill, to gain social acceptance, and to increase self-esteem. As we mentioned in Chapter 2, physical competence is one route to a favorable self-concept.

Sociological needs are closely associated with psychological needs. Sociological needs include the need for security, mastery, recognition, and belonging. These are needs that athletics can and should fulfill. Some athletes achieve security just by being a part of the team, regardless of how much time they spend in actual competition. For others, security is only achieved by first-string status, or at least by ample playing time. Mastery in athletics can be realized only through dedication and hard work. By drilling under varying environmental conditions and competing against various other players, an athlete continually strives to achieve mastery. Like security, recognition and belonging can be realized in athletics through mastery of sport skills. As noted earlier, those individuals who are highly skilled are likely to be accepted by their peers.

A properly structured athletic environment can meet many of the athletes' psychological and sociological needs. The mental and physical well-being of the athletes is a coach's first concern. Individuals who are made to feel comfortable in the company of peers, parents, and coaches are most likely to find fulfillment of their needs through athletics.

Our discussion of needs suggests that there are internal forces that cause an individual to seek self-actualization through participation in athletics. External motivation can encourage this inner drive to achieve.

INCENTIVES AND MOTIVES

Two other terms frequently used to explain motivation are *incentives* and *motives*. *Incentives* are justifications for goal-directed activities. Contracts in professional sport often include "incentive clauses." The incentives usually consist of sums of money to be paid if a player achieves certain objective levels of performance. A baseball player, for example, might receive extra cash for hitting thirty home runs or for batting .300 and getting 100 runs batted-in. A pitcher might receive extra pay for winning twenty games or pitching a no-hitter. Teachers and coaches often remark that students have no incentive to achieve. The fact is that so much emphasis has been placed on external incentives that students may not be intrinsically motivated to perform.

Motive is a concept often discussed, but rarely understood by those who use the term. A motive concerns the reasons for a course of action. In other words, what will be the result of a chosen course of action? What are an individual's motives for performance? Why does he or she continue to make personal sacrifices in order to perform? Receiving and enjoying the consequences of a particular action may be the motive for that action.

MOTIVATIONAL FACTORS AND SPORT

From our definition of motivation and our examination of its origins follows the conclusion that we are all capable of being motivated, and that motivation is necessary for learning—not only in athletics, but in other fields as well. Epuran and Horghidan have formulated three categories of motivational factors that can initiate or stimulate sport activity: movement need, need for self-assertion, and motor habits [11].

Movement need was defined earlier as a basic physiological need. The need for movement is an innate need that we must all fulfill through some kind of activity; athletics provides an opportunity for this need to be met. The importance of physical activity to women has not always been recognized by our society. This has, however, begun to change. Women are encouraged to exercise and to participate in athletics. Physical activity has become a way of life for women as well as men.

Self-assertion, the second category of need, is very evident in sport. Participants in athletics are continually placed in the limelight. This brings with it certain responsibilities, including accepting the consequences of one's actions. Most athletes accept the challenge to be responsible as well as self-assertive in their behavior.

The third category is that of *motor habits.* It has been said that sport, by its very nature, provides continuous motivation for athletes to use and improve their motor skills. Once motor habits have been acquired, the performer will probably continue to perform even after the need for extrinsic success has been fulfilled. An example of this phenomenon can be observed in runners who are apparently addicted to the habit of running daily. If prevented from running, these runners report physical and mental symptoms of withdrawal.

These three categories correspond to the needs that were discussed earlier. Although sport can provide an environment conducive to the fulfillment of needs, the potential athlete must first be motivated to take part in sport. Once the player has begun to participate, sport itself can become the motivation. In some instances, the coach or teacher must use motivational techniques to lure students to try a sport; this is necessary only when the internal drive to play is not strong enough. Some athletes need to be motivated and some motivate themselves. To be able to reach those who would benefit from external motivation, the coach must be familiar with the kinds of motivation and the impact of each technique on performance.

TYPES OF MOTIVATION

Most authors would agree that there are two types of motivation, although each prefers to attach his or her own label to each type. The two kinds in question are *intrinsic* and *extrinsic* motivation. Although it does seem clear that there are two types, we believe that the second type of motivation could not exist without the first. Simply stated, intrinsic motivation is motivation to perform an activity for its own sake: performance for the sake of enjoyment. Coleman Griffith, a pioneer in sport psychology, was a strong supporter of intrinsic motivation, as is evident in the following statement:

> When a game is played for its own sake—at the behest of the vigorous play spirit that we have inherited from our ancestors—and wholeheartedly, it yields physical, mental, and social rewards more generously than almost any other single activity in which we may engage. [12]

What Griffith describes corresponds to the fulfillment of Maslow's three categories of need, discussed earlier in this chapter. Griffith strongly believed that athletics provides the most ample opportunity for self-actualization.

Singer associates *ideal rewards* with intrinsic motivation. The rewards would be the fulfillment of the needs we have discussed [13]. Alderman has characterized the intrinsically motivated individual as one who *has to* participate because "there is an urgent need or compulsion within him to participate" [14]. For example, a person who participates might do so for a feeling of achievement, of belonging to a team, or for the physiological benefits afforded by physical activity.

Most coaches, when asked what types of athletes they would prefer to have on their team, would mention those who play because they "want to" or because they "like it." The athletes who want to play are often considered more valuable to a team than those who are there because of extrinsic motives. This is contingent, of course, on the athletes' having the physical ability necessary for adequate performance. An athlete must be intrinsically motivated to initiate participation in an activity.

In little league or other youth programs, there is little difficulty in motivating performance. At this age, children are eager to move, to achieve, and most of all, to be a part of the group. Athletics is an easy way to realize these goals. The sport itself provides the motivation to perform. Once children grow out of these programs, their intrinsic motivation may or may not be sufficient to enable them to continue in sport. There are several critical questions a coach must ask when selecting strategies to attract participants to his or her particular sport.

How can a coach promote intrinsic motivation? How can a coach cause an athlete to want to play? How can a coach cause an athlete to like sport—without the prospect of material gain? Although such questions cannot be answered for every case, Chapters 13 through 18 will describe several methods used by coaches from the youth to the college level. High school and junior high school coaches usually work with athletes who have voluntarily chosen to participate. Their reasons for volunteering may vary: their parents may actually have "volunteered" for them; their peers may have exerted pressure on them; or they may be there just because they need to support their self-concept. Once the athletes are there, how can they be kept interested? Motivational techniques will be discussed at length in Chapter 6.

Assuming that intrinsic motivation is present, it is possible· to examine the role of extrinsic motivation in athletics. Unlike intrinsic motivation, *extrinsic motivation* is performance for a material reward. Singer uses the term "materialistic" to describe extrinsic motivation [15]. Alderman combines intrinsic and extrinsic motivation in describing the athlete who "voluntarily chooses to participate in order to minimize certain losses to his psyche, while at the same time maximizing certain gains important to him" [16].

Athletes are becoming increasingly influenced by the prospect of rewards for performance. In some parts of the country, athletes are recruited into junior high sport with promises of conference championships, first-team status, or material gain. Then there are always possible fringe benefits such as being selected as an all-star or most valuable player. Such rewards are extrinsic in effect. Even in little league athletics, bidding on the basis of points is now being used to obtain player contracts; these kids are being "bought" and "sold" just as professional athletes are. In some sports, children win trophies that are too large for them to carry.

In junior high and secondary schools, extrinsic rewards have become more important than ever. Coaches feel that they must promise athletes certain things in order to ensure their best effort. An example from football is a star on the helmet. At the college level coaches have been known to promise rewards such as automobiles, extra money, clothes, or whatever else might appeal to the athletes. These athletes may eventually become motivated to continue performance for material gain. Whether intrinsic or extrinsic, motivation is a prerequisite to performance. There is a certain level of motivation that must be achieved before an athlete can hope to get the most from his or her ability. Level of motivation helps the athlete select appropriate courses of action.

Certain factors can determine the effectiveness of motivation. The coach who is familiar with these factors can help athletes derive the best possible results from motivation.

To most benefit the motivated individual, motivation must be directed toward a goal and must also be aroused at the most appropriate moment.

DETERMINANTS

Several authors have tried to determine which factors influence motivation. Alderman has suggested four determinants of motivation:

Availability—extent to which a particular situation makes available a certain kind of behavior.

Expectancy—anticipation that engaging in a particular action will lead to a particular goal.

Incentive—specific consequences that are attached to a particular course of action.

Motive—strength of repulsion or attraction to a general class of consequences . . . [17]

The last two determinants, incentive and motive, were discussed earlier as foundations of motivation. The first two—availability and expectancy—are critical to motivation. *Availability* concerns the opportunity that the activity affords the athlete to fulfill certain needs. If the opportunity to fulfill these needs is not present, the activity will be discarded in favor of an alternative. *Expectancy* is also an important factor. The athlete will ask, for example, what he or she can expect to get from the activity, intrinsically and extrinsically. Other kinds of expectation will be discussed under a separate section.

It is important to remember that these four determinants are based on the views of the participant. The participant decides whether to engage in the activity on the basis of his or her perception of the variables affecting participation.

The key word in the formulation of each determinant is "consequences." Once the activity has been chosen, then the prospective participant begins to weigh the consequences of participation in this activity as opposed to another. Levels of regard for the consequences of behavior are determined by cultural background, past experiences, and observation.

Our society rewards success. If we are successful in an activity, our desire for further participation is heightened; repeated failure diminishes the desire to participate. One serious fault in organized athletics is that youngsters are often placed in competitive situations that almost guarantee failure instead of success.

Beginning in the little leagues, less skilled children are often pitted against athletes who are more skilled than they are. Because youngsters mature at such different rates, it is unlikely that pairings on the basis of chronological age will be correlated to physical ability. On the high school level, the population and cultural background of the community can have a substantial effect on the level of skill that students achieve. Small communities will not have as many talented athletes from which to choose as will a large city. In regional competition, therefore, the smaller communities will be at a disadvantage.

Unlike the list of determinants proposed by Alderman, Singer's proposed list of determinants refers to coaches.

1. Nature of emotion inducing stimulant;
2. Type of skill;
3. Level of proficiency of participants;
4. Personality of participants . . . [18]

For a coach to motivate athletes, he or she must be aware of all aspects of the activity, as well as of the abilities of the participants. The complexity of the skill and the position played by each participant will usually determine the motivational technique chosen by the coach. There is far more to coaching than an above-average technical knowledge of the skills involved in a particular sport. The coach must also be familiar with the athlete. This includes knowledge of his or her past sport experience, whether the parents are active in sport, the number of children in the family, its socioeconomic status, and some familiarity with the intelligence and temperament of the student—to name only a few factors. These variables, along with countless others, will determine the kind of motivation that is best for a particular athlete.

The athlete's level of proficiency will affect the coach's approach to the situation. Rosenthal has extensively researched the subject of expectation [19]. A coach should expect different levels of performance from each athlete, depending in part on the abilities of each athlete. Personality is another important element in the choice of motivational technique, as we discussed in Chapters 3 and 4.

TIMING

Regardless of the kind of motivation used, timing is the most important aspect of motivation. Motivation at an inappropriate time is no more valuable than the entire absence of motivation, and may be more harmful to performance than no motivation at all. Mistimed efforts at motivation have an artificial air. To be effective, motivation must occur when the participant will most benefit from a feeling of recognition, belonging, or success. As was noted earlier, the activity itself often motivates the participant. Golf is a good example. Some people participate in golf not to compete against other players, but because golf itself presents a challenge: every shot is different. One good shot will motivate some players to continue to play; for others, only consistent success can sustain the desire to participate.

Tennis can be similarly viewed—with the added ingredient of competing against another player. Still, a good shot at the right moment can lead a participant to continue playing. In such situations, the participation itself acts as a motivator. But there are times, especially for beginning players, when there seem to be no good shots. It is at this point that the role of the coach is important. The coach's understanding of the role of timing in motivation can be invaluable to the performer.

There are several ways to motivate the apparently or temporarily unsuccessful performer. One way may be to remove the player from the present situation and review basic skills. Even this review can be motivating if properly presented: for example, games can be created to drill basic skills. Another approach is to have a skilled athlete help an unskilled athlete; both athletes can learn from the experience. Whatever the method used, timing is the key to success.

SKILL COMPLEXITY AND MOTIVATION

When planning motivational techniques for a particular sport, the coach must take into account the complexity of the skills to be performed. To understand the relationship of skill complexity to motivational level, the teacher or coach must first understand how motivation can be influenced by anxiety. Although the emotional aspects of anxiety will be discussed in Chapter 7, a brief overview is appropriate here.

Up to a point, anxiety rises in proportion to motivation. Research shows that highly anxious people perform less well in complex skill situations than do people with low to moderate levels of anxiety. Research also suggests that too high a level of motivation can impede performance of a complex skill, whereas in the performance of a simple skill motivational level can be high without having a marked effect on performance. This point is best expressed by the Yerkes-Dodson law, which states that there is an optimal level of motivation for performance in a particular skill [20].

As is clear in Figure 5.1, a theoretical relationship does exist between skill complexity and motivational level. Simpler skills can be performed more proficiently at a high level of motivation; more complex skills require a lower level of motivation for correct or efficient performance. The skills required for most sports are complex, and would therefore require lower motivational levels for optimal performance. This can be explained by the presence of competing correct and incorrect responses: if, in fact, a high level of motivation indicates a high level of anxiety, then an individual confronted in a complex skill situation with several incorrect responses and only one correct response will have difficulty choosing the correct response. In other words, the ability to make decisions can be impaired by a high level of anxiety. This situation does not hold true for simple skills. In the performance of simple skills, there are fewer incorrect responses than in complex skills; simple skills require less

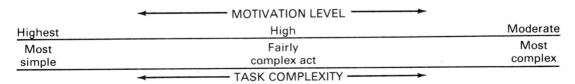

Figure 5.1. Skill complexity and motivational level

decision making during performance. Ruebush has reported that, in performances such as sports that require risk taking, subjects with relatively high levels of anxiety did significantly worse than subjects with lower levels of anxiety [21].

Another factor that must be considered when dealing with skill and motivational level is the primary emphasis of the skill, that is, whether the skill requires strength, power, or fitness. Activities that demand explosive strength—such as blocking or tackling in football— would require a high level of anxiety or arousal for execution. Other activities—such as sprinting—that require explosive power might also be aided by high levels of anxiety. Sports such as basketball or tennis might demand only a moderate level of anxiety and motivation for optimal performance.

Wechseler and Hartogs used a mirror-drawing task to study the effects of anxiety on a performance test. The results showed that coordination was adversely affected by anxiety [22]. Sports or positions in sports that rely on coordination for optimal performance would require that the participant have a relatively low level of anxiety. Examples would include tennis players, basketball players, and quarterbacks or defensive backs in football. If the level of anxiety is too high, muscular tension can impede coordination.

Some team sports clearly require different levels of motivation for different players. Football is an example: linemen should probably be at a high level of anxiety when going into a game; on the other hand, running backs and especially quarterbacks must be at a moderate level of motivation for adequate performance. Quarterbacks are constantly called upon to make quick decisions. The coach cannot afford to have the quarterbacks highly anxious before a game. Any sport in which some participants rely on explosive strength and others rely on coordination requires a special effort on the part of the coach: he or she must tailor the motivational technique to the individual.

Individualized motivation should actually be the mode of operation whatever the sport. Many variables other than skill complexity can affect motivation and performance. For example, certain participants may not need to be motivated or may be motivated at an inopportune time. Some athletes come to the field or court motivated and ready to play. The coach who takes pride in being a great motivator may overmotivate such athletes. The increased level of motivation can lead to increased muscle tension—which can inhibit performance. If a coach overmotivates, research shows that excessive anxiety and tension do act as deterrents to performance.

Johnson has explored the connections between emotion and competition in team activities [23]. He contrasted participants in a violent team sport—football—with participants in a combative team sport—wrestling. One of his findings was that excessive tension in wrestlers had harmful effects on their performance and on their feeling of well-being during and after competition. Wrestlers who demonstrated excessive excitement before matches rarely performed well. Johnson observed that worry seemed to impair control normally exerted by the higher brain centers. He also noted that in most cases, a condition of painful tension was characterized by high blood pressure accompanied by low pulse rate. Eysench and Gilliam obtained results similar to those of Johnson's study. They found that highly motivated subjects performed at a lower level on hand steadiness tests than did subjects at a lower motivational level [24].

Using the stabilometer performance of forty men, Ryan found that the experimental group, which was highly motivated, performed significantly better than the control group

[25]. In the case of complex activities requiring little complex decision making, high anxiety or a high motivation level may not deter performance. Complex decision making is certainly not necessary for successful performance on the stabilometer.

SUMMARY

It is clear that there is more to motivation than pep-talks, gimmicks, and other similar methods used to sustain attention levels in athletics. An exhaustive discussion of all subjects related to motivation is beyond the scope of this text. The preceding discussion should be sufficient to make a prospective coach or teacher aware of the complexity of the topic. A familiarity with certain principles of motivation can help coaches understand athletes and cope with specific situations. A few of the most important ideas are presented here for review:

1. Motivation is necessary for performance, either cognitive or physical.
2. Athletics can meet certain physiological, psychological, and social needs. But this "need-fulfilling environment" must be structured appropriately for the people it is meant to serve.
3. Intrinsic motivation is motivation to perform an activity for its own sake—for enjoyment.
4. Extrinsic motivation is performance for material gain. Athletes are increasingly influenced by prospects of reward for performance.
5. If a participant repeatedly fails, the desire to participate generally diminishes.
6. To adequately motivate athletes, coaches must be familiar with as many variables as possible that might influence performance.
7. Whatever the kind of motivation used, timing is probably the most important factor in motivation.
8. Research suggests that a high level of motivation can impede performance in a complex skill situation; a high motivational level will not have a marked effect on the performance of a simple skill. Most sports are complex and would therefore require lower motivation levels for performance.
9. Activities that require a great deal of explosive power and strength, such as blocking and tackling in football or sprinting in track, would require a high level of anxiety or arousal for execution.
10. Activities such as basketball and tennis might require only a moderate level of anxiety and motivation for optimal performance.

This is not an inclusive list of all the important concepts discussed in this chapter. The list does, however, present several issues with which the prospective coach should be familiar, in order to place the various motivational techniques in proper perspective. Finally, it should be noted that motivational techniques will usually be applicable to athletes of both sexes.

STUDENT LEARNING ACTIVITIES

1. Interview athletes in the community or school about their motivation to participate in sport. Construct a brief questionnaire that would include areas such as "personal physical fitness," or "recognition by peers" or "professional sport career goal." Compare differences in motivation between the casual recreation-seeker and the varsity college athlete on scholarship.
2. Compare motivation in men athletes and women athletes. What are their reasons for participating in sport?
3. Give examples of intrinsic and extrinsic motivators in sport participation.
4. Observe the levels of motivation of children participating in youth sport. Compare the levels at the beginning of the season to those at the end.

NOTES

1. Bryant J. Cratty, *Movement Behavior and Motor Learning* (Philadelphia: Lea & Febiger, 1973), p. 255.
2. R. B. Alderman, *Psychological Behavior in Sport* (Philadelphia: W. B. Saunders Co., 1974), p. 199.
3. Robert N. Singer, *Coaching, Athletics and Psychology* (New York: McGraw-Hill, 1972), p. 221.
4. Brent S. Rushall and Daryl Siedentop, *The Development and Control of Behavior in Sport and Physical Education* (Philadelphia: Lea & Febiger, 1972), p. 192.
5. G. F. Hansen, "Effect of Selected Motive-Incentive Conditions upon Development of Strength through an Isometric Training Program," *Research Quarterly* 38 (December 1967): 585-592.
6. B. L. Johnson and J. K. Nelson, "Effect of Different Motivational Techniques during Training and Testing upon Strength Performance," *Research Quarterly* 38 (December 1967): 630-636.
7. E. D. Ryan, "Effect of Differential Motive-Incentive Conditions on Physical Performance," *Research Quarterly* 32 (March 1961): 83-87.
8. J. K. Nelson, "An Analysis of the Effects of Applying Various Motivational Situations to College Men Subjected to a Stressful Physical Performance" (Doctoral diss., University of Oregon, 1962).
9. Alderman, *Psychological Behavior in Sport*, p. 194.
10. A. H. Maslow, "A Theory of Human Motivation," *Psychological Review* 50 (1943): 370-396.
11. Mihai Epuran and Valentino Horghidan, "Motivation Factors in Sport," in Gerald S. Kenyon, ed., *Contemporary Psychology of Sport: Second International Congress of Sports Psychology* (Chicago: Athletic Institute, 1970), pp. 143-148.
12. Coleman R. Griffith, *Psychology and Athletics* (New York: Charles Scribner's Sons, 1928), p. 258.
13. Singer, *Coaching, Athletics and Psychology*, p. 222.
14. Alderman, *Psychological Behavior in Sport*, p. 186.
15. Singer, *Coaching, Athletics and Psychology*, p. 222.
16. Alderman, *Psychological Behavior in Sport*, p. 186.
17. Ibid., pp. 186-187.
18. Singer, *Coaching, Athletics and Psychology*, p. 223.
19. Robert Rosenthal, *The Pygmalion Effect—What You Expect Is What You Get* (Chicago: Tiff-Davis Publishing Co., 1974).
20. Robert N. Singer, "Effects of Spectators on Athletes and Non-athletes Performing a Gross Motor Task," in William P. Morgan, ed., *Contemporary Readings in Sport Psychology* (Springfield, Ill.: Charles C. Thomas, 1970).
21. B. K. Ruebush, "Interfering and Facilitating Effects of Test Anxiety," *Journal of Abnormal and Social Psychology* 60 (January 1960): 205-212.
22. D. Wechseler and R. Hartogs, "The Clinical Measurement of Anxiety," *Psychiatry Quarterly* 19 (December 1945): 618-635.
23. W. R. Johnson, "A Study of Emotion Revealed in Two Types of Athletic Contests," *Research Quarterly* 20 (1949): 72-80.
24. H. J. Eysench and P. W. Gilliam, "Hand-steadiness under Conditions of High and Low Drive," in H. J. Eysench, ed., *Experiments in Motivation* (New York: Macmillan Co., 1964), pp. 82-89.
25. E. D. Ryan, "Relationship between Motor Performance and Arousal," *Research Quarterly* 33 (March 1962): 279-287.

Chapter 6
Techniques of Motivation

Having described the nature of the motivational process in Chapter 5, we can now present a variety of motivational techniques that can be used by coaches. Some of these techniques may be more successful than others. Their success will depend upon various factors, including the personalities of the coach and of the athletes and the anxiety traits of the athletes, to name just a few. Each coach should determine which of the following methods are appropriate to a given situation.

VERBAL COMMENTS

Verbal comments are perhaps the most familiar motivational technique. Pep talks or emotional pregame sessions have traditionally been considered some of the most effective motivators in sport. This technique was immortalized in the "win one for the Gipper" pep talk featured in the film about Knute Rockne, the famous Notre Dame football coach. Although this approach has been considered essential to the last-minute preparation of the team, it can in fact have a detrimental effect on performance. Talking with a team as a group can raise the anxiety level of players who are already sufficiently motivated to perform. To avoid the risk of overmotivation, coaches are beginning to have individual conferences with players just before a contest. The pregame talk is now a technical session devoted to strategy, rather than an opportunity to motivate players to perform.

Singer has proposed two kinds of comments, either of which can be effective at the appropriate time [1]. He says that coaches can have a tremendous influence on an athlete's performance through either *directive* or *incentive* comments. Most coaches make frequent use of directive comments—comments usually technical in nature that are aimed at improving performance. The goal of incentive comments, on the other hand, is to help the athlete develop a favorable attitude toward his or her performance. It is important for coaches to remember that verbal comments, whether directive or incentive, should be offered frequently and offered immediately after the action they refer to.

CHARTS AND GIMMICKS

Every coach, if asked, could describe various techniques of motivation that require verbal interaction. But motivational techniques are often nonverbal. For example, charts that follow the progress of an athlete's performance are one of the most commonly used techniques of motivation.

A possible drawback to the use of such charts is that charts that include the scores of all participants can inhibit performance. This difficulty is often unrecognized or neglected by coaches and teachers. In a study of the effects of reinforcement on elementary school students, Aune found that the students did *not* interpret the charts as reinforcement [2]. In fact, some students dropped out of the study because they did not want their scores compared to those of other students. These students had noticed that their scores were declining while those of the other subjects were improving. In any situation in which young children are competitors, comparing levels of achievement can be harmful to performance.

Young children tend to regard each performance as a success or a failure. According to the literature, children at the beginning levels of performance should be given as many opportunities to succeed as possible. As children grow older and advance to higher levels of performance, they view success and failure from a different perspective. Older children are less likely to judge performance on the basis of mistakes or errors in daily practice. They view success as overall achievement, either in a game or in an entire season. At the more advanced levels of performance, charts can be effective in motivating performers to improve. The coach or teacher must remember that different performers need different kinds of reinforcement; he or she should try to accommodate each participant.

Another method used successfully by coaches, especially at the secondary level, is posting newspaper clippings about the athletes' performances and the performances of their opponents. Even before the first game, one coach begins to post newspaper clippings on the walls of the dressing room; by the end of the season, the walls are completely covered with clippings. The clippings include write-ups on his teams, articles on opponents, and articles about outstanding teams that either have been or will be opponents. The same coach also paints slogans on the floor of the dressing room. Although such techniques may seem trivial to some coaches, others have found them very effective. These techniques are commonly thought of as *gimmicks* used for motivation.

A gimmick often employed by coaches in basketball is the technical foul. When a team is performing below expectations, the coach may, in an appropriate moment, cause the referee to charge the team with a technical foul. This gimmick can increase the anxiety level of the participants to the optimal level for performance. As is true of any motivative technique, timing is the key to the effectiveness of this method.

The technical foul technique can also be detrimental to performance. After all, it does give the opponents an opportunity to score. But most coaches use this method only when performance could not conceivably be worse than it already is. A similar technique in baseball, which must also be used very strategically, is the confrontation between the coach and the umpire. Again, this is a last resort, and should by no means be frequently employed. Similar techniques can be successful in any sport in which the coach is a visible factor during performance.

COMPETITION

The need to compete is generally accepted as a basic human need. Society contributes to the fulfillment of this need by promoting competition at all age levels. The need to compete is evident even in infants: possession of objects is important to infants. When children are later asked to share toys or other objects, they usually protest, and prefer to keep the desirable object for themselves. Children learn to cooperate, but the need to compete persists. Competitiveness manifests itself in almost every aspect of behavior. Youth sport programs offer a structured opportunity for children to fulfill their need to compete.

Research is inconclusive as to the relative effectiveness of competition and cooperation as motivators; indications are that pure competition, in which individuals compete one-to-one, is more effective than cooperation. Perhaps this is because competition is a basic or primitive instinct, whereas cooperation requires a greater degree of maturity and intellectual involvement.

At least three types of competition can serve as motivators: (1) competing against norms, (2) competing against one's own records, (3) competing against other people.

Competition against established norms is probably most common in physical education classes, where students' physical fitness is tested by activities prescribed by the American Alliance for Health, Physical Education, Recreation and Dance (AAHPERD). Norms have been established nationally for various age groups. In several instances in which the norms were not appropriate for certain geographical areas, school systems have collected enough data to establish their own norms. This is done, in part, to give students a greater sense of achievement than they might have if they were compared to the national norms. In track and field and in swimming, athletes also compete against standards. In these and other sports, certain established scores determine whether an athlete can qualify for regional or national competition. Although performers certainly try to win each time they compete, they are also constantly aware of the set standards for qualification.

Competition against one's own records is evident in almost any sport. Performers often use their best performance levels to establish their goals for the coming year. Track is a sport in which athletes often compete against their own records. A pole-vaulter who holds the school record will undoubtedly strive to match or exceed the established mark. In baseball, players can compete not only against their own records but against previous team records. In almost every sport where records are kept, the performer may be competing—either consciously or subconsciously—against his or her own past achievements.

Competition against other athletes is the most commonly discussed type of competition in sport. The drive to compete is evident in young children and is sustained or intensified as the child grows older. In a study comparing organized little league competition with competition in physical education classes, the findings showed that organizational status was not so much a motivator as was the competition itself [3].

Skubic tested the emotional responses of boys from little league and middle league baseball. Eight boys aged nine to fifteen who played highly competitive organized baseball were compared with a like number of boys playing softball in a physical education class. A galvanic study suggested that the youngsters were no more stimulated by competition in league games than they were by competition in physical education class games [4]. This study, completed in 1955, is still important today. Youth sport researchers such as Rainer Martens are continuing to investigate the effect of anxiety on performance in sport.

In a study using competition on a bicycle ergometer, Wilmore divided thirty male volunteers into two groups, and tested them on three work-capacity performances. A comparison between the groups on the first set of tests showed no significant differences in work capacity. The experimental group was then put into a competitive situation. In that group, both strength and endurance capacities were increased significantly under the motivation of competition. The control group did not improve as much [5].

In a study by Freischlag, thirty men and thirty women performed on a fine motor hand-eye coordination apparatus (rotary pursuit) under one of three conditions: (1) against an opponent of the same sex, (2) against an opponent of the opposite sex, or (3) with no opponent present. To enhance the competitive motive, every three subjects were offered a monetary reward for the highest individual total score. The results showed that competition had a positive effect on performance. The men were also found to be more motivated by competition than were the women. Scores were significantly higher in both competitive groups than in the group that was tested without an opponent. Of special importance to coaches who must deal with athletes of all levels of ability is Freischlag's conclusion that "the competitive motive, with noted differences between sexes, appears to be beneficial to the motor skill performance of both males and females at all ability levels" [6].

Singer et al. found that a placebo used to increase competitive drive in college subjects did not yield significantly higher scores than a placebo capsule or no incentive. The rotary pursuit apparatus was again employed to test three groups. Singer suggested that, unlike that of other kinds of skills, "perhaps the nature of psychomotor tasks is such that performance yields are usually high . . . due to subject motivation" [7].

There seems to be concensus that the innate need for competition makes it a natural motivator for sport. Interestingly enough, the need to compete can be observed at any level of performance—from sandlot sports to highly organized athletic programs.

KNOWLEDGE OF RESULTS

Knowledge of results (KR) has received considerable attention for many years from researchers concerned with variables that can affect learning. This research is of particular interest to educators, who have realized that access to the results of their performance can help students learn. Perhaps "practice makes perfect"—but not without knowledge of results. Technically speaking, no one ever achieves perfection in performance although "perfect" scores in gymnastics were recorded in the 1976 Montreal Olympics. Practice helps develop consistency in conditioned responses; if the athlete has been given feedback about performance, the conditioned responses should be correct. In other words, practice with knowledge of results leads to consistency. This should be kept in mind by those interested in teaching both cognitive and psychomotor skills.

Knowledge of results can be used not only as a part of the learning process, but as a motivator. Robb has suggested that motivation is one of the three purposes of feedback [8]. It could be claimed that the coach is not responsible for providing a knowledge of results, because each performer receives visual knowledge of results during the execution of a skill. Although this may be true in certain situations, research shows that some form of external knowledge of results is necessary early in the learning process. This is especially true with young, less skilled performers. As performers become more skilled, *internal* knowledge of results becomes more important than *external* knowledge of results. Either kind of KR can be valuable as a motivator.

When athletes are told or shown how their performance is correct or incorrect, they receive not only the technical cues necessary for improvement, but the attention of the coach. An athlete being advised on performance can be given a sense of belonging and achievement. When we are given reinforcing attention from those we look up to, we are motivated to learn and to perform. The basic human need for achievement can thus be indirectly fulfilled by a knowledge of results. What follows is a discussion of the kinds of knowledge of results that can be used as motivational techniques.

VISUAL KNOWLEDGE OF RESULTS

Research shows that visual knowledge of results has a greater effect on achievement than verbal knowledge of results. Most athletes, especially beginners, must be able to visualize the skill and visually gauge their performance. This visual KR can be presented in several ways. For example, if performance is timed, a coach can motivate athletes by showing them their times after each performance. The importance of presenting KR immediately after the execution of the skill cannot be overemphasized: research shows that immediate KR is more effective than delayed KR. Another important factor is the specificity of the KR; specific KR is more beneficial than general KR. An athlete who is told that he just did the 100-yard dash in 10.8 seconds will be more motivated than the athlete who is told, "Good time, now try to better that on your next try."

In football, offensive and defensive ratings can be used to motivate players, even though this type of KR is not available immediately after performance. An individual athlete may have performed very well, even though the team lost the contest. Although he may be disappointed by losing, his individual performance rating, presented at a later practice, can encourage further achievement. This method of visual KR would be especially appropriate for a beginning performer. The skilled performer is better able to gauge performance immediately after the contest.

In athletic situations where gross motor skills are predominant, participants have countless opportunities to receive visual KR. One of the coach's primary tasks is to create drills and other preparations that provide a motivating KR. The coach can institute a scoring system in practice. If the coach has access to film or videotape, instant replay can provide KR. Research has demonstrated that instant replay, by providing a very specific KR, can contribute to the improvement of performance. Since improvement is the goal of performers, any device that provides instructional feedback can serve to motivate participants.

VERBAL KNOWLEDGE OF RESULTS

Although visual KR may be preferable, verbal knowledge of results is also important as a motivator. Successful verbal KR relies more on the coach's ability to communicate than does visual KR. Verbal comments must not only be specific, but must be offered at the most appropriate moment. The coach should also realize that different athletes may be motivated by different kinds of KR.

Verbal knowledge of results is best used as a supplement to visual KR, or in situations where visual KR is impossible. Coaches often present verbal KR before visual KR because they mistakenly believe that the participants understand the verbal KR. In other words, coaches assume that participants can, on the basis of verbal comments alone, correctly conceptualize the proper execution of the skill. But verbal KR is usually more meaningful if participants have already received visual KR related to the skills in question. Research indicates that both visual and verbal KR are effective in motivating and subsequently improving performance.

KNOWLEDGE OF RESULTS AS REINFORCEMENT

It has been suggested that reinforcement is necessary for learning. Skinner, in studying operant conditioning, capitalized on reinforcement as a means of shaping behavior [9]. This and other research have demonstrated that reinforcement plays a significant role in learning situations. Positive verbal reinforcement is used to motivate exceptional children, students in "normal" classroom settings, and athletes. One difficulty in the application of reinforcement techniques is that educators—including coaches—often assume that the same kind of reinforcement is suitable for all participants. As we mentioned earlier, reinforcement should be specific to the skills involved and to the skill level and characteristics of each participant.

A coach giving instruction in complex skills may be confronted by athletes who have various levels of skill. Visual reinforcement presented to the entire group may be motivating for some athletes and discouraging to others. For example, good performers might be motivated to improve; but a visual reinforcement technique that compares the performance results of less skilled athletes with those of more skilled athletes can further discourage the less proficient performers. On the other hand, less skilled athletes might be motivated to reach the level of the better athletes. Yet another drawback is that skilled performers can become complacent and lose the motivation to improve. The coach can determine the most appropriate methods of reinforcement only if he or she is familiar with the skill level of the athletes, their athletic background, and other factors that can affect their response to motivational techniques.

REWARD AND PUNISHMENT

Both reward and punishment can be used to motivate. Reward, whose effects are longer-lasting than those of punishment, may take many forms. It can be terminal or concurrent. Winning a contest is an example of a *terminal* reward. An athlete can receive a *concurrent* reward by realizing that he or she performed well, even though the team was defeated. Prospective rewards or possible benefits of participation include extrinsic benefits such as a conference title, an individual award, or a winning season.

Other rewards, which may seem trivial to coaches but can be meaningful to athletes, are personal comments from the coach or nonverbal reinforcement such as a pat on the back. To be chosen team captain is also a reward. Experienced coaches could undoubtedly list other significant reward techniques.

Punishment can affect the immediate performance of some athletes. There is some question, however, as to the place of punishment in teaching and the kinds of punishment sometimes employed by coaches. Punishment can be either mental or physical. A participant who has made a mistake and is taken out of a contest might experience mental punishment. This technique could motivate some athletes *never* to make that same mistake again. Other athletes would respond to such punishment by losing the motivation to participate at all.

A method of physical punishment employed by coaches is exercise: "If you make another mistake, run ten laps around the gym." The value of the continued use of physical punishment is questionable. There is the risk that some athletes or prospective athletes will come to resent all forms of physical exercise or the athlete may become "punishment conscious." The participant may be so anxious about the possibility of making a mistake that his or her overall performance will suffer. A rule coaches can follow is: when in doubt, use reward.

With some effort, the coach can almost always find something that was acceptable in an athlete's performance. The coach should point out what the athlete did correctly, and use this as the starting point for the correction of mistakes.

SPECTATORS AND MOTIVATION

Coaches are often surprised by the difference between an athlete's performance during practice, and his or her performance in a game. Performance during games may be either better or worse than the levels achieved in practice. Sometimes players perform at precisely the same level, whether in practice or at a game. The difficulty of predicting how a player will perform in competition on the basis of practice performance has puzzled coaches. In an effort to identify the causes of such variation, researchers have measured the effects of spectators on performance. Because the variables involved in this research are difficult to control, the results have been inconclusive.

Research has dealt with audiences ranging in size from one or two people to large groups. The *size* of the audience seems to have an effect on performance. Another variable is the *mood* of the audience: whether the spectators are supportive or antagonistic, active or passive, knowledgeable or ignorant about the sport. A third variable is the *familiarity* of the athlete with the skill to be performed. Singer conducted a study measuring the effects of spectators on performance [10]. The subjects, who were both college athletes and nonathletes, performed a skill that was unfamiliar to both groups. In the presence of an audience, the nonathletes were the better performers. One of Singer's explanations was that the athletes were not capable of executing an unfamiliar skill.

Another explanation might be that the better performers suffer from the anticipation of being evaluated by the audience. This was shown to be the case when Paulus and Cornelius tested forty-five male gymnasts either alone or in the presence of an audience [11]. Those gymnasts who had been told that an audience would be present declined in level of performance; the better performers declined more than the less skilled performers did. Participants who are less skilled in a specific activity apparently feel little anxiety when performing before a group. On the other hand, outstanding athletes seem to feel uncomfortable executing unfamiliar skills in the presence of an audience.

Talk of the "home crowd" and "home court advantage" is common among coaches and athletes: they seem to agree that the home crowd motivates the athletes. But athletes can also be motivated by an antagonistic crowd. Many coaches contend that good athletes do not hear the crowd. This may occasionally be true, but the consensus is that the mood of the crowd has an important effect on performance; whether that effect is positive or negative depends on the perception of each athlete. Athletes whose performances are adversely affected by the yells and insults of the crowd are said to have "rabbit ears." Athletes who attend to such insults and try to respond to them only lead the crowd to become more rowdy. The coach should work with such athletes to help them learn to concentrate on their performance and screen out the distracting noise of an antagonistic crowd.

The proximity of the crowd to the sport arena is also an important variable. At a basketball game, spectators who sit at the edge of the court or on the balcony around the court have a greater influence on the athlete's performance than the crowds who are removed from the playing field. Now that glass backboards are used in basketball, it is common to see the spectators behind the backboard wave their arms and try to distract players during foul shots. The soccer fields in South America have been constructed with underground tunnels, moats, and high fences to separate the players and officials from unruly spectators. This became necessary to protect players, officials, and spectators from injury and even death during highly emotional soccer contests.

Although the effects of spectators on performance have been extensively researched, it is difficult to apply the results to practical situations. In an effort to eliminate extraneous variables, most of the research has been conducted in controlled laboratory situations. On the basis of observations coupled with research, the most appropriate advice for coaches seems to be that practices should be open to the public. This would allow athletes to experience the frustrations of performing in front of an audience before being required to perform in a game. An athlete who is accustomed to being watched during practice will be better able to concentrate during competition.

In 1924, Coleman Griffith devoted a major section of his early sport psychology text to the effect of the crowd on performance. His observations are summarized in the following passage:

> There are times, when, for all individuals, a crowd is a distinct source of encouragement. And then there are some individuals who cannot approach anywhere near their normal level of skill unless a good crowd is on hand to cheer. They feel like some public speakers feel who have to address a small audience. It may be doubted that athletes are always fully aware of the influence a crowd may be having on them while a game is actually under

way. Yet the coach who has seen a man practice on the day before a game and then play a game before a crowd, knows whether he is conscious of it or not; the mere presence of people is bringing the best there is in him out. Athletes sometimes play beyond themselves. They do better than they have any reason to expect considering the average level of their performance during practice. At such times, they may not recognize all the sources from which their eagerness and great skill spring; but if they were to search themselves they would no doubt find in the background of their minds a full appreciation of the fact that the crowd in the bleachers was on their side or against them. [12]

MUSIC AND NOISE

Crowds and spectators at athletic events provide one kind of noise during games. Music can also be used to affect performance during athletic contests.

Music has been used successfully for years as a motivational technique. In physical education, music has been used not only to encourage children to move, but to move in specific rhythmic patterns. In restaurants, pleasant, unobtrusive music seems to help customers enjoy their meals and eat at a leisurely pace. On the other hand, bars depend on multiple sales of alcoholic beverages; the music they provide is generally fast and lively. We all seem to be affected by music, both consciously and subconsciously.

Participants in sport are no exception. Basketball teams often use music during practice and during the warm-ups before games. Music can make time pass more quickly; the faster the music, the faster the task it accompanies will be performed. There was recently an incident in which a college was accused of using music to incite unruliness among the fans. The complaint may or may not have been justified.

The Harlem Globetrotters offer an excellent example of music as a motivator. Just hearing "Sweet Georgia Brown" brings to mind images of bouncing basketballs and fancy shooting drills. Several college coaches have emulated the Globetrotter's example by playing lively music before basketball games. Coaches believe the music motivates the players during both practices and games.

Coaches have also used tape-recorded "game noise" during preparation for games or matches. In the case of golf, the noise may include people talking, traffic sounds, or the murmur of planes. In other sports, the noise may be that of cheering, yelling crowds—both antagonistic and supportive.

In summary, it is clear that noise—music or not—can have an effect on athletic performance. Whether the effect is positive or negative depends on the individual. To use music or the shouts of spectators to the best advantage, the coach should ask team members how they respond to such influences.

ROUTINE AND MOTIVATION

Many coaches are so involved with motivational techniques that they overlook one of the most effective ways of motivating athletes: *changing routine.* A coach does not need to constantly create innovative techniques. Like anyone who has to perform repetitious tasks, athletes sometimes need to change the pattern of the tasks. This can be most effectively accomplished in practice. A change of routine is important in every sport in the development of both psychomotor and cognitive skills.

Once coaches have found effective drills, they tend to use the same drills day after day. Naturally, game plays are repeated in practice, to help players develop competence. But the same drills and same plays can become monotonous to the athletes. The monotony can be relieved if coaches simply change the order in which the drills or plays are executed. The motivational effects of change were demonstrated in a classic study conducted in 1939, in the Hawthorne plant of the Western Electric Company [13]. The research studied the effects of varying illumination in the plant. When the illumination was increased, production rose. Interestingly enough, production also rose when illumination was subsequently decreased. *Change* was the key factor in affecting the performance of the workers.

The inclusion of short drills within a practice session is another technique coaches use to sustain motivation. A team might spend five minutes or less on a particular skill before moving on to another skill. This practice method is very useful for several reasons. First, five minutes goes relatively quickly for athletes who are repeatedly executing the same skill. Second, repetition does not always insure perfection. A ten-minute drill is not necessarily more beneficial than a good five-minute drill. Third, if execution is incorrect after five minutes of repetition, chances are that repeated failure has made the athlete tense or anxious; his or her ability to learn will be inhibited until the level of tension or anxiety is lowered. Change or a brief break are efficient ways to lower tension.

Properly administered, drills can effectively improve athletic proficiency. We offer several suggestions for the most efficient use of drills. In 1967, Wickstrom described techniques of drill intended to sustain the athlete's attention.

1. Concentrate on drills until basically correct form starts to become automatic and thereby habitual. Drills need not be the only form of skill practice employed, but they should be emphasized.
2. Encourage students to concentrate on the correct execution of the skill or skills used in the drills. Drills which are performed sloppily are useless and probably far more harmful than beneficial.
3. Constantly make corrections during drills to keep attention on the proper technique of performance. Early corrections of a general nature made with enthusiasm and to the entire group are stimulating and effective. Along with the corrections, general comments on the correct fundamentals are positive in nature and of particular value. The students should be kept aware of the purpose and objectives of the drill while they are doing it.
4. Make drills game-like as often as possible. Drills of this sort are more interesting and challenging because they are similar to the actual game play.
5. Advance to the use of multiple-skill drills to emphasize the proper use of combined skills. The transition from drills to the game is easier if the drills have been devised to reflect the choices and problems actually encountered in games.
6. Make extensive use of modified games to create the much desired competitive atmosphere. Most games can be modified to emphasize one or two skills and still

offer controlled practice. The modified game is one of the easiest ways to maintain high interest and still retain the spirit of the drill.

7. Keep drills moving at a brisk pace and involve as many participants as possible. This procedure will increase the amount of individual participation and practice. As motor learning involves the factor of trial-and-error, the student needs many opportunities to participate, evaluate, and change. One or two chances per individual in a drill will have little impact on learning. [14]

Another motivational technique is to allow the players to plan a practice session. Given the opportunity, players often design a practice session that is physically demanding and beneficial to the team. If the athletes decide their fate for the day, they seem more willing to give their best effort to the activities.

Practicing at different times of day is another way to provide change in routine. Participants might enjoy the prospect of varying practice time from week to week: from noon, to afternoon, to evening, and if possible, to morning. Rotating practice schedules have become a necessity. Few athletic facilities can accommodate the increasing demands for practice time and space made by both men's and women's teams.

EXPECTATIONS AND MOTIVATION

Expectations in athletics are influenced by parents, peers, and coaches. The expectations or aspirations of athletes are important variables in physical and psychological performance. Robert Rosenthal has extensively researched expectations and performance [15]. For the purposes of this text, expectation will be discussed only as it relates to athletes and coaches.

Student athletes of all ages have a unique ability to intuit what is expected of them. If an athlete sees that the coach does not expect a high level of performance, research has shown that the athlete will not perform at his or her best level. In other words, the athlete will usually match performance to level of expectation. It is therefore important that coaches expect all athletes to perform proficiently.

The coach must also understand that athletes differ in ability. Those athletes with good self-concepts can accurately judge their ability to perform. Realistic expectations can only be established if the coach knows the athlete and the athlete knows himself or herself. The expectations of the coach can be tremendously motivating to athletes. A coach who is familiar with the potential of each athlete is in an ideal position to help the athlete establish realistic goals.

Singer has suggested four techniques that coaches can use to set goals in sport: (1) not saying anything, (2) offering negative criticism, (3) giving positive qualitative directions, and (4) giving positive quantitative directions [16].

Singer's first suggestion, "not saying anything," might seem peculiar, but is actually a technique appropriate to the needs of some athletes. Coaches are often confronted by athletes who are capable of setting their own goals. In this case, the coach can do more harm than good by trying to help the athlete set objectives. The coach can be more helpful by saying nothing.

Many coaches believe that negative criticism is the most effective motivational technique. But negative criticism is helpful only in a limited number of cases. Few people can be motivated by negative criticism to achieve long-range goals. The coach should exhaust the alternatives before using negative criticism.

Singer's third suggestion, "positive qualitative directions," is probably the most frequently used means of motivating an athlete to set goals. Well-meaning coaches often tell athletes "Run faster," "Try harder," or "Shoot better shots." Such qualitative comments are usually effective in motivating athletes to improve. But in most sports, athletes need to have specific goals, and such goals can be established more easily in quantitative terms.

Giving positive quantitative directions is usually the most effective way to help athletes establish their objectives. Coaches who are familiar with their athletes' abilities can help them establish quantitative aims. Using the preceding qualitative directions as models, and assuming the athletes are capable of meeting the goals, a coach might say, "Try for ten seconds," instead of "Run faster"; or "Try to shoot a seventy-six," instead of "Try harder."

Whether the coach uses qualitative or quantitative directions to help establish goals, he or she will want to remember these suggestions from Singer:

> The implication is that the coach should provide external incentives relevant to the status of each athlete. A hard goal for one person is not necessarily hard for another. Specific, hard, and reasonably attainable goals apparently have a stronger influence on output than the general encouragement given to all athletes. [17]

SUMMARY

As we mentioned earlier, the list of techniques discussed in the chapter does not and could not include all the methods that various coaches may have found successful. Creative and imaginative coaches are constantly developing motivational techniques that they find effective in specific situations. But the list did include many influences that coaches neglect because they are not easily recognized as motivators: an example is the presence of spectators during performance. Perhaps coaches should encourage spectators to observe practice, so that the practice environment will be more like the game environment.

Charts and gimmicks can also be effective if used properly. Improperly used, these techniques can be detrimental to performance. Several methods can be used to stimulate intrinsic motivation in athletes, including competition, knowledge of results, music, change in routine, and expectation. Used strategically, all of these factors can benefit learning and performance in athletics.

STUDENT LEARNING ACTIVITIES

1. Prepare and present a pep talk by a coach whose team record is zero wins and seven losses; by a coach in the finals of a qualifying tournament; or by a coach whose team has won thirty consecutive games.
2. Interview a coach to obtain his or her techniques for motivating athletes.

3. Debate in class the advantages or disadvantages of reward and punishment as motivators in sport.
4. Compile a list of ways to make skill practices more interesting and motivating for athletes in a variety of specific sports.

NOTES

1. Robert N. Singer, *Coaching, Athletics and Psychology* (New York: McGraw-Hill, 1972), pp. 227-228.
2. Dennis Aune, "Effects of Visual Versus Verbal Reinforcement in Learning a Gross Motor Skill" (Master's thesis, Mankato State University, 1976).
3. Jerry Thomas, "Reward Systems and Youth Sport" (Paper presented at National Youth Sport Directors' Meeting, Washington, D.C., February 1979).
4. Elvera Skubic, "Emotional Responses of Boys to Little League and Middle League Competitive Baseball," *Research Quarterly* 26 (May 1955): 342-352.
5. J. H. Wilmore, "Influence of Motivation on Physical Work Capacity and Performance," *Journal of Applied Physiology* 24 (June 1968): 459-463.
6. Jerry Freischlag, "A Comparison of the Effects of Sex, Competition, and Ability on a Perceptual Motor Task," *Research Quarterly* 44 (March 1973): 178-184.
7. Robert N. Singer, Jack H. Llewellyn, and Ellington Darden, "Placebo and Competitive Placebo Effects on Motor Skill," *Research Quarterly* 44 (March 1973): 51-58.
8. Margaret Robb, "Man and Sports, the Acquisition of Skill," *Quest* 14 (1970): 50-55.
9. B. F. Skinner, *Contingencies of Reinforcement* (New York: Appleton-Century-Crofts, 1969).
10. Robert N. Singer, "Effects of Spectators on Athletes and Non-athletes Performing a Gross Motor Task," *Research Quarterly* 36 (1965): 473-482.
11. Paul B. Paulus and William L. Cornelius, "An Analysis of Gymnastic Performance under Conditions of Practice and Spectator Observation," *Research Quarterly* 45 (March 1974): 56-63.
12. Coleman Griffith, *Psychology and Athletics* (Champaign, Ill.: University of Illinois Press, 1924), p. 240.
13. F. J. Roethlisberger and W. J. Dickson, *Management and the Worker* (Cambridge: Harvard University Press, 1939) cited in Robert N. Singer, *Coaching, Athletics and Psychology* (New York: McGraw-Hill, 1972), p. 230.
14. R. L. Wickstrom, "In Defense of Drills," *The Physical Educator* 24 (1967): 38-39.
15. Robert Rosenthal, *The Pygmalion Effect—What You Expect Is What You Get* (Chicago: Tiff-Davis Publishing Co., 1974).
16. Singer, *Coaching, Athletics and Psychology*, p. 225.
17. Ibid.

Chapter 7
Anxiety and Performance

The study of the effect of anxiety on motor performance has become a major topic of interest to sport psychologists in recent years. Before reviewing the extensive literature on the subject, it is first necessary to define the terms used by researchers in discussing the concept of anxiety.

Anxiety is an emotion that is difficult to define and even more difficult to reliably detect in performers. "Nervousness" is often used synonymously with anxiety. At one time or another, almost everyone has been nervous. Nervousness can be experienced at various levels of intensity. "Tension" is another term used to describe the chronic, usually low-level anxiety to which we all seem to be susceptible.

Fear, a still higher level of anxiety, can have a serious effect on sport performance. Walker describes fear as "intense anxiety experienced in response to a specific threat" [1]. Anxiety can take the form of *unconscious anxiety,* an anxiety of which we are not consciously aware, or *free-floating anxiety,* intense anxiety that appears and disappears—only to return again later. Coaches should be aware that in the case of free-floating anxiety, the anxious person realizes that he or she is under pressure, but cannot attach a specific cause to the anxiety attacks.

Panic is the most serious level of anxiety. We would never want panic to be a part of the athletic environment. It is a condition in which "the anxiety has become so great that the person loses complete control of himself and the situation" [2]. The key to dealing with someone who is suffering from panic is gentleness and patience.

We have summarized the view of anxiety proposed by Eugene Walker, a clinical psychologist. To add to the confusion, still other terms have been used synonymously with anxiety, or to describe anxiety. *Stress* and *arousal* are also used in literature concerned with anxiety. Cratty attempts to clarify the terms with the following definitions:

> Anxiety appears to be a general fear or foreboding, a personality trait marked by a lower threshold to stressful events. Stress is an internal reaction, an intervening variable between situation and performance. . . . Tension, on the other hand, is overt muscular contraction caused by an emotional state or by increased effort . . . [3]

Martens has defined arousal as "intensity dimension of behavior" [4]. He also says that "the arousal manifested by a stressful or threatening situation is called state anxiety."

Over the years, coaches and athletes have often used other, less technical terms to describe anxiety in competitive athletic situations. Expressions such as "choking," "psyched up," "psyched out," "having butterflies," "four-o'clock player," and "getting high" vividly describe the various effects anxiety can have on athletes. A close examination of the meanings of these expressions reveals an interesting phenomenon: although anxiety has a negative effect on the performance of some athletes, it enhances the performance of others.

Athletes who choke or get psyched out during athletic competition are those who cannot cope with the anxiety that is always present in sport. Anxiety in sport is produced mainly by what Spielberger calls the fear of failure [5]. In athletic competition, athletes are not only afraid of losing a contest or scoring fewer points than usual, but of not performing as well as they had expected to.

"Four-o'clock player" is the term used to describe an athlete who gives an excellent performance during practice sessions, when there is no risk of winning or losing. But the four-o'clock athlete participating in an actual game will fail to perform up to his or her potential. In light of the athlete's demonstrated abilities, the explanation for this variation in performance must lie in the athlete's anxiety and his or her inability to cope with it.

The expressions, "psyched up," "getting high," and "having butterflies," are closely related to the definition of arousal given in Martens's discussion of anxiety [6]. Coaches readily admit that athletes must be motivated to do their best in competition. But there seems to be a fine line between being psyched *up* and being psyched *out*. If athletes become too emotionally aroused before a competition, they may experience excessive muscular tension; this will inhibit their performance rather than enhance it. This phenomenon is explained by the "inverted-U hypothesis," discussed later in this chapter.

The term "gamesmanship" can be used to summarize the psychological facets of athletic competition, including motivation and anxiety. Gamesmanship was coined to refer to psychological techniques used to gain a competitive advantage over an opponent. Bobby Riggs, the famous tennis player, can be identified as one of the early experts in the art of gamesmanship. Jimmy Connors and Ille Nastase are two more recent proponents of this technique. In boxing, Muhammed Ali was an expert gamesman who tried to psych out his opponents before a match.

Although gamesmanship seems more prominent in individual sports such as tennis and boxing, where the physique and psyche of one person are pitted solely against those of another, it has certainly been used in team sports as well. In football, for example, the player who has scored a touchdown and "spikes" the ball at the feet of a vanquished opponent is making a not-too-subtle attempt to "psych" the opponent: to injure his self-concept and produce anxiety, anger, or shame that may inhibit his performance in the rest of the game. When the opposing coach calls a succession of time-outs just before a free-throw attempt in the final seconds of a closely contested basketball game he is illustrating yet another example of gamesmanship. The intentional use of a technical foul is another gimmick used. A basketball coach might call a technical foul to change the momentum of a game.

In baseball, the constant verbal harrassment that goes on between fanatic supporters ("bleacher bums") and the opposing team illustrates the psychological competition that is part of present-day athletics at almost every age and level of skill. Coaches of little league and pee-wee teams in every sport have been known to encourage their bench players to taunt the opposing team—in an effort to gain advantage by shaking up the inexperienced young athletes. Examples of gamesmanship are frequent in today's athletic competition. It is significant that this is largely a phenomenon of modern sport. Athletes in the past who tried to use such techniques were considered devious and were criticized by their peers. An example would be the famous baseball player Ty Cobb, who in his many attempts to steal base, invented the foot-first slide intentionally to frighten the player covering the base. It has been said that Cobb was despised by his fellow players.

STATE AND TRAIT ANXIETY

To better understand the various effects of anxiety on athletes, it is essential to have a more complete understanding of the phenomenon of anxiety itself. The following discussion should be helpful for this purpose.

Spielberger, a psychologist noted for his extensive work in the area of anxiety and behavior, was the first researcher to clearly differentiate between two types of anxiety: *state* and *trait anxiety*. In a 1970 publication, Spielberger defined state anxiety (A-state) as "a transitory emotional state or condition of the human organism that is characterized by subjective, consciously perceived feelings of tension and apprehension, and heightened autonomic nervous system activity" [7]. Trait anxiety (A-trait) is defined by Spielberger as the "relatively stable individual differences in anxiety proneness, that is . . . tendency to respond to situations perceived as threatening with elevations in A-state intensity" [8]. In other words, trait anxiety (A-trait) is comparable to any relatively stable personality trait (as described in Chapter 3 under the Cattell 16PF) whereas state anxiety (A-state) is a temporary condition caused by one's immediate perception of the environment.

Research has shown that the personality characteristic identified as A-trait is present in all of us, including athletes, in varying degrees. Those who have higher levels of A-trait tend to be more anxious in situations identified as anxiety-producing, such as academic testing situations, athletic competitions, and frightening situations. Efficiency of performance on certain mental or motor tasks has usually been used to measure anxiety.

In athletics, certain competitive situations naturally produce more anxiety than others. For example, the pressure on a basketball player taking a free throw in the first minute of a close game is considerably less than the pressure on the same player taking a free throw in the last minute of a close game. Both A-trait level and state level will affect how a player copes with pressure. Remember that a high level of anxiety is not always detrimental to performance. For example, anxiety may be helpful in tasks that require strength or power. Newspapers often report feats of remarkable strength executed by people in anxiety-producing situations: elderly women, for example, who have rescued relatives trapped under cars. A high level of anxiety may be detrimental, however, to the execution of skills that rely on cognition and manipulation for optimal performance.

In the past decade, sport psychologists have studied the variable of anxiety and its effect on athletic competition. The results of these and future studies will help both coaches and athletes recognize and cope with the sometimes helpful and sometimes harmful variable known as anxiety.

ANXIETY AND ATHLETIC PERFORMANCE

In his discussion of competitive anxiety, Spielberger relates the concept of anxiety specifically to athletics. He defines competitive anxiety as the "tendency to perceive competitive situations as threatening and to respond to these situations with feelings of apprehension or tension [9]. According to Spielberger, fear of failure and fear of physical harm appear to be the most prevalent determinants of A-state in competitive sport.

Rainer Martens has expanded Spielberger's work by developing a specific test to assess the level of anxiety in sport participants. The test was based on the model depicting the relationship between competitive A-trait and the competitive process shown in Figure 7.1 [10].

The rationale underlying Martens's Sport Competition Anxiety Test (SCAT) is based in part on the following concepts:

1. People who have high A-trait levels will often react to sport competition with higher A-state levels; they perceive situations to be more threatening than would those with lower A-trait levels.
2. Athletes will probably differ from nonathletes in A-trait as assessed by a specific competitive sport test; the two groups would probably have similar scores on a test of general A-trait.
3. The intensity of changes in A-state brought about during competition are influenced by such factors as the athlete's past practice and competitive experiences, the athlete's level of skill, and the athlete's perception of the importance of the event—whether there would be a possible loss of self-esteem, for example.

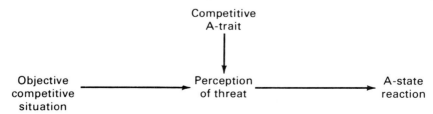

**Figure 7.1. Martens model of competitive A-trait as a mediator
between competitive stimulus and response**

(Adapted from Rainer Martens, *Sport Competition Anxiety Test,* Champaign, Ill.,
Human Kinetics Publishers, 1977, p. 33)

4. The development of Martens's SCAT test should provide the basis for valuable future research in the field of athletic competition. There are many ways of using such a test to provide practical information to coaches.

DETECTING ANXIETY

Without administering a written anxiety test, a coach or teacher can learn to recognize the influence of anxiety on learning and competitive situations. The influence is usually negative and results in less efficient performance. For example, good athletes who give consistently poor performances in competitive situations may be suffering from anxiety. An excessively anxious football player who repeatedly fumbles the ball may be literally "squeezing" the ball out of his grip through excessive muscular tension.

Poor performance in high-pressure situations may be yet another symptom of anxiety in athletes. Game statistics can show the coach which performers fail in the "clutch": consistently miss free throws in the last minute of a basketball game; serve double faults to end tennis matches; serve a fault at game point in volleyball; or fail to hit the ball when there are baserunners in scoring position in softball or baseball. These are just a few examples of the kinds of situations that test the athlete's ability to handle anxiety.

A third example of anxiety is illustrated by athletes who seem to freeze or forget their strategic assignments during a game. In cases of extreme anxiety, some athletes momentarily lose touch with reality and are unable to function in high-pressure competitive situations.

The player who is prone to injury is another example of the way anxiety can manifest itself in athletic competition. Players who are repeatedly injured during practices and games are often highly anxious individuals who have an ambivalent attitude toward competitive athletics. They want to play, but they are afraid of failure. Consequently, they may seek the only acceptable way of not playing: they choose the role of the injured athlete, willing but unable to participate.

The athlete who is afraid of winning is similar to the injury-prone athlete. Whereas the injury-prone athlete is afraid to compete, the athlete who is afraid to win does compete, but prefers to lose. This fear of winning is a manifestation of the athlete's anxiety. According to Vanek and Cratty, the athlete who is afraid to win fears the responsibilities attached to winning, among them the "responsibility to continue winning"—to meet one's own expectations and those of the spectators [11]. This theory can perhaps explain the meteoric rise and fall of "champion" athletes in individual sports such as golf, tennis, and boxing.

ANXIETY RESEARCH

Our review of the research on anxiety is limited to those studies assessing motor performance. It is interesting that much of this research has been conducted within the past decade, demonstrating the relatively recent interest in this particular psychological aspect of sport competition.

Hutson studied the relationship between level of anxiety and the learning of skills in beginning horseback riding [12]. The Parallel Anxiety Battery was used to assess levels of anxiety in six women enrolled in a beginning riding class. The findings showed that, as the students increased in skill, their anxiety tended to decrease.

Slevin used Spielberger's test of state and trait anxiety (STAT) to assess the effect of anxiety on the performance of an unfamiliar gross motor skill [13]. While being observed by researchers, eighty high school nonathletes executed a modified fencing lunge and recovery under experimental conditions of competition. Results from the study showed that individuals with low levels of trait anxiety performed better in the novel skill than those who had been classified as having high levels of trait anxiety.

In a study using a college basketball team, Nelson and Langer examined some of the psychological variables present among athletes in competitive situations [14]. They assessed anxiety levels of the team members by using the Taylor Manifest Anxiety Scale. The results showed that the performance of athletes with extremely high levels of anxiety was poor. Nelson and Langer also found that athletes who scored extremely low in anxiety did not perform well, either—perhaps because of a lack of dedication.

The results of Nelson and Langer's study support the results of an earlier study on the effects of anxiety on learning. In an extensive review of the literature on anxiety, Reed concluded that both high and low levels of anxiety tended to disrupt the learning process, whereas moderate levels of anxiety created an ideal atmosphere for learning [15].

Hollingsworth conducted a study to determine the effects of special performance and encouragement on the acquisition of a gross motor skill. She also investigated the relationship between levels of trait anxiety, state anxiety, and the performance of this same task [16]. Ninety male and female junior high school students who had scored either "high anxious" or "low anxious" on Spielberger's Trait Anxiety Inventory (STAI) were randomly divided into a "performance goal group," a "verbal encouragement group," and a control group. The subjects practiced a two-ball, one-hand juggling task for five minutes on twelve consecutive school days. They took the STAI just before each practice session. The average number of catches per trial was recorded for each subject and each session. All subjects were given knowledge of results. Subjects in the "verbal encouragement group" were told to do their best. Subjects in the "performance goal group" were given a goal based on their previous trial. Apart from the data on anxiety, no significant differences in performance levels occurred. A strong relationship was found to exist between state and trait anxiety. It was also found that as the performance level increased with practice, the anxiety level tended to decrease.

Another issue that is often discussed by coaches is the effect of the actual competitive situation on the anxiety levels of performers. Novaczyk dealt with this issue by investigating the differences in trait and state anxiety levels among individuals participating in three divisions of junior high school competitive ice hockey [17]. The subjects were 103 eighth and ninth grade athletes. Both the Sport Competition Anxiety Test (SCAT) and the short form of the State Anxiety Inventory (SAI) were administered to all subjects. Subjects were given tests before and after practice, games, and playoff games. The results are presented in Figure 7.2. There were significant differences among competitive situations and between pretest and posttest situations.

Several researchers, including Singer, have examined the relationship between anxiety and learning [18]. The relationship can be illustrated by the inverted-U hypothesis, which states that "performance improves with increasing levels of arousal (anxiety) to an optimum point, whereupon further increases in arousal (anxiety) cause performance impairment." The inverted-U hypothesis is graphically presented in Figure 7.3.

Tutko has found supporting evidence for the inverted-U hypothesis in his research measuring the effect of anxiety on the performance of athletic teams [19]. His results showed that the level of anxiety felt by an athlete determined the extent to which he learned. For example, the athlete who was not anxious about the upcoming athletic competition paid less attention to the information given by the coaching staff. On the other hand, the athlete who was concerned about an approaching competition became excessively anxious; this also interfered with learning. Tutko suggested that the athlete who could maintain a moderate level of anxiety would be the most efficient performer.

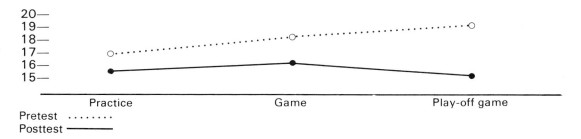

Figure 7.2. A-state means for each of three competitive situations

(Adapted from Todd D. Novaczyk, "A Comparison of Trait and State Anxiety Levels between Three Divisions of Youth Ice Hockey Participants and Trait Anxiety Levels between Athletes and Non-Athletes," master's thesis, Mankato State University, 1977, p. 41)

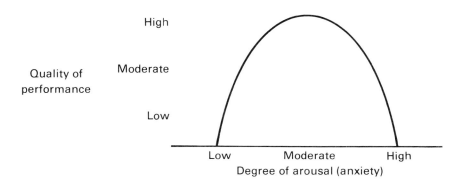

Figure 7.3. The inverted-U hypothesis of the arousal (anxiety) performance relationship

(Adapted from Robert N. Singer, *Motor Learning and Human Performance,* 3rd ed., New York, Macmillan Publishing Co., 1980, p. 249)

DEALING WITH ANXIETY LEVELS OF ATHLETES

How can coaches effectively cope with the anxieties of their athletes? First, they can use one of the anxiety inventories to identify the A-trait levels of their athletes. (Examples of anxiety inventories are shown in Figures 7.4, 7.5, and 7.6.) Second, coaches can familiarize themselves with the A-state levels of individual athletes in a variety of competitive situations: low-pressure situations, moderate-pressure situations, and high-pressure situations. A coach who knows the specific effects of anxiety on his or her athletes can make more strategic decisions during a game. A coach should know, for example, *whether* to substitute players in the last tense moments of a game—and *which* players to substitute.

Having identified high A-trait and A-state athletes, coaches can use one or more of the following techniques to help reduce anxiety during competition.

1. Have the team practice in situations that artificially create pressure. In football, for example, have players practice the "two-minute drill"; in basketball, chart free throws made in the last minute of the game; in baseball or softball, use base runners to simulate tying or winning runs so that outfielders can practice throws and infielders can practice double plays.
2. Use verbal and nonverbal positive reinforcement to build the athlete's confidence and self-concept during all phases of practice and competition.
3. Give the athlete sufficient practice and playing time, so that he or she has the variety of experience and skill necessary to succeed in every aspect of the sport. Techniques for accomplishing this are discussed in Chapter 11, which deals with methods of instruction.
4. Motivate the athlete to the optimal level for performance. Coaches should avoid excessive motivation, which can inhibit performance by creating muscle tension. Remember that adequate levels of motivation may vary for each athlete.
5. Maintain a consistent and stable emphasis on the importance of each athletic competition. The pressure for play-off games should be the same as the pressure for regular league games. John Wooden, a successful former basketball coach at UCLA, was said to regard each game with equal emotion.
6. Help the athletes set goals for individual accomplishment that are realistic and that can be attained in the course of the competitive season.
7. Coaches should conceal their personal fears and anxieties about certain games or competitive situations. If a coach's anxieties are communicated to the team, the athletes cannot help but be affected by them.

SUMMARY

It is clear that anxiety plays an important role in the acquisition of motor skills as well as in athletic performance. Anxiety can either enhance or inhibit performance. Whether its effect is positive or negative depends on how an individual athlete perceives the situation.

People with low A-trait levels have been known to perform better in selected motor skills than those with high A-trait levels. There is also a positive relationship between the A-trait and A-state levels of participants in athletic competition.

A moderate level of anxiety seems best for the acquisition and performance of motor skills. Levels of anxiety either too high or too low tend to inhibit learning and performance.

Written assessment techniques are available for coaches who want to identify anxious athletes. Experience can also help coaches learn to recognize the signs of anxiety during competition. Coaches can also use a variety of techniques to counteract some of the detrimental effects of anxiety.

Athletic participation has often been touted as a means of relieving anxiety and tension. But it is clear that athletic competition can also *produce* anxiety.

Figure 7.4. Illinois Competition Questionnaire (Form A)

	Hardly Ever	Sometimes	Often
1. Competing against others is socially enjoyable.	A	B	C
2. Before I compete I feel uneasy.	A	B	C
3. Before I compete I worry about not performing well.	A	B	C
4. I am a good sportsman when I compete.	A	B	C
5. When I compete I worry about making mistakes.	A	B	C
6. Before I compete I am calm.	A	B	C
7. Setting a goal is important when competing.	A	B	C
8. Before I compete I get a queasy feeling stomach.	A	B	C
9. Just before competing I notice my heart beats faster than usual.	A	B	C
10. I like to compete in games that demand considerable physical energy.	A	B	C
11. Before I compete I feel relaxed.	A	B	C
12. Before I compete I am nervous.	A	B	C
13. Team sports are more exciting than individual sports.	A	B	C
14. I get nervous wanting to start the game.	A	B	C
15. Before I compete I usually get up tight.	A	B	C

(From Rainer Martens, *Sport Competition Anxiety Test,* Champaign, Ill.:
Human Kinetics Publishers, 1977, p. 93)

Figure 7.5. Illinois Competition Questionnaire (Form C)

	Hardly Ever	Sometimes	Often
1. Competing against others is fun.	A	B	C
2. Before I compete I feel uneasy.	A	B	C
3. Before I compete I worry about not performing well.	A	B	C
4. I am a good sportsman when I compete.	A	B	C
5. When I compete I worry about making mistakes.	A	B	C
6. Before I compete I am calm.	A	B	C
7. Setting a goal is important when competing.	A	B	C
8. Before I compete I get a funny feeling in my stomach.	A	B	C
9. Just before competing I notice my heart beats faster than usual.	A	B	C
10. I like rough games.	A	B	C
11. Before I compete I feel relaxed.	A	B	C
12. Before I compete I am nervous.	A	B	C
13. Team sports are more exciting than individual sports.	A	B	C
14. I get nervous wanting to start the game.	A	B	C
15. Before I compete I usually get up tight.	A	B	C

(From Rainer Martens, *Sport Competition Anxiety Test,* Champaign, Ill.:
Human Kinetics Publishers, 1977, p. 94)

Figure 7.6. Sport Evaluation Questionnaire

1. I feel	Very calm	Calm	Not calm
2. I feel	Very nervous	Nervous	Not nervous
3. I feel	Very pleasant	Pleasant	Not pleasant
4. I feel	Very jittery	Jittery	Not jittery
5. I feel	Very rested	Rested	Not rested
6. I feel	Very scared	Scared	Not scared
7. I feel	Very relaxed	Relaxed	Not relaxed
8. I feel	Very worried	Worried	Not worried
9. I feel	Very sure	Sure	Not sure
10. I feel	Very frightened	Frightened	Not frightened

(Modified from C.D. Spielberger)

STUDENT LEARNING ACTIVITIES

1. Describe athletes who were observably affected by anxiety during competition.
2. List specific examples of gamesmanship being used in athletics.
3. Administer one of the anxiety inventories to a group of athletes during practice and game situations and compare the results.
4. Observe a coach in several competitive situations. Estimate the coach's level of anxiety on the basis of his or her actions. What effect did the coach's anxiety have on the players?

NOTES

1. Eugene Walker, *Learn to Relax: Thirteen Ways to Reduce Tension* (Englewood Cliffs, N.J.: Prentice-Hall, 1975), p. 115.
2. Ibid.
3. Bryant J. Cratty, *Movement Behavior and Motor Learning,* 3rd ed. (Philadelphia: Lea & Febiger, 1973), p. 288.
4. Rainer Martens, "Arousal and Motor Performance," in Jack Holman, ed., *Exercise and Sport Science Review,* vol. 2 (New York: Academic Press, 1974), pp. 155-188.
5. C. D. Spielberger, "Theory and Research on Anxiety," in C. D. Spielberger, ed., *Anxiety and Behavior* (New York: Academic Press, 1966), pp. 3-19.
6. Martens, "Arousal and Motor Performance," pp. 155-188.
7. C. D. Spielberger, R. L. Gorsuch, and R. E. Lushene, *STAI Manual for the State-Trait Anxiety Inventory* (Palo Alto, Calif.: Consulting Psychologists Press, 1970), p. 3.
8. Ibid.
9. Ibid.
10. Rainer Martens, *Sport Competition Anxiety Test* (Champaign, Ill.: Human Kinetics Publishers, 1977), p. 33.
11. Miroslav Vanek and Bryant J. Cratty, *Psychology and the Superior Athlete* (London: Macmillan & Co., 1970).
12. Margaret Hutson, "The Relationship of Anxiety Level to Learning Skills in Beginning Horseback Riding" (Master's thesis, University of North Carolina at Greensboro, 1966), cited in *Abstracts* of *Completed Research in Health, Physical Education and Recreation* (Washington, D.C.: AAHPER, 1966), p. 29.
13. Robert Lee Slevin, "The Influence of Trait and State Anxiety upon the Performance of Novel Gross Motor Tasks under Conditions of Competition and Audience" (Doctoral diss., Louisiana State University, 1970).
14. D. O. Nelson and Philip Langer, "Getting to Really Know Your Players," *Athletic Journal* 44 (September 1963): 88-92.
15. Horace B. Reed, Jr., "Anxiety: The Ambivalent Variable," *Harvard Educational Review* 30 (Spring 1960): 141-153.
16. Barbara Hollingsworth, "Effects of Performance Goals and Anxiety on Learning a Gross Motor Task," *Research Quarterly* 36 (May 1965): 162-168.
17. Todd D. Novaczyk, "A Comparison of Trait and State Anxiety Levels between Three Divisions of Youth Ice Hockey Participants and Trait Anxiety Levels between Athletes and Non-Athletes" (Master's thesis, Mankato State University, 1977).
18. Robert N. Singer, *Motor Learning and Human Performance,* 3rd ed. (New York: Macmillan Co., 1980), p. 249.
19. Thomas A. Tutko, "Anxiety," in Leonard A. Larson, ed., *Encyclopedia of Sport Sciences and Medicine* (New York: Macmillan Co., 1971), pp. 932-933.

Chapter 8
Information Processing

Assuming that a prospective athlete has the physical ability necessary to execute various athletic skills, a coach should be familiar with other variables that can influence learning and performance. A critical factor that can determine how much and how fast we learn is our ability to receive and process information. How does an athlete decide what action to take in a given situation? Take an example from baseball: there are players on first and third bases; it is the second inning with one out; the ball is hit to the shortstop. How does the shortstop decide whether to throw to second base, home plate, or first base? To make a decision, the shortstop must receive, organize, and process many pieces of information. On the basis of information stored from previous experience as well as a quick analysis of the present situation the shortstop must quickly decide where to throw the ball—most likely to second base, to begin a double play.

Similar examples can be cited from almost every sport, particularly those sports that might be called "perceptual," sports in which successful execution depends on the athlete's quick perception and analysis of a situation. Athletes receive information from the environment and make decisions on the basis of past experience or other feedback supplied by a coach, instructor, or other athletes.

How does an elementary school child know in which direction to kick the ball in a kickball game? Children visually survey the situation and then make decisions based on what they see and what they have experienced in the past. How do athletes in a complex sport know the correct sequence of actions for the successful execution of a given skill? They have learned and practiced the skill in various sequences over a period of time. In other words, execution has become automatic. How did they initially learn the correct sequence? They probably learned the skill in parts, taking one bit of information and linking it to another, until the sequence was complete. Golf is such a sport. Certain skills required in golf must be learned before other skills can be mastered. Any sport in which skills are acquired progressively would be in the same category as golf.

Athletes are able to execute skills because of *information processing*, a complex operation that can be simply understood. Several models of information processing have been proposed. The model in Figure 8.1 shows the sequence of events that must be completed if an athlete is to learn how to perform a given skill [1]. This model assumes that learning occurs according to a logical sequence of events. In baseball, for example, there are specific skills that a young athlete must learn in order to be successful. Each skill must be learned according to a logical pattern; a related series of skills must be learned in sequence. Coaches must ensure that students have mastered the skills of the first level before they go on to the second level.

The central nervous system is capable of processing only one bit of information at a time. Although this might appear to be a slow process, it is actually very quick—so quick that an athlete processing and implementing instructions from a coach can do so almost instantaneously. The presentation and reception of instruction is a major aspect of *input*, the first part of the model.

INPUT

Input concerns the instructional environment and the methods used to present information to athletes. Probably the first task of the coach is to structure the environment so that the information presented to athletes will be given their undivided attention. There are several ways to make the environment conducive to learning:

1. Hold practice where games are to be played. If athletes become familiar with the court or field during practice time, they will be more comfortable in game situations.
2. When instructing the team, eliminate distractions. Nothing is more disruptive to learning than a background of noise and activity.
3. Have all the necessary equipment ready when the team reports for practice. This allows teaching and learning to progress smoothly and without interruption.

There are undoubtedly many other points to consider when structuring the coaching environment. But these three will make the task easier both for the coach and the athlete. Specific examples will be offered later in the chapter.

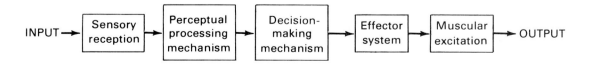

Figure 8.1. Model of information processing

The methodology of coaching and teaching is the second aspect of input. Coaches need sound methods of instruction if athletes are to receive the maximum benefits from their teaching. Before beginning to instruct the team, the coach should be familiar with the athletic backgrounds of the players: what kinds of experience have the athletes had in the sport before coming to this particular setting? If they have played the game before and have practiced fundamental skills, the coach can first review the fundamentals, then move on to more complex activities. If the athletes are unfamiliar with the skills involved in the sport, the coach must begin by teaching basics. Coaches should remember that mastery of fundamental skills is necessary to the execution of complex activities.

Once the coach is familiar with the past athletic experience of the players, he or she can formulate the material to be presented. The arrangement of information should be logical and sequential. There are several ways to help athletes process the information they receive:

1. Be sure the material is organized logically and stated simply.
2. Present the material in sequence: begin with basic skills and progress to more complex skills.
3. Be specific in words and actions or demonstrations.
4. Give athletes time to think about the material before moving on to a new skill or technique. At the end of a practice, a review session that includes problem-solving questions can help the coach assess the athletes' understanding of the material.

Clearly stated expectations and goals are necessary even before the actual teaching process has begun. Athletes must enter the sport arena knowing what is expected of them—by the coaches and by the other athletes. As we discussed in Chapter 6, specific goals can be excellent motivators. Clear expectations and goals help athletes focus their attention on what is important, and ignore what is irrelevant to performance.

Once the coach has structured the environment and prepared the material for presentation, the athletes are in a position to receive and process information, and to execute skills. The second step in the processing model is *sensory reception* of information.

SENSORY RECEPTION

Athletes receive information from the coach by means of sensory reception. When presenting information to athletes, coaches should make use of all the athletes' sensory receptors. There are four kinds of receptors or nerve endings that can be used to receive information: exteroceptors, interoceptors, proprioceptors, and distance receptors [2].

Exteroceptors are nerve endings located near the surface of the skin. They provide the central nervous system with information about heat, cold, pressure, size, shape, texture, and "feel," including information that is important in sport. Baseball pitchers use exteroceptors to inspect the baseball: some pitchers like seams that stand up from the ball; others prefer a ball with smooth seams. A football player must maneuver the ball into a position that feels good before he passes it. Different hitters prefer to use bats of different weights and grip sizes. Because the use of exteroceptors is so important in sport, coaches should encourage hands-on activities—active physical participation.

Interoceptors are nerve endings located in the internal organs. They provide information about feelings such as hunger and internal pain. Whenever athletes perform for an extended time, interoceptors signal information to the brain.

In athletics and physical education, *proprioceptors* are the receptors most frequently referred to. These nerve endings, located in the muscles and joints, provide the central nervous system with information about body and limb position. It is not uncommon to hear both coaches and athletes refer to the "feel" of a certain skill. In other words, the correct execution of a skill must feel natural or comfortable to the athlete. The feeling of comfort comes from repeated and correct skill execution; performance can be consistent only when the feeling is consistent. In physical education, kinesthesis or body awareness is a term used synonymously with proprioception. Athletes must at all times have complete control of their bodies. Coaches should comment freely on an athlete's performance, particularly in the early stages of his or her career. Unless they are watched and guided by the coach, young athletes can become comfortable with incorrect techniques of execution.

Distance receptors are the fourth kind of receptors. These nerve endings, located in the eyes and ears, provide information about distance. Coaches must make sure the environment is free of distractions so that these receptors can effectively pick up cues to learning and performance.

Once the bits of information are received, the athlete must form a mental conception of the skill. The information can be received for processing in at least four different ways. *Visual reception,* which relies on distance receptors, is one method. Everything that is presented visually should be easy to see and to inspect. The background should not be cluttered with moving objects or other things that might distract the athletes from whatever they are meant to observe.

A picture is certainly worth a thousand words in sport instruction. To have a mental picture of correct performance, athletes must be able to see correct execution of the skill. When presenting information visually, the coach must be sure the team is not distracted by the coach's verbal instructions—if these instructions are of secondary importance to the visual materials.

While observing visual materials, athletes also process information using the *auditory sense* of the distance receptors. Listening is of primary importance to instruction. As was mentioned earlier, auditory information must be presented in a logical, sequential manner. The environment should be free of distracting noise. Extraneous noise can prevent an athlete from hearing valuable information about the use of specific equipment or a strategy necessary for successful performance. The coach must remember that not every athlete who is listening is understanding the verbal instructions. Athletes must be given time to think about the information. Time should also be set aside to discuss particularly complex topics.

The sense of touch, or *tactile perception*, relies on exteroceptors for information; exteroceptors receive what tactile perception processes. Athletes, like most people, seem to appreciate and understand things that they can touch. Tactile perception gives the athlete an awareness of such things as pressure, texture, size, and shape. The baseball coach can talk about bat size and weight, but the players have to touch, lift, and swing bats if this information is to have meaning. The basketball coach can talk about the difference between the "feel" of a leather basketball and a rubber basketball, but players must hold, pass, and shoot the two basketballs to appreciate the difference. Information received through the sense of touch is of primary importance in sport.

The fourth means of receiving information is through *kinesthesis,* which relies on proprioceptors. Kinesthesis is body awareness. Like the sense of touch, it is developed through active participation. A good kinesthetic sense is necessary for successful participation in any sport. Athletes must be in control of their movements; an uncomfortable athlete will not perform well, no matter what the sport. There are right and wrong ways to position the body for each sport. The correct positions should be taught as early in the learning process as possible, to prevent athletes from feeling comfortable using incorrect techniques. Playing golf for the first time is a good example. If there is no one available to instruct a player in proper form, it won't be long before he or she feels comfortable using improvised techniques. One only has to visit the local golf course to see the variety of unorthodox golf swings.

Players using incorrect techniques may experience some early success, but they will find it difficult to achieve any consistency in performance until the mistakes are corrected. Another example can be found in basketball. Young athletes often push the ball up to the basket by shooting from the hip. This method of shooting eventually feels comfortable to the player. But placed in a competitive environment, the athlete won't be able to shoot over other players until he or she has mastered the correct technique.

These examples illustrate why it is imperative that coaches teach young athletes correct fundamental movements. The athletes should be encouraged to develop a "feel" for correct execution. Raw talent isn't enough; execution has to be based on correct fundamental technique.

The four methods of receiving information—visual, auditory, tactile, and kinesthetic—are seldom used independently. Most activities require the use of two or more receptors. Once the information has been received by the central nervous system, it must be strategically organized. The organization and processing take place in the mechanism of *perceptual processing.*

PERCEPTUAL PROCESSING MECHANISM

Perception includes the receiving, organizing, and processing of information. The organized information is sent to the higher brain centers to be stored until it is needed. For the perceptual mechanism to work properly, the receptors must first efficiently receive the information. It is the responsibility of the coach to provide athletes with information that can be effectively processed.

A detailed discussion of perception is beyond the scope of this text. Coaches should remember that the athlete's perception of the sport and the environment will in part determine his or her degree of success in that sport. Perceptions are stored in the brain and become the foundation for decision making.

DECISION-MAKING MECHANISM

The decision-making mechanism allows decisions concerning skill execution to be made. The ability to make appropriate decisions is critical in sport. On the basis of the stimuli, received information, and perceptions, the athlete selects a course of action; one would hope that he or she has several alternatives from which to choose. An athlete's ability to make decisions depends on *experience*. The role of the athlete's past experience was discussed in Chapter 7. If athletes have had previous experience in a particular sport their ability to make decisions is relatively efficient. We can assume that they have received information and stored it in their memories for future use.

Each time an athlete learns a new way to execute a skill, the method is added to a growing repertoire of methods. The experienced athlete has had more opportunities to make decisions and can be more successful in the future. The storing of experience enables athletes to put their physical and cognitive abilities to best use. The recognition of sounds offers a practical example. We can distinguish a siren from a horn because we have stored these sounds in our memory. When we hear a siren, we can quickly decide to pull the car to the side of the road. We know this is not necessary when we hear a horn. Athletes also have to make quick decisions. A hitter in baseball must quickly adjust his swing to the pitches; the adjustments will be based on his past experience and conditioned responses.

Coaches must remember that responses are not retained after brief or infrequent exposure to skill, but after repeated practice in the skill. Coaches must be willing to use repetitive practice techniques and teaching methods to ensure that athletes receive, process, and store the skills necessary for a particular sport. Techniques such as drill, whole or part, and massed or distributed practice are discussed in Chapter 11.

Once an appropriate response to the stimulus has been chosen, the information is conveyed from the decision-making center through the *effector system* to the the appropriate muscle groups.

EFFECTOR SYSTEM

The effector system oversees the transmission of information from the central nervous system to the muscles. For the complete skill to be executed, various messages must be sent simultaneously to all the appropriate muscles. The last process in the model is *muscular excitation*.

MUSCULAR EXCITATION AND OUTPUT

For coaches, this is it! This is where athletes show how much they have learned. If a player has made the appropriate decisions, the appropriate muscles will be stimulated to produce the desired movement.

Once the athlete has executed the skill, he or she should be given knowledge of results. Athletes should be made aware not only of what they did right, but of what they did wrong. Theorists in the field of education believe that some kind of external reinforcement is essential to the learning process. The role of knowledge of results was discussed in Chapter 6.

Perhaps an example would help illustrate how the various parts of the processing model can work together to produce correct performance. The following example describes one way of teaching the skill of batting in baseball or softball.

1. Prepare the environment.
   a. Get the field ready. Prepare the batter's box, pitcher's plate, etc.
   b. Make sure the background is conducive to hitting. The background behind the pitcher should be dark, so that the batter can easily follow the ball.
   c. Get the equipment ready. Provide bats of various sizes and weights. Provide plenty of balls, preferably new ones that are easy to see.
2. Prepare instructional strategy.
   a. Help the athlete select a bat of the right weight and length.
   b. Explain the grip and let the athlete try the grip.
   c. Describe how each part of the body moves to prepare for and execute the swing.
   d. Explain the strike zone.
   e. Allow students to practice the swing without a pitched ball.
   f. Make sure the pitcher throws consistently in the strike zone—or use a pitching machine.
   g. Allow at least ten consecutive swings at one trial for each athlete.
   h. Be sure each athlete has more than one trial in the course of the practice.
   i. Teach students to recognize the difference between the sound the bat makes on a successful hit and an unsuccessful hit.
   j. At future practices, review the batting techniques.
3. Encourage learning.
   a. Be liberal with verbal and nonverbal reinforcement.
   b. Use positive reinforcement.
   c. Give specific feedback.
   d. Use constructive criticism.
4. Review at the end of each session, leaving time for questions and answers on technique.

SUMMARY

We described the seven stages of an information-processing model: input, sensory reception, perceptual processing mechanism, decision-making mechanism, effector system, muscular excitation, and output. We gave examples from sport to illustrate the role of each stage in the process. To help coaches understand the importance of such a model, we described a method of teaching batting that is based on the concepts of information processing.

These suggestions by no means cover all the aspects of teaching batting. They do, however, include the major categories of information processing. For example, clearing the environment of distractions allows the batter to receive visually relevant information about hitting the ball. The use of new balls during practice also facilitates *visual reception*. The faculty of *auditory reception* allows athletes to receive the coach's verbal instructions and criticisms. Auditory reception also enables the athlete to distinguish between the sound of a good hit and an unsuccessful hit. When the players try various bat sizes and actually practice the swing, they rely on *tactile reception*. Finally, *kinesthetic awareness* makes it possible for the athlete to repeat the swing technique until the correct sequence of movements becomes automatic.

NOTES

1. Ronald G. Martenvik, *Information Processing in Motor Skills* (New York: Holt, Rinehart & Winston, 1976), p.5.
2. Ibid.

Chapter 9
Aggression and Performance

Aggression is a term that is used extensively in sport. If coaches were surveyed and asked to identify the characteristics of successful athletes, aggression would be high on the list. What is meant by aggression in sport? Aggressive plays are used in football, for example when the defense executes a fierce tackle. In basketball, good rebounders, good defensive players, and the players who consistently drive to the basket are all described as aggressive. Aggressive tennis players rush to the net at every opportunity. The volleyball player who dives to the floor to attempt an apparently impossible save is playing aggressively. In these and other examples from sport, aggressive acts can be defined as those in which the athlete (1) is highly motivated, (2) demonstrates a great release of physical energy, and/or (3) is not inhibited by fear of potential failure or injury.

In recruiting athletes, coaches often describe the desirable athlete as one who is "hungry, aggressive, and a competitor." The legendary football coach of Florida A & M University, Jake Gaither, often said that he wanted athletes who were *"mobile, agile, and hostile"* [1]. Aggressive athletes seem to be desirable athletes.

On the other hand, teachers often describe trouble-making or disruptive students as aggressive. It seems that while aggressive behavior is desirable in athletes and demanded by coaches, it may be discouraged in students and prohibited by teachers. Student athletes, especially those in junior and senior high schools, are constantly shifted from an environment where aggression is rewarded to an environment where aggression is punished. What both teachers and coaches must realize is that there are two types of aggressive behavior: one deserves discipline; the other deserves reinforcement.

Both teachers and coaches can probably defend their definitions of aggression. Much of the research on the manifestations of aggression supports the teachers' view of aggression as an undesirable trait. Aronson describes aggression as behavior intended to cause harm or pain [2]. The key to this definition is the word "intend." If an athlete fractures another athlete's nose by accident, the fracture is not the result of aggression. But if the athlete intended to fracture the nose, he or she was being aggressive in the negative sense of the word.

From 1978 to 1979, when over 70,000 teachers were physically assaulted by students, the students were demonstrating aggression as defined by Aronson [3]. Such harmful or destructive acts are rightly termed acts of aggression. But a basketball player who gets fifteen rebounds and twenty points in a game could be described as "aggressive" in a positive sense.

THEORIES OF AGGRESSION

What follows is a review of the origins and characteristics of aggressive behavior. Familiarity with theories of aggression can help coaches put aggressive behavior in the proper perspective. Bandura describes three theories of the causes of aggression in children: the instinct theory, the drive theory, and the social learning theory [4].

According to the *instinct theory,* aggressive behavior is used for protection. Infants are born with certain instincts and needs—one of which is the instinct of self-protection. Certain reflexes in infants are examples of aggressive behavior that is intended for protection [5].

The *drive theory* states that aggression is caused by frustration—the frustration, for example, of not being able to reach a chosen goal. Potentially frustrating situations should not necessarily be avoided. Children need to learn to cope with frustration. Because frustrating situations cannot be eliminated from sport, athletics offers a good opportunity for players to learn to tolerate frustration. Bandura's description of frustrating instructional techniques would be of interest to coaches: "poor teaching strategies, poor planning, insensitivity to various ability levels, and distracting mannerisms are considered sources of frustration resulting from weak instructional concerns" [6].

The *social learning theory* probably has more implications for coaches than the first two theories. According to the theory, the causes of aggression originate in three modeling influences: family, subculture, and symbolic modeling [7].

The effects of *family* modeling are determined by three kinds of influence: power assertion, love withdrawal, and induction. Parents can assert power by physically punishing children, or by depriving them of privileges or material objects. Ignoring or isolating children constitutes withdrawal of love. Reasoning with children to encourage them to change behavior is an example of induction. Whenever possible, coaches should use the third type of influence. Withdrawal of love can have harmful effects on the psychological development of young athletes. With older athletes, coaches can use any of the methods to motivate aggressive behavior, if aggression is in fact desirable in the sport situation.

According to Bandura, the *subculture* is a primary determinant of aggression in certain socioeconomic groups [8]. In some subcultures, aggressive behavior is not only condoned but encouraged. Studies of cultural and subcultural patterns of violence have shown that certain groups within society are socialized differently with respect to aggression. McKee and Leader have found that preschool children of lower socioeconomic background are more aggressive—more likely to injure another child—than children with higher socioeconomic status [9]. In addition, children from lower socioeconomic backgrounds were shown to have more freedom to express aggression and to engage in physical violence than children from higher socioeconomic backgrounds [10].

Considering these and other data, it would not be surprising if individuals of lower socioeconomic background tended to gravitate to more combative sports. In an early study of this subject, Weinberg and Kirkson found that nearly all boxers are recruited from the poorest segment of society [11]. From 1957 to 1962, data were collected on male athletes at Michigan State University. Eleven sports were ranked according to the gross family income of the participants and the occupational status of the fathers of the athletes. Football and ice hockey, two of the most combative sports, were located at the low end of the socioeconomic rankings [12]. Wrestlers ranked low according to their fathers' occupational status, but high on family income [13].

From a study of young Canadian hockey players, Vaz has reported a correlation between lower-class background and aggressive behavior, a relationship that becomes stronger as players become older and the hockey more competitive [14]. Vaz has suggested that players from the lower social classes gravitate to hockey because their value system corresponds to the value system prevalent in that sport.

The third influence on the development of aggression, *symbolic modeling,* may be the most familiar to children and athletes. Symbolic models of all kinds are constantly provided by the media.

Many young people regard the athletes they see on television as models. Of course, some athletes might not be the best models for young people. It is believed by some people that television can cause violent or destructive behavior, especially in young children and people suffering from emotional illness. Television was in fact used in the trial of a young man accused of murder. The lawyer for the defense contended that television had "brainwashed" the young man to commit murder [15].

This brief examination of modeling influences reflects an interesting phenomenon: aggression can be instigated by almost any agent in the environment. As was mentioned earlier, most aggressive behavior is viewed as undesirable behavior. At least one writer, however, has tried to place aggression in a positive context. Berkowitz has said that there are probably two types of aggression: goal and instrumental [16]. *Goal aggression* is behavior directed toward a goal; the behavior may include intent to harm someone along the way. Boxing is an example of goal aggression. Although goal aggression is not appropriate in sports such as football and ice hockey, some coaches teach their athletes that the end of winning justifies the means; the means can include techniques intended to inflict injury on the opponent. Coaches of youth football teams have been heard to scream in the heat of a game, "You have to hurt someone to be a winner" [17]. Another frequent comment is, "If we can get Number 16 out of the game, we can easily win." Encouragement of goal aggression is unacceptable in sport.

Instrumental aggression, on the other hand, is pursuit of a goal *without* the intent to harm anyone or anything along the way [18]. Sport should be a training ground for the development of instrumental aggression.

AGGRESSION AND ATHLETIC COMPETITION

Orlick has presented a summary of aggressive behavior that may help prospective coaches understand the various kinds of aggression present in sport [19]. Orlick has placed the physical aggression found in sport on a continuum that ranges from violent acts of brutality to assertive behavior for goal achievement. This continuum is presented in Table 9.1.

Regardless of the kind of aggression demonstrated by a player, the amount of aggression is usually determined by the level of frustration produced by the particular situation. Competition can be frustrating, particularly when we lose. But even in an undecided contest, frustration can arise from the anxiety of anticipating possible defeat, and the demands upon one's behavior created by the competitive conditions [20]. Berkowitz has said that the level of the anger or aggression produced by a frustrating situation will be affected by at least three traits [21].

The first determinant, *drive strength,* is influenced by the intensity of the satisfaction obtained by winning, or the intensity of the disappointment incurred by losing. For example, the drive to win a practice game would probably not be as strong as the drive to win the league championship game.

The second factor, *degree of interference,* refers to the interference with one's activities that can result from the conditions of the competition. Games that are rained out heighten the anxiety and frustration of the athletes, who then have no outlet for the excess energy created by anticipation.

Table 9.1. Physical Aggression Continuum

BEHAVIOR CATEGORY	ORIENTATION	PRIMARY MOTIVATION
Violence	Antihuman	To destroy another through extreme brutality or extreme force. Satisfaction in destroying others.
Destructive aggression	Antihuman	To hurt, to inflict harm, to injure another. Satisfaction in hurting others.
Expressive aggression	Self-oriented	To make a good hit, to wipe someone out. Satisfaction in hitting rather than in hurting or destroying. Pleasure associated with the hit itself.
Instrumental aggression	Goal-oriented	To achieve a goal or accomplish a task. Hurtful act is the means to a goal. No intent to hurt or destroy and no satisfaction in the aggressive act itself.
Accidental aggression	Unintentional	Injurious contact occurs by accident with no intent and no satisfaction in the act itself or in the outcome of the act.
Assertive behavior	Goal-oriented	To achieve a goal or accomplish a task effectively. No aggression and no intent of aggression involved. Individual initiative provides the means to the goal. Not classified in the realm of aggression unless it involves injury, intent to injure, or both.

From Terry Orlick, *Winning through Cooperation* (Washington, D.C.: Acropolis Books, 1979), pp. 126-127.

The number of *thwarted response sequences* is the third trait. The longer the sport contest, the greater the number of opportunities for response. If a player is not performing well, the level of his or her frustration will increase with each successive failure.

A coach should help each athlete understand and deal with frustration and aggression. Hellison has said that whether participation leads to aggression depends on the conditions of the activity [22]. His approach is not unlike that of Berkowitz—but Hellison does interpret aggression as undesirable. According to Hellison, the conditions of an activity that can lead to aggression are:

1. The amount of frustration experienced by the participant in expressing aggression in response to a stronger opponent or rules of conduct which encourage sportsmanship.
2. Whether the participant wins or loses.
3. The degree of emphasis on winning.
4. Whether hostility is carried over after the activity has ended. [23]

It is clear that aggression can be interpreted either as a positive or a negative trait. The goal of athletic competition should be to develop aggression as a positive trait. Berkowitz has said that "competitive games provide an unusually satisfactory social outlet for the instinctive aggressive drive, but that some discharge could be obtained even from sports involving sedentary intellectual competition, such as chess and checkers" [24].

SEX DIFFERENCES AND AGGRESSION

There is evidence that men tend to be more aggressive than women. Differences in aggressive behavior are probably the result of influences that begin in childhood. In a review of the literature on this topic, Zoble has found that girls are consistently more punished for aggressive behavior than are boys [25]. In our culture, aggression has traditionally been viewed as a desirable trait for men but not for women.

Early sex-role training discourages aggression in girls but encourages it in boys [26]. Tutko and Neal have said that women learn to *not* be aggressive, to *not* win, to *not* get into situations where there is the risk of pain, and to *not* be taught—or they will lose their femininity [27].

It seems that such cultural influences may be changing. Today, girls who are interested in sport are not afraid to develop the aggressive tendencies that will enable them to be successful athletic competitors. With the increased availability of athletic scholarships for women, more high school girls are defying tradition in order to receive the financial benefits of participation in sport.

INSTRUCTION AND AGGRESSION

Zaichkowsky et al. have designed a model that relates decision making to aggression [28]. This model is appropriate to athletics because athletes are affected by every decision made by the coach. The model shows that when athletes have some part in making decisions, the level of aggression in the learning environment is reduced. The model, modified for athletics, is presented in Figure 9.1.

Decision making dictated entirely by the coach or entirely by the athletes creates a chaotic, aggressive climate. The best decision-making combination is marked by the third arrow from the left in the model. The placement of the third arrow slightly to the left of center indicates that although the athletes are active in decision making, the coach makes the final choice. There is always potential for frustration in the sport environment. Giving athletes a role in making decisions gives them an opportunity to control at least some of the variables that can produce frustration.

SUMMARY

In this chapter, we have examined the role of aggressive behavior in athletics. Evidence is contradictory as to whether such behavior is desirable or undesirable in sport. There is conclusive research about the correlation between the socioeconomic status of athletes and aggressive behavior.

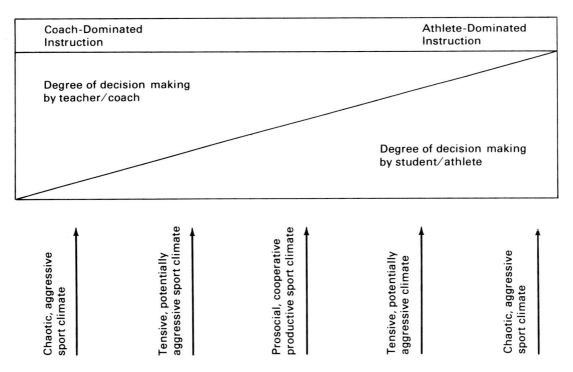

Figure 9.1. Teacher/coach-student/athlete decision-making instructional model

(Adapted from L. Zaichkowsky et al., *Growth and Development: The Child and Physical Activity,* St. Louis, Mo., C. V. Mosby Co., 1980, p. 197)

Bandura's three theories of aggression are the *instinct theory,* the *drive theory,* and the *social learning theory.* The social learning theory and the three modeling influences that can affect the development of aggression have the most relevance for coaches. Of the two types of aggression, *goal aggression* and *instrumental aggression,* instrumental aggression is more appropriate in athletic competition.

To prevent angrily aggressive responses from athletes, coaches should be aware of the conditions that can lead to frustration and aggression. Coaches should also be prepared for differences between men and women with respect to aggressive behavior. Such differences are cultural and not biological in origin. The chapter offered a model for reducing aggression in the athletic environment. Prospective coaches can use the model to help ensure that aggressive behavior in sport is positive in nature.

STUDENT LEARNING ACTIVITIES

1. Formally debate in class the topic of aggression: is it a trait caused by sport or cathartically relieved by sport?
2. Observe a boys' and girls' basketball game. Contrast the aggressive behavior displayed by the boys with that displayed by the girls.
3. Discuss the difference between aggressive and violent behavior in sport.

NOTES

1. Personal knowledge of Judy Blucker, who has heard Jake Gaither speak on several occasions in Florida.
2. E. Aronson, *The Social Animal* (San Francisco: W. H. Freeman & Co., 1977).
3. Leonard Zaichkowsky, Linda B. Zaichkowsky, and Thomas J. Martinek, *Growth and Development: The Child and Physical Activity* (St. Louis, Mo.: C. V. Mosby Co., 1980).
4. A. Bandura, "Social Learning Analysis of Aggression," in E. Ribes-Mesta and A. Bandura, eds., *Analysis of Delinquency and Aggression* (Hillsdale, N.J.: L. Erlbaum, Associates, 1976).
5. Ibid.
6. Ibid., p. 194.
7. Ibid.
8. Ibid.
9. J. P. McKee and F. Leader, "The Relationship of Socioeconomic Status and Aggression to the Competitive Behavior of Preschool Children," *Child Development* 26 (1955): 135-142.
10. Robert Sears, Eleanor Maccoby, and Harry Levin, *Patterns of Child Rearing* (Evanston, Ill.: Row, Peterson Co., 1957).
11. S. Weinberg and Arond Kirkson, "The Occupational Culture of the Boxer," *American Journal of Sociology* 57 (1956): 460-469.
12. Harry S. Webb, "Reactiontology," in *Aspects of Contemporary Sport Sociology,* Gerald S. Kenyon, ed., (Chicago: Athletic Institute, 1968), pp. 124-128.
13. Ibid.
14. Edmund W. Vaz, "The Culture of Young Hockey Players: Some Initial Observations," *Canada* (October 1970).
15. This defense was used in the 1978 murder trial of a seventeen-year-old boy, Ronnie Zamora, who was subsequently found guilty of murdering an elderly neighbor woman in Dade County, Florida. His attorney, Ellis Rubin, claimed that television had given him the idea for the murder. (Personal knowledge of Judy Blucker.)

16. Leonard Berkowitz, *Aggression: A Social Psychological Analysis* (New York: McGraw-Hill, 1962), p. 361.
17. Personal observation of Jack Llewellyn in his study of youth sport.
18. Berkowitz, *Aggression: A Social Psychological Analysis.*
19. Terry Orlick, *Winning through Cooperation: Competitive Insanity—Cooperative Alternatives* (Washington, D.C.: Acropolis Books, 1979), pp. 126-127.
20. Berkowitz, *Aggression: A Social Psychological Analysis,* p. 181.
21. Ibid.
22. Don Hellison, *Humanistic Physical Education* (Englewood Cliffs, N.J.: Prentice-Hall, 1973).
23. Ibid., pp. 25-26.
24. Berkowitz, *Aggression: A Social Psychological Analysis,* p. 204.
25. Judith Zoble, "Femininity and Achievement in Sports," in A. Yianakis et al., eds., *Sport Sociology: Contemporary Themes* (Dubuque, Iowa: Kendall/Hunt Publishers, 1976), pp. 185-193.
26. Zaichkowsky et al., *Growth and Development: The Child and Physical Activity,* p. 195.
27. Thomas A. Tutko and Patsy Neal, *Coaching Girls and Women: Psychological Perspectives* (Boston: Allyn & Bacon, 1975).
28. Zaichkowsky et al., *Growth and Development: The Child and Physical Activity,* p. 197.

Chapter 10
Mental Preparation and Performance

Mental preparation is essential to any competitive event: coaches continually urge players to "think!" or to "concentrate!" Games are said to have been won as a result of mental preparation—or lost for the lack of it.

Athletes who are not mentally prepared for competition sometimes experience mental lapses during a game. Examples of the effects of insufficient mental preparation occur at all levels of sport. In professional as well as amateur tennis, certain players cannot sustain their concentration long enough to win a tie-breaker. In baseball, many players can pitch "major league pitches" on the sidelines but cannot throw the same pitches during a game. Also in baseball, some hitters settle into a state of mind that renders them unable to hit a certain pitch, even though they have the physical ability to do so. In basketball, players who lose the ball to an opponent often lose their concentration as well.

It is easier to understand lack of mental preparation among athletes in youth sport. Young athletes have limited attention spans. If they are distracted by things outside the game, the competition can take on secondary importance. The authors once saw a little league baseball outfielder kneeling in centerfield searching for four-leaf clovers. Another outfielder was looking into space, enjoying nature. Their environment had obviously become more interesting to these athletes than the game itself.

During a close game of soccer, a five-year-old boy sat in the goal tying his shoelaces, a process that required several minutes. Another young boy refused to enter a youth soccer game because he was busy playing with his pet snake. It could not be said that these two athletes were suffering from mental lapses. Their concentration was simply on something other than soccer.

Although the inability to concentrate can hinder sport performance, there is evidence that *too much* concentration can also be harmful to performance. One college baseball player who was having difficulty executing certain skills said that he was "concentrating too much on concentration." The phrase "paralysis by analysis" illustrates the potential danger of excessive mental concentration.

Not only is adequate mental preparation desirable for optimal performance, it is essential. As we mentioned in the chapters on motivation and anxiety, there is an optimal level of arousal necessary for successful performance. The athlete who is too relaxed about the game is likely to make errors of omission; the overanxious athlete tends to make errors of commission.

METHODS OF MENTAL PREPARATION

In an effort to achieve a psychological state conducive to successful sport performance, athletes are using techniques that are still new to the sport world. Methods such as hypnosis, meditation, yoga, self-hypnosis, and progressive relaxation are being used at all levels of competition, but especially by professional athletes. A detailed discussion of each technique is beyond the scope of this text. But we will offer an overview of several methods, so that prospective coaches will be familiar with their basic characteristics.

The successful use of techniques of mental preparation depends on two factors: first, the athlete must possess the physical ability necessary to execute the skill. Mental preparation cannot enable athletes to execute skills that are beyond their ability. By reducing or eliminating the mental inhibitors of performance, such methods can help athletes achieve their physical potential. An example is the baseball pitcher who throws "major league pitches" on the sidelines. Mental preparation would help him throw the same pitches during actual competition; it could not assist him if he did not possess the innate ability.

The second factor that can influence the success of mental preparation is the attitude of the athlete. He or she must believe that the technique can improve performance. Athletes who approach a program of mental preparation with a positive attitude will be benefited in some way.

HYPNOSIS

Hypnosis is one of the most misunderstood concepts in psychology. There are many mistaken notions about the use of hypnosis in athletics. This section is not intended to prepare prospective coaches to be hypnotists; it is instead an attempt to acquaint the reader with the meaning and use of hypnosis in sport.

Several authorities have attempted to define hypnosis. Perhaps a review of these definitions will convey the confusion surrounding hypnosis as a method of achieving self-realization. LeCron and Bordeaux define hypnosis as the uncritical acceptance of suggestion by a subject who is in a trance [1]. Salter has described hypnosis as nothing more than a conditioned reflex [2]. A conditioned reflex is a learned response acquired through repetition and subconsciously controlled. Regardless of the definition one chooses, hypnosis is generally regarded as hypersuggestibility—an exaggerated form of suggestibility [3]. The key to hypnosis is the extent to which an individual is susceptible to suggestion. Everyone is susceptible to some degree; athletes, like other people, vary in their degrees of suggestibility.

There are essentially two types of hypnosis: *heterohypnosis* and *autohypnosis* [4]. Both types will be examined in this chapter. In the first case, the hypnotic state is induced in the subject by someone else. Autohypnosis or self-hypnosis is the induction of the hypnotic state by oneself. Athletes have been known to use both methods [5]. As a practicing sport psychology consultant, the author (JHL) prefers to instruct athletes in self-hypnosis, primarily because the athlete does then not become dependent on someone else for suggestion.

There are several elements essential to the successful use of hypnosis. Subjects must *want* to be hypnotized; they must have *confidence* in the hypnotist; and they must train their minds to *accept* suggestions [6]. Some hypnotists also consider absolute freedom from fear essential [7].

COMMON FALLACIES ABOUT HYPNOSIS

Before discussing hypnosis and sport, it is necessary to mention some common misunderstandings about hypnosis.

1. *Under hypnosis you are apt to do anything, good or bad. You obey the hypnotist automatically, no matter what you are told to do.* Actually, subjects under hypnosis will not do anything contrary to their moral principles, nor will they commit an antisocial act. They act only on those suggestions that they accept [8].
2. *Under hypnosis you are asleep and unaware of your surroundings.* This is not true. Under hypnosis, awareness is actually heightened [9].
3. *Being hypnotized means lapsing into a state of unconsciousness.* Being hypnotized, even in a deep state, is not the same as being unconscious. The subject under hypnosis is aware of everything that is going on [10].

These three misconceptions about hypnosis are only a few of those believed true by opponents of hypnosis or those who are ignorant of the nature and purposes of hypnosis. We mentioned the fallacies in an effort to allay any fears the reader may have about hypnosis.

HYPNOSIS IN SPORT

Hypnosis in sport has only recently begun to receive publicity; it is used by athletes such as Steve Carlton, Mark Fidrych, and Eric Soderholm, all in professional baseball. But it has been used by athletes in various sports since the 1964 Olympics. Naruse used hypnosis during the 1964 Olympic Games to treat athletes suffering from stage fright [11]. Since then hypnosis has been used extensively by athletes at various levels of sport.

Hypnosis, which has been applied to swimming, archery, and gymnastics, as well as other sports, has occasionally had unexpected effects. Naruse reported that "image rehearsal with slight physical practice showed its utility not only for champions, but also for the other ordinary members of school, because it heightened their motivation, interest, and self-confidence toward sport participation in school hours" [12]. Naruse, *In Hypnosis in the Seventies,* presents a detailed outline of the possible uses of hypnosis in sport.

Unestahl, sport psychologist for the Swedish Olympic Team, has been quite successful in the use of hypnosis [13]. He has outlined several ways in which hypnosis can improve the performance of athletes:

1. Helping the sportsman to use his real ability, by abolishing or diminishing different blocking factors (such as negative expectations, disturbing factors).
2. To get better control over such important variables as activation, arousal, tension, and motivation.
3. To establish the imagination of a good result without too much conscious effort.
4. To program in a winning state or winning feelings. This can be accomplished by having the sportsman describe in detail how it felt to have a very successful performance. If this is difficult for the athlete, then hypnotic regression can be used to get a better description of the successful performance.
5. To try to get a faster recovery from fatigue after exercise, for instance in the halftime break in a match. [14]

There are two means of achieving such results. One is the use of posthypnotic suggestions: giving instructions under hypnosis that will go into effect once the subject has awakened. The second method is to give instructions as direct suggestions under hypnosis; for instance, a subject could perform in competition under the influence of hypnosis [15].

Along with Naruse and Unestahl, others have successfully applied hypnosis to the learning of both simple and complex motor skills. As a result of his work with sport performance and hypnosis, Ulrich has made some interesting observations. He believes hypnosis is not used as extensively in sport as it could be, perhaps because many athletes have misconceptions about the purpose of hypnosis. They tend to think of hypnotic treatment as magical and capable of bestowing magical powers [16]. Although it is the athlete's belief in hypnosis that helps improve performance, there is an optimal level of suggestibility for effective results.

A perhaps more realistic and modern analysis is that offered by Gale, a medical hypnotist who extensively researched hypnosis and sport [17]. He claims that hypnosis relaxes athletes and can help them more efficiently learn a skill. He has also said that if the hypnotist uses sufficiently specific suggestions to change performance, build the athlete's confidence, or complement the athlete's existing skills, the athlete can be helped to improve his or her skill.

Kroger, a clinical hypnotist, has cited several examples in which hypnosis was used to correct performance faults in sports such as golf, baseball, and football [18]. A professional baseball player used as one example had been severely "beaned" by a pitched ball. The player became "plate shy," and chose a more protective batting stance. His batting average dropped significantly. The player went to a hypnotist, who first asked about the player's background and other pertinent facts, then gave the player a posthypnotic suggestion: he reminded the athlete how remote the possibility was of his ever being hit again. The player's batting average quickly rose to its usual level.

Another example given by Kroger was that of a professional golfer who became extremely anxious when playing in front of large crowds and against tough opposition. He was especially nervous while putting. The player was instructed in the use of self-hypnosis and imagery. He overcame his anxieties, learned to ignore the spectators, and improved his performance. After extensive practice in hypnosis, he could actually see a dotted line between the ball and the hole when putting.

Citing other literature would only serve to support the studies just mentioned. The point is that hypnosis can be effective if properly used by qualified individuals working with willing athletes. Everyone can experience hypnosis; its degree of effectiveness depends on the suggestibility of the subject and the specificity of the instructions.

The discussion has so far centered on heterohypnosis, with only occasional reference to self-hypnosis. Technically speaking, the two methods are separate. But as one learns more about self-hypnosis, it becomes apparent that *all hypnosis is actually self-hypnosis* [19].

SELF-HYPNOSIS

In hypnosis, the subject responds to the suggestions of the hypnotist. The subject permits the hypnotist to bring about a state of calm and relaxation because the subject *desires* this mental state. All hypnosis involves three things: motivation, relaxation, and suggestion [20].

Many sport psychology consulting programs now in operation offer variations of the basic techniques of self-hypnosis. *Self-hypnosis* or *autohypnosis* is the induction of the hypnotic state by oneself [21]. It has been pointed out that an athlete must be *motivated* for hypnosis to be effective. The second phase of hypnosis, *relaxation,* can also be self-induced. There are several means of achieving the optimal state of relaxation for *self-suggestion.* These will be discussed later in the chapter.

Self-hypnosis is basically the "voluntary acceptance and application of one's own suggestions" [22]. Self-hypnosis can be effective in almost every aspect of our lives: it can help us stop smoking; it can improve physical skills. This section will examine self-hypnosis and athletic performance.

Before using self-hypnosis, it is important that the athlete understand exactly what he or she wants to accomplish through self-hypnosis. For example, an athlete who is having difficulty executing a certain skill must be sure that he or she is familiar with the fundamentals of the skill. As in the case of mental practice, the skill must be visualized in its correct form, not in an incorrect form.

Caprio and Berger have formulated the "4-A's" method of self-hypnosis [23]. The four steps are: autorelaxation, autosuggestion, autoanalysis, and autotherapy.

There are several ways to achieve *autorelaxation.* One technique is to find a quiet place, lie down, take several deep breaths, close your eyes, and relax. Another is to use the progressive tension-relaxation technique: this means alternating complete muscle contraction or tension with complete muscle relaxation. Deep breathing exercises are part of the tension-relaxation technique. A subject who has learned to recognize complete or partial tension should also be able to recognize complete or partial relaxation.

Most people may not, and probably will not, be able to achieve complete relaxation in their first attempts at self-hypnosis. The number of relaxation sessions necessary to achieve full relaxation will depend on the individual. But once a subject has accomplished and practiced self-relaxation, he or she should be ready to use the "rapid method of autorelaxation" [24]. With training, relaxation can be quickly achieved by the repetition of a word or phrase that acts as a signal to relax.

Autosuggestion is the second step in self-hypnosis. The voluntary acceptance of a suggestion is essential to successful self-hypnosis. There are several suggestibility tests that can enable potential subjects to determine their level of suggestibility: these include the eye-closure test, the swallowing test, and the hand-tingling test [25].

The third stage in self-hypnosis is *autoanalysis.* By this stage, the subject should be receptive to suggestion. To accomplish the chosen goal, the subject must be able to analyze the source of the problem; this applies to any sport or any basic skill. For example, if you are a hitter who is in a batting slump, what are some of the things that you did before the slump that you are doing differently now? What sequence of movements did you follow when you made a successful hit? Once the problem has been analyzed, the subject is ready to work on the solution.

The fourth part of the process, *autotherapy,* is difficult for many athletes to complete. In this step, positive thinking is used to increase the efficiency in skill. It is a difficult process for most athletes because they visualize the skill as a whole and are unable to form an image of its component parts. Often, coaches are also unable to visualize each part of a skill. Self-hypnosis will be of little value to the athlete who cannot detect the individual faults in execution that contribute to failure in performance. Successful self-hypnosis requires the intelligent application of self-knowledge and the repeated practice of self-discipline [26].

The technique of self-hypnosis has been used successfully in sport, but not always under the label of self-hypnosis. There have been several programs in the past few years that would be of interest to athletes and prospective coaches. Two such programs have been used by Suinn and by Llewellyn. Suinn has worked primarily with skiers and track-and-field athletes [27]. Llewellyn has used self-hypnosis with baseball players and golfers, primarily at the college level [28]. A brief review of these programs may be helpful for athletes and prospective coaches.

VISUO-MOTOR BEHAVIOR REHEARSAL

Suinn, a clinical psychologist, used a combination of approaches to develop what he calls "visuo-motor behavior rehearsal" [29]. VMBR is divided into three basic steps: relaxation, the practice of imagery, and the use of imagery to strengthen cognitive or motor skills. In his relaxation program, Suinn uses progressive relaxation techniques similar to those previously discussed. According to Suinn, imagery seems to come more easily to subjects who are deeply relaxed. In Suinn's program, the imagery is of a practical nature.

> The imagery of visuo-motor behavior rehearsal apparently is more than sheer imagination. It is a well-controlled copy of experience, a sort of body-thinking similar to the powerful illusion of certain dreams at night. Perhaps, the major difference between such dreams and VMBR is that the imagery rehearsal is subject to conscious control. The final step is to use

imagery to practice a specific skill. What makes this type of practice so useful is its similarity to an actual competitive event. [30]

Suinn has been very successful in carrying out this program with various teams, primarily because the effects of hypnosis on performance are almost immediate. His three rules for structuring the program are worth mentioning here:

> First, all . . . recommendations were couched in terms of specific actions. Second, recommendations had to be stated in ways that could be used immediately. . . . Third, the recommendations had to involve known principles systematically related to behavioral change. [31]

Suinn's program has been successful for both the Colorado State University and the United States Nordic Ski Teams, as well as the United States Biathlon teams. He has worked with athletes in other sports as well. A more extensive discussion of his program and others can be found in Suinn's book on sport psychology [32].

MENTAL SELF-IMPROVEMENT

Llewellyn has worked primarily with baseball players, using a program based on the principles of both heterohypnosis and self-hypnosis [33]. The program begins with a conference to determine the athlete's degree of suggestibility. Influences that can help the athlete relax are determined at this time: these may be music, quiet, body position, darkness, and so on. During the second session, the athlete decides which aspects of performance need improvement. Llewellyn and the athlete list both the strengths and weaknesses of the player's skills. They discuss strengths so that the experience will be a positive one for the athlete; this also helps the athlete relax and think positively about the program.

Once the strengths and weaknesses are determined, the weak aspects of execution are analyzed. Each skill is listed step by step. For example, if a hitter has difficulty hitting a certain pitch, every step is listed which, if executed correctly, would enable the player to hit that pitch. If the athlete is unable to list the skills in sequence, then the coach is asked to do so. It is imperative that the skills be correct and in the proper sequence.

Once the list is complete, the program is begun. During succeeding sessions, the athlete practices progressive relaxation with the assistance of Llewellyn. Developing the ability to relax may require more than one session, as noted earlier. Once relaxation is achieved, Llewellyn reads the list to the athlete. As the list is read, the athlete visualizes each step. If any step is not clear to the athlete, the session is stopped and started again. After a few sessions, the athlete is able to use the program on his or her own time. The player is eventually able to relax and visualize the entire skill, including everything he or she expects to do during the contest. A pitcher, for example, should be able to visualize each pitch as it travels to the desired location. During the game he should be able to take the signal and instantaneously visualize the pitch before actually throwing the ball.

This program has been successful with both hitters and pitchers in baseball. It has also been effective with golfers. A description of two case studies might help illustrate the impact of the program.

A college baseball player was unable to hit a low inside pitch, a difficult pitch for many players. It was clear that he had the power to pull the ball and to adjust to that particular pitch. After several sessions in the program, the player began to hit the inside pitch with power to left field.

A second case concerned a pitcher who had trouble throwing a curve over the plate during games. He did, however, have a very good curve ball on the sidelines. The program emphasized two aspects of performance: improving the player's ability to visualize the curve ball during competition and shutting out variables that seemed to interfere with optimal execution. After several sessions, he was successfully throwing the curve ball during games. Other athletes are now participating in the program.

Remember that in order to execute a skill, the athlete must have the requisite physical ability. You can't make a .300 hitter out of a player who can't hit. If, however, an athlete has demonstrated physical talent, there is no reason why he or she cannot be taught the proper techniques of mental preparation.

SUMMARY

Mental preparation is a topic of increasing importance to both coaches and athletes. The safe and efficient use of techniques of hypnosis and self-hypnosis requires training. The reader should be aware of the potential hazard of using these methods without sufficient instruction. Research substantiates the positive effects of a well-organized mental preparation program on the execution of sport skills. Coaches should realize that simply yelling "concentrate!" to their players is not enough; methods of concentration must be explained by the coach and practiced by the athletes.

STUDENT LEARNING ACTIVITIES

1. Read and report to the class on a contemporary newspaper or magazine article that discusses an athlete's mental preparation for a game, tournament, or season.
2. List and contrast suggested mental preparation techniques that could be used in each of the following sports:
   a. Golf
   b. Basketball
   c. Baseball
   d. Swimming
3. Review the suggested steps for self-hypnosis, and try the technique for total relaxation. Can you achieve total relaxation?

NOTES

1. Leslie M. LeCron and J. Bordeaux, *Hypnotism Today* (New York: Grune and Stratton, 1947).
2. Andrew Salter, *What Is Hypnosis?* (New York: Farrar, Straus, and Co., 1955).

3. Frank S. Caprio and Joseph Berger, *Helping Yourself with Self-Hypnosis* (Englewood Cliffs, N.J.: Prentice-Hall, 1963).
4. Ibid., p. 12.
5. Ibid.
6. Ibid., p. 17.
7. Dave Elman, "Reference Notes for the Course in Medical Hypnosis," cited in Caprio and Berger, *Helping Yourself with Self-Hypnosis*, p. 17.
8. Caprio and Berger, *Helping Yourself with Self-Hypnosis*, p. 17.
9. Ibid.
10. Ibid., p. 19.
11. Gosaku Naruse, "On the Application of Hypnosis in Sport," in Lars-Eric Unestahl, ed., *Hypnosis in the Seventies* (Orebro, Sweden: Welins Tryckeri Eftr. AB, 1975), pp. 171-175.
12. Ibid., p. 172.
13. Lars-Eric Unestahl, "The Use of Hypnosis in Sport and Art," in Lars-Eric Unestahl, ed., *Hypnosis in the Seventies*, pp. 176-178.
14. Ibid.
15. Ibid., p. 178.
16. Richard P. Ulrich, "The Effect of Hypnotic and Non-Hypnotic Suggestions on Archery Performance" (Doctoral diss., University of Utah, 1973).
17. C. K. Gale, "Hypnosis May Help Athletes Learn Skills," *Scope Weekly*, 9 March 1969, p. 15.
18. W. S. Kroger, *Clinical and Experimental Hypnosis* (Philadelphia: J. B. Lippincott, 1963).
19. Caprio and Berger, *Helping Yourself with Self-Hypnosis*, p. 19.
20. Ibid.
21. Ibid., p. 12.
22. Ibid., p. 19.
23. Ibid., p. 27.
24. Ibid., p. 28.
25. Ibid., pp. 29-32.
26. Ibid., p. 39.
27. Richard Suinn, "Body Thinking: Psychology for Olympic Champs," *Psychology Today* 10 (July 1976): 38-42.
28. Jack H. Llewellyn, "Mental Preparation in Sport," in press, *Journal of Sport Behavior*, 1981.
29. Suinn, "Body Thinking: Psychology for Olympic Champs," p. 40.
30. Ibid., p. 41.
31. Ibid., p. 42.
32. Richard Suinn, *Psychology in Sports: Method and Application* (Minneapolis: Burgess Publishing Co., 1980).
33. Based on an ongoing program conducted by Jack H. Llewellyn at Florida International University since 1978.

Chapter 11

Practice Factors

Practice in a variety of forms has been shown to be of value in the acquisition of motor skills. From 1900 to 1940, experimental psychologists extensively researched the effects of various practice variables on motor learning [1]. During this time, studies were conducted that are still considered classics. The results of the research were applied by practicing physical educators. Although there was a lull in research during the forties, the development of specialized fields within the physical education profession led to renewed interest in the effects of practice on the acquisition of motor skills. During the 1950s and 1960s, sport psychologists and motor learning specialists began to research such effects and relate them specifically to sport. A review of the research literature of the 1970s, however, shows that interest in practice and its influence on motor learning has decreased.

PRACTICE VARIABLES

Among the variables that have been investigated by researchers are whole versus part methods of practice, massed versus distributed practice, and mental practice. A review of the research of these three topics yields conflicting results. In the following discussion, the reader should be aware of the problems associated with comparing and evaluating results of individual research studies. Rarely do the methods, procedures, or variables used in two different studies precisely coincide. It is consequently difficult to generalize or synthesize results obtained in several areas of research.

WHOLE VERSUS PART PRACTICE

Ascertaining the value of practicing the whole task as opposed to first practicing its parts is a topic that was of early interest to researchers. The *whole method* of practice requires that the motor skill be repeated in its entirety until it is mastered. The *part method* is used in several ways: (1) the whole skill is separated into parts, each of which is practiced and learned before a new part is learned, or (2) parts are added to partially mastered skills, to help the student achieve a smooth execution of the overall sequence. The second part method is known as *progressive-part*.

Much of the early research by psychologists in this field investigated the learning of cognitive tasks or novel physical tasks. The discussion that follows covers only the motor skills commonly encountered in coaching and teaching sport.

In an early physical education study, Cross found that the whole method of practice proved best for ninth grade boys learning the simple skills of passing and catching in basketball [2]. But he also found that the progressive-part method was more effective in the acquisition of more complex basketball skills, such as the "stop-pivot-shoot."

By studying students learning to execute a kip on the high bar, Shay found the whole method of practice superior to the part method [3]. In a later study of eighteen gymnastic and tumbling skills, Wickstrom found only one significant difference between the whole and part methods of practicing these skills: the whole method was superior to the part method in learning the "back roll-snap down" [4].

Niemeyer conducted a study of 336 students learning the skills of swimming, volleyball, and badminton using either the whole or part method of practice [5]. His results showed that the whole method was more efficient in teaching students to swim. Acquisition of swimming skills was measured by how fast the students learned, how fast and how far they swam, and how good their form was. In volleyball, the group using the part method showed greater improvement than the group using the whole method. Students in the first group acquired each individual skill—serving, setting, spiking—before playing the game of volleyball as a whole. There was no difference in skill acquisition among badminton students. Niemeyer concluded that the whole method was superior for learning skills in individual sports—sports that, like swimming, do not require interaction with opponents. In the case of team sports, which do require contact with the opponent, Niemeyer found that the part method might be more effective.

SUMMARY OF WHOLE VERSUS PART METHODS OF PRACTICE

A review of the extensive literature comparing the whole to the part method of practice yields several generalizations:

1. The whole method seems preferable when the skill to be learned consists of a chained sequence of movements—such as the tennis serve—that could not be efficiently broken into parts [6].
2. Students using the whole method generally learn faster, although the part method can be helpful in quickly eliminating errors [7].
3. The part method seems to be more appropriate for complex motor skills. It can also be used to overcome boredom or fatigue during long practice sessions [8].
4. The whole method seems preferrable when the learners are older, more intelligent, highly motivated, and/or have a prior knowledge of the task. The part method is preferable in the early stages of the learning process and when practices are massed [9].

The efficiency of either the part or the whole method depends on the nature of the motor skill to be learned and the characteristics of the learners. Teachers and coaches should remember these variables when planning their practice sessions.

Coaches of youth sport, for example, would find the progressive-part method more useful for several reasons. First, breaking the sport skills into parts makes them easier for inexperienced players to acquire. Second, the progressive-part method continuously introduces the students to new skills. This method can help sustain the interest of young athletes, who tend to have relatively short attention spans.

Coaches deciding on a method of instruction should consider the type of sport skills they will be teaching. In basketball, dribbling is a *whole* task, best mastered in its entirety. But coaches teaching the jump shot can divide the skill into two parts: the jump and the shooting technique. These must ultimately be practiced whole for the skill to be successfully executed.

Some sport skills require continuous, rhythmic movements that are difficult to break down into parts for the purposes of instruction. The golf swing, for example, must be learned as a whole skill for maximum efficiency. Many gymnastic skills also require whole practice techniques.

Niemeyer's research illustrated the importance in volleyball of learning the individual skills of serving, setting, and spiking as parts before playing the game as a whole [10]. This seems to hold true for almost any sport that combines a variety of skills.

MASSED VERSUS DISTRIBUTED PRACTICE

A basic assumption about the learning of any motor skill is that increased practice ensures increased skill. Research studies in the fields of psychology and physical education have tried to determine *frequency* and *length* of practice necessary for efficient learning.

Many of these studies have dealt with mental tasks or novel motor tasks, and have been conducted in laboratory situations designed to control variables such as prior knowledge, motivation, and skill level. For the most part, this review of the relative efficiency of massed versus distributed practice will give major emphasis to those studies investigating the gross motor skills likely to be of importance in sport.

In reviewing the research on massed and distributed practice, one problem arises—that of precisely defining terms. Each study has determined and defined the frequency and/or length of practice and rest intervals in its own way; this makes comparisons among studies difficult. For example, in a recent review of research on the teaching of physical education, the authors question the very use of the term "massed" practice. They believe that massed practice might be better described as a degree of distributed practice [11].

In a review of psychological research, Mohr published a summary of the results of forty-five studies contrasting the effects of massed and distributed practice on a variety of tasks [12]. She reported that forty studies produced results favoring distributed practice, three studies favored mass practice, and two studies found no significant differences.

Wagner studied the effects of practices of various lengths on the learning of basketball skills by junior high school boys [13]. As might have been expected, he reported that the group that practiced longer developed higher levels of skill at a faster rate than either of the two groups that practiced for shorter periods. But after the initial practices, the groups given less practice time seemed to learn as much as the others.

Scott studied the learning rate of beginning swimmers [14]. He reported that swimmers who practiced four days a week learned faster than those who practiced two or three days a week. A second study using swimming as well as badminton and volleyball found that students on a distributed practice schedule learned faster than did those on a massed practice schedule [15]. These results were achieved despite the fact that the massed practice group had thirty minutes more total practice time per week than did the distributed practice group. (The first group practiced for sixty minutes, twice a week; the second for thirty minutes, three times a week.)

Singer compared two distributed practice groups with one massed practice group in the learning of a novel basketball skill: attempting to score a basket by bouncing a basketball off the floor [16]. He found that the skill of the distributed practice group with twenty-four hours' rest between practices was significantly higher than that of the other two groups. There was no significant difference between the distributed practice group with five minutes' rest between practices and the massed practice group.

In a study using elementary school girls, Austin investigated the effect of distributed and massed practice on a velocity throwing skill [17]. Over a period of six weeks, the massed practice group practiced fifty consecutive throws each Wednesday. The distributed practice group practiced ten consecutive throws each day, Monday through Friday, and the control group did not practice. The performance of the distributed practice group was superior to that of both the massed practice and control groups. In the distributed practice group, learning continued to increase with time spent in practice.

SUMMARY OF MASSED VERSUS DISTRIBUTED PRACTICE

The research on massed versus distributed practice shows some conflicting results. In the acquisition of gross motor skills, it does seem that distributed practice promotes faster learning, as demonstrated by skill performance. Researchers have used—among other reasons—the theory of inhibition, the fatigue factor, and the motivation and maturity of the learner to account for the superiority of distributed practice [18].

But the superior value of distributed practice has recently been questioned by researchers. Whitley summarizes these doubts:

> Even though there is little experimental support for the traditionally accepted belief that distributed practice is superior to massed practice in motor learning, it continues to be commonly accepted. . . . Almost without exception, studies of this nature have been concerned with determining the effects of practice distribution on motor performance . . . rather than on motor learning. . . . While there remains little doubt as to the superiority of distributed practice over massed practice in *motor performance*, it is quite possible that this is not the case for motor learning . . . [19].

Dunham has also noted the distinction between learning and performance. He claims that "observed performance must be considered at best a relative estimate of true learning" [20].

IMPLICATIONS FOR COACHES

On the basis of the literature, we offer the following generalizations about the length and frequency of practice:

Longer practices can benefit acquisition of motor skills if one or more of the following conditions is met:

1. The learner's level of skill is above that of a beginner.
2. The learner is highly motivated.
3. The learner is a mature individual.
4. The activity itself is of such a nature that learners have short intervals of rest between performances.

It is clear that longer practices would be more appropriate for high school and college athletic teams than for youth sport teams, because of the advanced skills and greater maturity of the older participants. But whatever the sport, it is important to organize the longer practices so that there are short rest periods distributed throughout the practice. This helps prevent fatigue from interfering with learning.

Coaches can efficiently organize longer practices by carefully outlining a time plan for the two- to three-hour practice. For example, the coach should organize the instruction, demonstration, and practice of skills into time blocks. Coaches can use rest intervals for a review discussion of the skills, to help athletes practice problem-solving skills, or to present new skills and techniques.

Distributed practices seem to promote learning and performance more efficiently than massed practices do. Shorter, distributed periods of learning enable athletes to assimilate the learning and reinforce the skill between practices. Because massed practices tend to be less frequent, athletes may find it more difficult to retain what they have learned. The fatigue that can occur during a massed practice may also hamper performance. An athlete who is tired is less likely to execute skills efficiently. Injuries occur more frequently when athletes are fatigued.

In the case of certain motor skills, massed practices are more appropriate and will enable students to learn more quickly than distributed practices. Because it takes time to set up the necessary equipment, massed practice is most appropriate for gymnastics. In sports that require long periods of sustained activity, massed practice can help athletes develop the endurance necessary for actual competition. This is especially important in sports such as soccer, football, and baseball, in which a game can last between two and three hours.

Sports such as golf and bowling require the use of unusual facilities for practice and play. Because of the time required for transportation to the facility, and the expense of using the facility, massed practices are more feasible for such sports.

Closely spaced practices early in the learning process allow students to learn more efficiently and to retain what they have learned. Daily practices give the coach the opportunity to review and reinforce the skills and techniques. Frequent practices also help the athletes retain the skills and techniques.

MENTAL PRACTICE

Mental practice can be defined as the mental rehearsal of a motor skill. This concept has been actively investigated by researchers for many years, but much of the research has been conducted since 1960. The results show that mentally practicing a motor skill can facilitate the learning of such a skill.

That skills can be improved through mental rehearsal should not come as a surprise to those who are experienced in motor skills and athletics. Coaches and physical education teachers have stressed the mental side of movement—concentration and cognitive skills— since the beginning of organized instruction in sport.

Clark studied high school boys learning to shoot fouls in basketball, and compared the effects of mental and physical practice [21]. After fourteen days during which the physical practice group shot thirty goals per day and the mental practice group imagined shooting thirty goals per day, a retest of shooting skill showed significant gains for both groups.

Start conducted a second basketball study assessing the effect of intelligence and mental practice on the learning of a novel skill: the underhand free throw [22]. Although the group of boys improved significantly in skill after nine daily mental practice sessions, Start could find no significant relationship between level of intelligence and degree of improvement achieved through mental practice.

Egstrom studied the effect of mental practice, physical practice, and several combinations of the two on the learning of a novel paddleball skill by college men [23]. He reported that physical practice and a combination of physical and mental practice were superior to mental practice alone.

In a study using college women, Shick found that in the performance of the volleyball serve, a group using only mental practice improved more than a group that did not practice at all [24]. She also reported that mental practice for three minutes had a greater effect on the acquisition of the skill than did mental practice for one minute.

Richardson, in a comprehensive review of mental practice studies, concluded that mental practice was associated with improved performance—despite a variety of inadequacies in the research methods used in these studies [25]. In a later review, Corbin reported that, under optimal practice conditions, "there is little doubt that mental practice can positively affect skilled motor performance" [26].

SUMMARY OF MENTAL PRACTICE

A review of the literature on mental practice yields the following generalizations:

1. Mental practice is of more benefit to learners with some previous experience or acquired competence in the motor skill than it is to beginners.
2. Combinations of mental practice sessions with physical practice sessions seem to be more effective than mental practice sessions alone.
3. For mental practice sessions to be most helpful, the coach should provide guidance as to the content of the sessions.
4. Mental practice has been shown to be more effective in improving simple motor skills than complex motor skills.
5. Learners must be highly motivated in order to successfully improve their skills through mental practice.

IMPLICATIONS FOR COACHES

It is clear that coaches of all sports can help athletes learn skills by teaching them mental practice techniques. Training procedures should rely on a combination of physical and mental practice.

Mental rehearsal can be used to enhance the learning of all sport skills and techniques, but it seems to be most effective with those that require intense concentration for successful execution: these include shooting a free throw in basketball, hitting various pitches in baseball and softball, executing the swing in golf, receiving a pass in football, performing a high jump in track, and serving in volleyball—just to name a few.

Mental practice can also be used to reinforce the acquisition and application of strategies used in sport. Examples include assorted offensive and defensive plays used in team sports, such as the "rundown" play in baseball and softball. The principles of the rundown can be practiced mentally so that the play can be successfully executed in the heat of a game. Players should not have to stop and think about a strategic procedure during the game. Mental as well as physical practice makes perfect.

How can a coach use mental practice? The coach can establish a practice pattern that makes the maximum use of all practice time. For example, players could be asked to mentally rehearse select skills or techniques during the physical rest times scheduled during practice. In addition, coaches could schedule ten- to fifteen-minute classroom sessions for review and mental practice at the beginning or end of each practice. For coaches of outdoor sports, select skills and strategies could be mentally rehearsed for one or two hours on rainy days.

It is essential that the coach make the specific objectives of the mental rehearsal sessions clear in advance, and that the sessions themselves be carefully planned and conducted. If the athletes see that the coach is not genuinely committed to mental practice techniques, they will fail to take the sessions seriously and will derive little, if any, benefit from them.

SUMMARY

Practice is an important variable in motor learning. This chapter discussed the benefits and implications of *whole* versus *part* methods of practice, *massed* versus *distributed* practice, and *mental* practice. Because of the obvious importance of practice factors in motor skill development and coaching, the reader is encouraged to review carefully the generalizations and implications found at the end of each section in the chapter. The practice implications vary for the different age and sport groups in coaching, and coaches should apply the practice principles most appropriate for their sport and age group.

STUDENT LEARNING ACTIVITIES

1. Choose a specific sport skill and lead the rest of the class through a mental practice session of that skill.

2. Develop a written plan for a practice session in a specific sport. The plan should be efficient in its use of available time and space. Good coaches, like good teachers, use lesson plans to maximize their effectiveness.
3. Observe the practice sessions of several high school coaches. Analyze the efficiency of the sessions by recording the percentage of practice time taken up by: (a) noninstructional activities—drinking water, waiting for instruction to begin, (b) verbal instruction, (c) physical instruction and/or practice.

NOTES

1. George Sage, *Introduction to Motor Behavior, A Neuropsychological Approach*, 2nd ed. (Reading, Mass.: Addison-Wesley Publishing Co., 1977), p. 389.
2. T. J. Cross, "A Comparison of the Whole Method, The Minor Game Method, and Whole-Part Method of Teaching Basketball to Ninth Grade Boys," *Research Quarterly* 8 (1937): 46-54.
3. C. T. Shay, "The Progressive-Part Versus the Whole Method of Learning Motor Skills," *Research Quarterly* 5 (1934): 62-67.
4. R. L. Wickstrom, "Comparative Study of Methodologies for Teaching Gymnastics and Tumbling Stunts," *Research Quarterly* 29 (March 1958): 109-115.
5. R. K. Niemeyer, "Part versus Whole Methods and Massed Versus Distributed Practice in the Learning of Selected Large Muscle Activities," *Sixty-Second Proceedings of the National College Physical Education Association for Men* (1959): 122-125.
6. Sage, *Introduction to Motor Behavior, A Neuropsychological Approach.*
7. Bryant J. Cratty, *Movement Behavior and Motor Learning*, 3rd ed. (Philadelphia: Lea & Febiger, 1973), p. 362.
8. John N. Drowatzky, *Motor Learning Principles and Practices* (Minneapolis: Burgess Publishing Co., 1975), p. 215.
9. Joseph Oxendine, *Psychology of Motor Learning*, 3rd ed. (Philadelphia: Lea & Febiger, 1973), pp. 214-215.
10. Niemeyer, "Part Versus Whole Methods and Massed Versus Distributed Practice in the Learning of Selected Large Muscle Activities," pp. 122-125.
11. John E. Nixon and Lawrence F. Locke, "Research on Teaching Physical Education," in Robert M. Travers, ed., *Second Handbook of Research on Teaching* (Chicago: Rand McNally, 1973), pp. 1210-1242.
12. Dorothy Mohr, "The Contributions of Physical Activity to Skill Learning," *Research Quarterly* 31 (1960): 321-355.
13. C. G. Wagner, "The Effect of Different Lengths of Practice on the Learning of Certain Basketball Skills among Junior High School Boys" (Master's thesis, Temple University, 1962).
14. M. G. Scott, "Learning Rate of Beginning Swimmers," *Research Quarterly* 25 (March 1954): 91-99.
15. Niemeyer, "Part versus Whole Methods and Massed versus Distributed Practice in the Learning of Selected Large Muscle Activities," pp. 122-125.
16. Robert N. Singer, "Massed and Distributed Practice Effects on the Acquisition and Retention of a Novel Basketball Skill," *Research Quarterly* 36 (March 1965): 68-77.
17. Dean A. Austin, "Effects of Distribution and Massed Practice upon Learning of a Velocity Task," *Research Quarterly* 46 (March 1975): 23-30.
18. Oxendine, *Psychology of Motor Learning*, pp. 214-215.
19. Jim D. Whitley, "Effects of Practice Distribution on Learning a Fine Motor Task," *Research Quarterly* 41 (October 1970): 576-583.
20. Paul Dunham, Jr., "Learning and Performance," *Research Quarterly* 42 (May 1971): 334-337.
21. L. V. Clark, "The Effect of Mental Practice on the Development of a Certain Motor Skill," *Research Quarterly* 31 (October 1960): 560-569.
22. K. B. Start, "The Relationship between Intelligence and the Effect of Mental Practice on the Performance of a Motor Skill," *Research Quarterly* 31 (October 1960): 644-649.

23. G. H. Egstrom, "Effects of an Emphasis on Conceptualizing Techniques during Early Learning of a Gross Motor Skill," *Research Quarterly* 35 (October 1964): 472-481.
24. Jacqueline Shick, "Effects of Mental Practice on Selected Volleyball Skills for College Women," *Research Quarterly* 41 (March 1970): 88-94.
25. A. Richardson, "Mental Practice: A Review and Discussion, Parts I and II," *Research Quarterly* 38 (March, May 1967): 95-107, 263-273.
26. C. B. Corbin, "Mental Practice," in William P. Morgan, ed., *Ergogenic Aids and Muscular Performance* (New York: Academic Press, 1972), pp. 93-118.

Chapter 12
The Coach as a Counselor

Although counseling techniques are rarely mentioned in books on coaching, coaches are often called upon to be counselors to their athletes. Sabock explains that athletes often bring their problems or personal concerns to a coach "because of the special rapport that develops between athletes and coaches" [1]. What causes this "special rapport" between athletes and coaches? It is difficult to pinpoint any one reason, but there are several possible causes.

1. First, the atmosphere in sports is more relaxed than the atmosphere encountered in most classrooms. Athletes usually feel more relaxed with their coaches than with other teachers or members of the school staff.
2. Mutual respect generally exists between athletes and coaches. Athletes, like other people, are likely to trust those they respect.
3. There seems to be a bond between coaches and athletes that is related to the cooperative struggle inherent in any sports competition. The bond produced by athletics is like that felt by any group of people who have had to cooperate over time to achieve a goal. Examples of this undefinable bond can also be seen among veterans from the same army unit during war or persons who have survived a common disaster. The common bond in sport encourages the athletes to view the coach as a counselor.
4. Finally, leaders in athletic achievement are viewed positively by society. Young athletes admire and often idolize sport heroes and heroines. Coaches and other leaders in sport can greatly influence the lives of maturing young athletes. Because they feel respect and admiration for leaders in sport, young athletes often seek their counsel.

LIMITS TO THE COACH'S ROLE AS COUNSELOR

Athletes do tend to bring their problems and concerns to their coaches. Coaches working in the schools have an ethical and moral responsibility to try to help their students, just as any teacher would. Coaches should realize, however, that there are limits to the extent and kind of counseling that they can offer athletes. Most coaches and teachers do not have the formal training in psychology necessary to counsel students who have severe emotional or psychological problems. Coaches should learn to recognize the symptoms of such problems and seek the aid of professional counselors when that seems appropriate.

Failing to place limits on their counseling can be dangerous for coaches as well as for athletes. Coaches often fail to seek additional help for a seriously troubled athlete because they are afraid to betray the trust of the athlete concerned. But by not alerting an outside professional to the athlete's problem, the coach can only do more harm than good. To retain his or her trust, the coach should try to convince the athlete that additional help is essential to the resolution of the problem. With the athlete's full knowledge, the coach should then secure professional assistance. If the coach is not completely honest with the athlete, the bond of trust will be broken.

COUNSELING TECHNIQUES

The counseling techniques a coach will use depend on the kind of problem the athlete has. For the majority of problems that athletes bring to coaches, *listening* is the necessary technique. Being a concerned but unbiased listener is an important skill for coaches, especially those who work with adolescents. During their teenage years, youngsters experience difficulties that are a natural part of the process of becoming adults. Because of the pressures of participation in sport, being an athlete can sometimes increase the number and magnitude of these problems.

In many instances, merely giving the athlete the opportunity to talk about a problem can help alleviate its severity. By listening without making judgments, the coach can assure the athlete that (1) the problem is probably not as serious as he or she originally thought; (2) there is hope for resolution of the problem; and (3) the coach is genuinely concerned for the welfare of the athlete.

As a counselor, the coach must first listen to the athlete's problems, then guide the athlete to a solution. This can be done by suggesting that the player pose various solutions to the problem; the coach should be careful *not* to suggest specific solutions. Once the athlete has offered several solutions, the coach can help the athlete determine the consequences of each course of action. The athlete must make the final decision alone. Once that decision has been made, the coach can help the athlete carry out the decision by suggesting a specific way to implement it and by checking back with the athlete later to see that everything went well.

A second technique that can be used to counsel athletes is *values clarification* [2]. This technique is especially appropriate for athletes whose problems have ethical or legal implications. Values clarification is a systematic approach to teaching people how to make their own value judgments. The coach will *not* be imposing his or her value system on the athlete. The approach assumes that the process of making value judgments enables people to develop a consistent and reasonable value system.

The values clarification approach can be used in counseling athletes who have problems of an ethical or legal nature such as:

1. Chemical abuse
2. Premarital sexual encounters
3. Cheating in school
4. Stealing, fighting, or other antisocial behavior
5. Sportsmanship issues

Over a period of time, the coach would guide the athlete through the four phases of values clarification: examining, affirming, choosing, and acting. In the first phase, the coach would encourage the athlete to *examine* his or her beliefs and behavior. In the second phase, the athlete would be expected to *affirm* his or her values publicly—perhaps in a group team session, if this were appropriate to the situation. During the third phase, the coach and athlete identify alternative courses of action and examine the various consequences of such actions. After weighing the consequences, the athlete alone must *choose* a course of action. In the fourth and final phase, the athlete must *act* consistently with the values that have been chosen.

During the entire process, the coach serves as a guide, helping the athlete identify alternatives and consequences, and pointing out any discrepancies that might exist between what the athlete says he or she believes and what the athlete actually does. Once the athlete has completed the process, the coach will remain available to help the athlete reaffirm his or her choices should similar situations occur in the future. Although values clarification as an individual counseling technique can require quite a commitment of the coach's time, it can also be successfully applied to team situations. Without isolating individuals, the coach can help the group tackle problems common to all the members.

ETHICAL ISSUES IN COUNSELING

As noted earlier in the chapter, the potential influence of coaches is so great that they must make a conscious effort to avoid imposing their values on their athletes. Young athletes blinded by faith in and respect for the coach cannot judge whether the coach's own value system is right or wrong. This is especially true of athletes in youth sport or high school competition. Older, more mature athletes in college, club, and professional sport have probably already developed their own value systems. The potential influence of the coach is offset by the maturity of the athletes. But coaches of younger athletes have a moral and ethical responsibility to allow the athletes to establish their own values.

The following hypothetical situation offers an example of a potentially "unfair" influence. The coach of a junior high girls' tennis team smokes marijuana. Apart from the legal issue, this is a personal decision of the coach. But if she reveals this to her team, she risks imposing her own values on the athletes. Because these young and immature athletes view the coach with such respect, she has a potentially unfair influence on the values of the team members. With respect to the issue of smoking marijuana, the coach can maintain a neutral influence on her team only by concealing her personal decision. The young athletes would then be able to weigh the consequences of various decisions and choose the values that are appropriate for them.

DEALING WITH PROBLEM ATHLETES

Coaches occasionally encounter highly skilled athletes with behavior problems. In some instances, coaches may prefer counseling these athletes to expelling them from the team. A technique known as *reality therapy* has been used successfully with students who have behavior problems in school [3]. Reality therapy offers a means of interacting with and helping problem students. It is based on the idea that a student, or in this case an athlete, is able to identify the behavior problem and its consequences, make a judgment about it, plan a change, and make a commitment to carry out that change.

This model places sole responsibility for change on the athlete, not on the coach. The coach should not moralize or preach to the athlete. The coach should neither ask for explanations nor tolerate excuses for the athlete's behavior. Throughout the process, however, the coach should show the athlete that he or she cares about the athlete, has concern for the athlete's future, and genuinely values the athlete as an individual.

Siedentop has identified seven basic principles for the use of reality therapy with problem students [4]. These principles can easily be modified for use with athletes as well.

1. The coach should focus on the *present* behavior problem, avoiding any reference to past problems.
2. Both the coach and the athlete should deal with the problem rationally, *not* emotionally.
3. The athlete should be asked to make value judgments about the behavior in question; the coach should *avoid* making such judgments.
4. The coach should help the athlete identify the consequences of the behavior. Avoid asking why the behavior occurs; instead, ask what happens as a result of the behavior.
5. The coach should continuously demonstrate that the athlete is valued as a person. Reinforce the fact that it is the behavior, not the person, that is undesirable.
6. The coach should help the athlete make a commitment to a change in behavior. The direction of the change and the identification of consequences should be determined primarily by the athlete.
7. Once the commitment is made, the coach should never accept an excuse for breaking the commitment.

Applying the principles of reality therapy to problem athletes can help a coach be consistent in dealing with other athletes as well. This model for coping with behavior problems can also prevent a coach from making a serious mistake in the heat of a moment.

To illustrate this point, consider a typical problem in coaching. Several members of a boys' high school basketball team are continually late for practice. To resolve the problem, the coach, in anger, announces that anyone late to practice will not play the next game.

During the next week, a player with a legitimate reason is late for practice—for the first time all season. Because of the coach's earlier decision, made in anger, the player and in fact the entire team are penalized for something that could not have been avoided.

In this example, the coach could not have reversed the rule without losing the respect of the athletes. Instead of helping the team as it was intended to, the rule only hurt the team. If the basketball coach had used a reality therapy model, the few players who were continually late for practice would have been counseled when the problem occurred. If successfully counseled, the players would have realized the potential consequences of their behavior to the morale of the team. Once the players had recognized and discussed the seriousness of the problem, they could then have determined—with the coach—the consequences of continuing to be late. They would then have made a commitment to change, with full knowledge of the results of failing to meet the commitment—not being permitted to play the next game, for example. The coach could then have dealt separately with the single player who was late for the first time all season and who had a legitimate excuse.

One should not assume from this example that rules that apply to the entire team are bad or unnecessary. On the contrary, team rules for behavior are essential to the welfare of any team. Such rules, established jointly by the coach and the athletes, serve as the foundation for the efficient functioning of the team, just as laws serve as the foundation for the efficient functioning of society.

But these rules must be fair, and ensure the consistency of the coach's behavior toward the athletes. Consistency does *not* mean inflexibility on the part of the coach; it does mean the equitable application of all rules to all athletes. By being both consistent and fair, coaches can sometimes prevent behavior problems, many of which arise when athletes feel that the coach is playing favorites. Counseling problem athletes can help the coach avoid decisions that are hasty or unfair.

SUMMARY

Coaches are often called upon by athletes who want help with a problem. *Listening* will alleviate many of the problems. The coach has a responsibility, especially if he or she works in a school, to seek professional counseling for those athletes who have serious emotional or behavioral problems. *Reality therapy* and *values clarification* are two additional techniques that can be used to counsel athletes.

There are ethical boundaries that should be respected by coaches who work with athletes of high school age or younger. The respect they are accorded by our society places a serious moral responsibility on coaches for the development of values in young athletes.

NOTES

1. Ralph J. Sabock, *The Coach,* 2nd ed. (Philadelphia: W. B. Saunders Co., 1979), p. 59.
2. Louis Raths et al., *Values and Teaching* (Columbus, Ohio: Charles E. Merrill, 1966).
3. Daryl Siedentop, *Developing Teaching Skills in Physical Education* (Boston: Houghton Mifflin Co., 1976), p. 159.
4. Ibid, pp. 311-312.
5. Bruce C. Ogilvie and Thomas A. Tutko, *Problem Athletes and How to Handle Them* (London: Pelham Books, 1966).

Chapter 13
Coaching Girls and Women

In order to better understand the psychology of coaching girls and women in sport, it is essential to be familiar with the recent history of girls' and women's sport in the United States. Although girls and women have participated in sporting events since the beginnings of recorded civilization, it has only been in the past twenty years that girls and women have been encouraged to participate in sport and have responded to that encouragement by participating in larger numbers than ever.

HISTORICAL DEVELOPMENTS

Western culture has historically regarded sport as a masculine activity. This attitude is the primary reason for the limitations placed on women's participation in sport. A second reason for the slow development of female participation in competitive sport has been the resistance of women physical educators themselves. From the 1920s to the 1950s, the national governing association of women physical educators espoused a philosophy that supported participation in sport for the "joy and love of play, not for the purpose of beating an opponent" [1].

It was only in 1962, with the creation of the women's advisory board to the Olympic Development Committee, that what was then the Division of Girls' and Women's Sports of the AAHPER was persuaded to change its philosophy to favor competition for the highly skilled girl [2].

In the first half of the twentieth century, there were a few women pioneers in the world of competitive sport. Women such as Babe Didrikson Zaharis in track-and-field and Maureen Connally in tennis defied prevailing attitudes toward women in sport and were instrumental in gaining the attention and tolerance—if not the acceptance—of the public.

These two women athletes became sport heroines of their time primarily because the news media gave extensive coverage to their extraordinary accomplishments.

Movies produced in the 1970s about the lives of these two athletes recently reinforced our memory of their achievements. Although the athletic achievements of early women athletes such as Zaharis and Connally may have been surpassed by modern women athletes, women's sport today probably receives relatively less news coverage than Zaharis and Connally did.

Although a few outstanding women athletes have won the respect and admiration of the public, society has continued, for the most part, to reject the idea of women in sport. Spears points out this paradox:

> Sport for women has been more a myth than a reality because the western world has both accepted and rejected women in sports. Society has always been enthralled by the athletic skill and prowess of a few women. . . . But, for most women society has created a role which excludes them from sport. [3]

It is easy to find examples of the truth of Spears' observation. While most of the public readily accepts a Chris Evert or a Nadia Comaneci, it is still ready to reject the young girl who wants to play little league baseball.

What are the causes of this rejection? Society has traditionally dictated that it is all right for girls to participate in dance, tennis, and other "feminine" physical activities, but that it is *not* all right for girls to participate in "masculine" physical activities such as baseball.

With the general social changes of the 1960s, the traditional role of girls and women began to change as well. Women demanded the right to do their own thing—right along with men. For some women, "their own thing" meant sport. Despite the continued influence of cultural restrictions, the participation of girls and women has increased tremendously in *all* sports in the past decade.

What has been primarily responsible for the tremendous growth of girls' and women's sport in recent years? The achievements of earlier women athletes undoubtedly laid the foundation for the developments in sport today. But growth can be primarily attributed to four sources of influence: the change in women's roles fostered by the women's movement; the growth of national and international sport for women fostered by the Olympics; increased television coverage of women's sport events; and the sport "civil rights" law: Title IX of the Educational Amendments Act of 1972.

FACTORS CONTRIBUTING TO THE GROWTH OF GIRLS' AND WOMEN'S SPORT

It is obvious that the women's liberation movement has had a tremendous impact on the role of women, particularly since the 1960s. The publication of Betty Friedan's *The Feminine Mystique* can be considered a major catalyst of the movement [4]. Today, more and more women feel free to challenge established cultural values and norms.

Girls and women participating in competitive sport today have made remarkable progress in a relatively short time. Since women's national sport championships were first initiated by the forerunner of the Association of Intercollegiate Athletics for Women, the number of collegiate championships has increased from three in 1969 to thirty-nine in 1980

[5]. There has also been phenomenal growth in the number of girls competing on interscholastic sport teams in high schools. From 1971 to 1980, the number of girls competing increased from 300,000 to 1,800,000 [6].

Sport feminism is an outgrowth of the women's movement. Two recent books have made this topic their central theme [7]. Girls and women are becoming increasingly militant in demanding their right to compete in sport.

Along with the women's movement, the Olympics has fostered women's participation in sport, both on the national and the international level. Since the modern Olympics were renewed by Baron Pierre de Coubertin in 1896, women's competitive events have gradually been added [8]. Davenport points out that 45% of the United States Olympic Team of 1976 were women, a total of 137 women competitors [9]. But there is still much progress to be made in other countries of the world, as Vernacchia notes:

> Women's participation in the Olympic movement, as both athletes and administrators, has been limited. Approximately 15% of all participants in the summer and winter Olympics of 1976 are women. [10]

Since the onset of the cold war in the 1950s, the political impact of the Olympics has indirectly influenced the quality and quantity of women's sport programs at the high school and college levels in the United States. The countries of Eastern Europe and the Soviet Union have developed extensive youth training programs in sport for both men and women. These countries seem intent on using sport success in the Olympics as a means of promoting their political ideologies. With coverage of the Olympics available to a worldwide audience, such nations do have an opportunity to realize their intent. In an editorial about the United States' boycott of the 1980 Olympic Games, Hempstone discussed this issue:

> Nowhere in the world, both internally and externally, have sports been more thoroughly politicized than in the Soviet Union. . . . Abroad, the party saw that Soviet athletic excellence could "convincingly demonstrate that socialism opens up the greatest opportunities for man's physical and spiritual perfection." [11]

While the United States has had an excellent youth sport program for boys sponsored by schools, civic organizations, and public agencies, it is now promoting one for girls—in an effort to offset the competitive advantage of the Eastern European countries and the Soviet Union. An example is the national volleyball training camp that was established in 1978 to prepare our women's Olympic volleyball team for the 1980 Games.

The third factor in the increased participation of women in sport is the increase in television coverage of women's sport events. Much of this coverage has obviously been devoted to the Olympics themselves. Television has made international and national heroines of women athletes such as Olga Korbut and Nadia Comaneci in gymnastics, Chris Evert and Tracy Austin in tennis, and Nancy Lopez in golf.

It does seem that increased media coverage would bring with it an increasing acceptance of women in sport. Successful women athletes can serve as role models for young girls interested in athletics. In addition, parents of young girls have become more aware of the financial benefits available to outstanding women athletes. In a country such as the United

States, where the ability to earn money is equated with success, the media has helped convince parents that participation in sport can be both an acceptable and profitable way for their daughters as well as their sons to attain success.

The success in recent years of the American gymnastic teams—both male and female—in international competition can be traced to the growth of competitive youth gymnastic groups. This increase in the number of young athletes training to be gymnasts seems directly related to the television exposure given the Olympic gymnastic competition since 1960.

The development of youth soccer in this country has also been influenced by the media. Television's coverage of soccer stars such as Pele and Kyle Rote, Jr. has provoked the interest of both young boys and young girls. The popularity of girls' youth soccer is demonstrated by the addition in September 1978 of girls' soccer as a varsity sport in the high schools of Dade County, Florida, the fifth largest school system in the United States [12].

The last and most significant factor in the growth of girls' and women's sport has been Title IX of the Educational Amendments Act of 1972. This act declares that "no person in the United States shall, on the basis of sex, be excluded from participation in, be denied the benefit of, or be subjected to discrimination under any education program or activity receiving Federal financial assistance" [13].

The first guidelines for the application of Title IX to athletic programs were developed by the Department of Health, Education and Welfare in June 1975. The original guidelines said that women could not be discriminated against with regard to availability of teams, coaches, practice facilities, funding, equipment, medical services, publicity, or financial aid. Additional guidelines were published in the *Federal Register* of December 1979, to further clarify the definition of sex discrimination in intercollegiate sport.

Schools failing to meet the requirements of the Title IX guidelines by 1 July 1978 faced the potential loss of all federal funding. Several institutions have been and are continuing to be investigated by the former HEW Office for alleged violations of Title IX in athletics. As of December 1978, ninety-three lawsuits charging discrimination against women in athletics under the Title IX guidelines had been reported [14].

There is little doubt that Title IX has been the greatest single impetus for the growth of girls' and women's sport in the schools of America. With this sudden growth, however, have come several problems.

PROBLEMS ARISING FROM THE GROWTH OF GIRLS' AND WOMEN'S SPORT

One major problem is that there are not enough well-trained women coaches to meet the sudden demand of girls' and women's teams at every level. Because there were few intensive sport programs in the past for women, there are now relatively few female coaches or potential coaches with experience in highly competitive sports. In the past, most women coaches were physical education teachers who may or may not have had competitive experience themselves. Although these women had the technical knowledge necessary to train athletes in the development of skill and strategy, they were often unfamiliar with the psychological aspects of coaching.

This trend is changing today as many of the top women college athletes are graduating to become coaches. These young women have gained firsthand knowledge of the psychological stresses of competition. In addition, many college programs now offer a psychology of coaching class for young men and women who plan a career in physical education and/or coaching.

Disagreement about the philosophy of women's sport has been a problematic accompaniment to its growth. At the beginning of this chapter, we mentioned that the position first held by the governing association of the AAHPERD promoted "joy and love of play," not just beating an opponent [15]. This group, the Division of Girls and Women in Sport (DGWS), is now the National Association of Girls and Women in Sport (NAGWS) of the American Alliance for Health, Physical Education, Recreation and Dance (AAHPERD).

NAGWS was the founder of the collegiate governing body for women's athletics now known as the Association of Intercollegiate Athletics for Women (AIAW). In 1968, NAGWS was responsible for drafting the original statement of philosophy for the governance of the developing athletic programs for women. The statements censured athletic scholarships for women and prohibited young women holding such scholarships from competing in national championships sponsored by the CIAW, now the AIAW. The original intent of the ban on scholarships was to "avoid the pitfalls and evils of men's athletics." It was generally believed by the leadership of NAGWS that, by prohibiting athletic scholarships for women, it was protecting women's sport from unethical recruiting practices, illegal payments to athletes, and the pressure of winning at any cost.

But by the 1970s, the ban on athletic scholarships for women was viewed not as protection but as discrimination. In 1973, the women tennis coaches of two Florida colleges filed a lawsuit against NAGWS and AIAW, resulting in a procedural—if not philosophical—change in the AIAW governance rules for women's collegiate athletics [16]. With certain restrictions, AIAW now allows athletic scholarships and recruiting of athletes.

The original intent of the leaders of the AIAW was to build a model of collegiate athletics that was philosophically different from the existing men's model. This model, as described in the published procedures of the AIAW, remains different in many ways from the model presented by the National Collegiate Athletic Association.

PHILOSOPHICAL DIFFERENCES BETWEEN WOMEN'S AND MEN'S ATHLETICS

The basic difference between the men's and women's models of sport lies in the philosophical foundation of organized competitive sport itself. Gruneau has identified two antithetical philosophical positions from which sport can be viewed: a meritocratic ideology and an egalitarian ideology [17].

These conflicting ideologies have been defined by Malmisur:

The meritocratic ideology:
(a) coincides more so with mainstream values of modern capitalistic societies;
(b) is more concerned with open and ample opportunity to compete for rewards than inequality of rewards;

(c) is founded in the belief that the most qualified will "attain" the most important positions;

(d) and finally views inequality as inevitable and non-problematic.

The egalitarian ideology:

(a) critically describes western industrial capitalistic societies by the widespread differences of reward that accrue to positions and roles;

(b) is more concerned with benefits based upon equal social need;

(c) is founded upon the belief that inequality is created and maintained by those in power;

(d) and finally views inequality as an area of constant conflict . . . [18]

It is Malmisur's contention that men in sport have traditionally followed a meritocratic ideology, whereas the brief history of women in sport is an example of "sports behavior guided more by an egalitarian rather than meritocratic ideology" [19].

The contrast between men's and women's sport is similar to the contrast between "big-business athletics" and "educational athletics," defined in relation to college sport by Celeste Ulrich, former president of AAHPERD. Men's collegiate athletic programs could be viewed as the "big-business" side of athletics: particularly in football and basketball, huge expenditures are made to promote not only the athletic success of the team, but its public image as well. College teams compete to win games; they also compete for media coverage and the increased recognition it brings. In the past, women's collegiate programs have had to rely on participants playing for the love of the sport: there were no college scholarships; there were limited budgets for uniforms, travel, and equipment; publicity and media coverage were almost nonexistent.

As women's sport programs gain increasing financial support through the influence of Title IX, the programs may undergo a philosophical change. Greater emphasis may come to be placed on *winning* than on *participation*. The administrators of the programs may be among the potential causes of this change. The administrators, most of whom are men, may demand that the women's sport programs adhere to the same ideology as the men's programs—if they are receiving comparable financial support. Malmisur poses pertinent questions about this issue:

> Are women prepared to convert play into display; mass-participatory oriented objectives into spectator-oriented and finally emphasize the process of development and honor more objective achievement? . . . Are men willing to encourage equal treatment for women in sport while allowing them an egalitarian based program? Do women want a meritocratic sports program . . . [20]

HUMANISTIC SPORT

A philosophical discussion of sport would be incomplete without reference to humanistic sport. The issue of humanistic sport has been given extensive publicity by authors such as Jack Scott *(The Athletic Revolution)*, Dave Meggysey *(Out of Their League)*, and Gary Shaw *(Meat on the Hoof)*, just to mention a few [21]. Proponents of humanistic sport believe that the athlete is more important than the sport itself. This philosophical commitment implies that each participant should be dealt with as an individual, rather than as a member of a group. Sport is viewed as a means to an end, not as an end in itself. In other words, the values derived from sport participation should be those that are deemed valuable in all aspects of life, not just on the playing field or court.

With these concepts in mind, it is easy to identify humanistic sport with the "educational" model of sport, as opposed to the "big-business" model of sport. Most scholastic and collegiate athletic directors would publicly espouse the values of humanistic sport in an educational environment. But in many schools and colleges, sport is conducted more on the model of "big business"; that is, the athletes are viewed as factors that can be manipulated to produce wins, gain publicity, and bring financial benefit to the school or coach.

As the reader progresses through the remaining chapters, it should become clear that this book has been written to guide coaches who adhere to the educational model of athletics. The ideas presented are those that have proven successful for coaches working in a humanistic sport environment.

SUMMARY

The history and philosophy of girls' and women's participation in sport in the United States provides insight into current developments. The cultural bias has been against women's involvement in athletics, but in recent years several factors have helped to counteract this bias:

1. The change in cultural roles fostered by the women's liberation movement of the early 1960s
2. The growth of national and international sports for women through the Olympics
3. Increased television coverage of women's sporting events
4. The legislation of Title IX of the Educational Amendments Act of 1972

Among the problems that have arisen from the sudden growth in girls' and women's sport are the lack of well-trained women coaches and the change in ideology in girls' and women's athletics. Humanistic sport was proposed as the appropriate model for athletics conducted in an educational environment.

NOTES

1. Betty Spears, "Prologue: The Myth," in Carole Oglesby, ed., *Women and Sport: From Myth to Reality* (Philadelphia: Lea & Febiger, 1978), p. 12.
2. Sara Staff Jernigan, "Women and The Olympics," *Journal of Health, Physical Education, and Recreation* 33 (April 1962): 25.
3. Spears, "Prologue: The Myth," p. 3.
4. Betty Friedan, *The Feminine Mystique* (New York: Dell Books, 1963).
5. Carrie Haag, *National Championship Advisory Newsletter,* 23 September 1980 (Washington, D.C.: AIAW), p. 2.

6. *1980-81 Handbook of National Federation of High School Activities* (Kansas City, Mo.: National High School Activities Association).

7. Carole Oglesby, ed., *Women and Sport: From Myth to Reality* (Philadelphia: Lea & Febiger, 1978); Stephanie L. Twin, ed., *Out of the Bleachers* (Old Westbury, N.Y.: The Feminist Press, 1979).

8. William H. Freeman, *Physical Education in a Changing Society* (Boston: Houghton Mifflin Co., 1977), pp. 178-180.

9. Joanna Davenport, "The Women's Movement into the Olympic Games," *Journal of Physical Education and Recreation* 49 (March 1978): 58-60.

10. Ralph Vernacchia, "Problems of Modern Olympics," *Journal of Physical Education and Recreation* 49 (March 1978): 70-71.

11. Smith Hempstone, "Sports Act as Propaganda in USSR," *Hollywood Sun-Tattler,* 18 July 1980.

12. Information obtained from Russie Tighe, coach at Miami Jackson Senior High School, Miami, Florida.

13. *Federal Register* 40 (5 June 1975): 24084-24451, Library of Congress Publication.

14. Don Shoemaker, "Count to Title Nine . . . and Punt," *Miami Herald,* 29 December 1978.

15. Spears, "Prologue: The Myth," p. 12.

16. The original lawsuit was filed by Elaine Gavigan, tennis coach at Broward Community College, Ft. Lauderdale, Florida, and Peachy Kellmeyer, tennis coach at Marymount College, Boca Raton, Florida. The lawsuit was settled out of court by AIAW agreeing to change its rules to allow scholarship athletes to participate in national tournaments.

17. R. Gruneau, "Sport, Social Differentiation, and Social Inequality," in D. Ball and J. Loy, eds., *Sport and Social Order* (Reading, Mass.: Addison-Wesley Publishing Co., 1975), pp. 121-184.

18. Michael Malmisur, "Title IX Dilemma: Meritocratic and Egalitarian Tensions," *Journal of Sport Behavior* 1, no. 3 (August 1978): 130-138.

19. Ibid., p. 133.

20. Ibid., pp. 136-137.

21. Jack Scott, *The Athletic Revolution* (New York: Macmillan Co.: 1971); Dave Meggysey, *Out of Their League* (Berkeley, Calif.: Ramparts Press, 1971); Gary Shaw, *Meat on the Hoof* (New York: St. Martin's Press, 1972).

Chapter 14

Coaching Youth Sport

In this country, youth sport opportunities have been vastly different for boys and girls. Whereas such organizations as little league have been sponsoring programs for young boys for approximately forty years, it has only been in the past decade that similar opportunities have been available for young girls in communities across the United States.

It has been estimated that twenty million boys and girls between the ages of eight and sixteen are now involved in sport programs outside school [1]. Obviously, a great many coaches are required to work with these twenty million boys and girls.

Youth sport coaches need two kinds of competence: the technical competence to teach the skills of the sport; and the emotional competence to deal with young people. A capable technician will not be successful with young athletes unless he or she can cope with their emotions. On the other hand, the coach who is sensitive to the feelings of young people but knows very little about technical skills would be destined to failure. Lack of adequate preparation for coaching has been the most serious weakness of the youth sport programs in this country. But with an increasing number of youth sport clinics devoting time to the psychology of coaching, this seems to be changing [2].

The American Alliance for Health, Physical Education, Recreation and Dance has recently published a book to help educate the millions of coaches and parents who are actively involved in youth sport programs. This book, *Youth Sports Guide for Coaches and Parents,* was one of the first to present information intended to increase the value of sport participation for children [3].

DESIRABLE CHARACTERISTICS OF A YOUTH SPORT COACH

What are the desirable characteristics of a youth sport coach? How do these differ from the characteristics of a high school or college coach?

Anyone who has worked with young children in a learning situation knows that *patience* is not only a virtue, it is an essential skill for coaches of young, unskilled, and inexperienced but aspiring athletes. Patience is one of the most important characteristics of a youth sport coach.

A youth sport coach should have a *humanistic approach* to sport. A coach who is interested only in the win-loss record of a team has no business working with the fragile egos of young children. Coaches should be humanely interested in how the children develop under their guidance, not only physically, but emotionally as well.

Honesty is yet another important characteristic of coaches. Young children have an almost uncanny ability to detect dishonesty. This does not mean that coaches should be honest to the point of cruelty. Coaches should take account of the children's level of emotional maturity, and be considerate of their feelings.

Youth sport coaches must also have a *sense of fairness*. Each athlete on the team should be treated equitably and consistently by the coach. This would include the initial selection procedures for the team, the assignment of playing positions, and the playing time accorded each athlete. Coaches should never forget that children know which positions are the most critical. Consistently playing certain children in noncritical positions will do little to build their confidence or self-concept. At the early stages of skill development, children should learn about and be allowed to try every position.

A coach must also be a *good teacher*. He or she must understand the critical learning periods of children, as well as the appropriate methods of teaching skills.

Finally, *knowledge of the sport* is essential for a coach of a youth sport team. The coach must actually teach all of the necessary skills, techniques, and rules of the sport to these aspiring young athletes. In many instances, the youth sport coach provides the athlete's first exposure to the sport. The skills and techniques the young athletes acquire will influence their future performance in the sport. It is consequently of importance that the *correct* skills and techniques are taught by the coach.

One could undoubtedly name many other personal qualities that are important to the success of coaches of youth sport. This success should not necessarily be measured by win-loss records; it should be assessed by less quantifiable criteria, by the actions and attitudes of the players themselves. If each youth sport participant has fun, "while developing physical skills and emotional maturity in a positive interaction with other children," then the coach can consider himself or herself highly successful [4].

Those aspiring to be coaches in youth sport should ask "Who is the successful coach? (a) one who has an undefeated season and has only three children return to play again next year, or (b) one who has a mediocre win-loss record and who has every child return to play next year?" For the benefit of the children, (b) should be the correct answer. After all, youth sport programs are organized and conducted for the benefit of children. Only where misconceptions exist about the goal of youth sport programs would (a) appear to be the correct answer.

Coakley has made several excellent suggestions on how to organize youth sport programs to most benefit the participants and ensure success of the programs [5]. We have summarized his suggestions:

1. *Eliminate the symbolic association with professional teams.* Coakley advises that youth sport teams not be named after professional teams; behavior of professional teams is rarely compatible with the goals of organized youth sport.

2. *De-emphasize or eliminate league standings, play-offs, and awards for victory.* Research has shown that if the athletes' motivation in youth sport can be sustained only by a sophisticated award system, future involvement in the activity may directly depend on the continuation of such awards [6].

3. *Eliminate tryouts and institute procedures to eliminate lopsided scores in games.* Several youth leagues are now using a selection process to balance the teams in ability and skill. Team rosters can also be shifted during the season to ensure the enjoyment of all the participants.

4. *Do not keep individual records for players.* Each youngster can set individual goals and work toward them during the season. Placing emphasis on personal achievement records at such an early age can distort the purpose of youth sport programs, which is to encourage participation for all.

PSYCHOLOGY OF COACHING YOUTH SPORT

How important is psychology at this level of coaching? Because of the young age of the participants, it is extremely important. Children who are emotionally immature can be psychologically damaged by an authority figure such as the coach.

Parents can't always give children the time they need. The structured playtime provided by sport can be of great value to children. Many participants in youth sport programs view the coach as a substitute parent. Youth sport coaches sometimes play more than one role in the lives of young athletes. They are teachers, counselors, and friends. These roles were examined in earlier chapters of the book.

There are several reasons for the psychological influence that coaches may have over youth sport participants. First, the status our society accords those who are successful in sport is recognized by children at an early age, thanks to the media coverage of athletic events. Coaches of youth sport teams are often idolized by their young players. Second, because these sport programs are usually set up outside the school, they provide a less formal environment in which the coach and athlete can interact. This informality encourages the athletes to view the coach as a friend and counselor. Finally, the physical skills of the young players are at a beginning level. The young athletes therefore see the coach as an "expert" in the sport.

MOTIVATION

It is obvious to even the most casual observer that young children are highly motivated to participate in sport. At least in the past, youngsters were so self-motivated that they required less extrinsic encouragement than athletes of any other age. But as youth sport programs have expanded and become more organized, elaborate reward systems modeled after those used in high school and college sport have become more common. Rewards in the form of trophies and awards are the rule rather than the exception for youth sport participants. Coaches should remember that children need to play and to compete; a little creativity on the coach's part can contribute significantly to sustaining children's interest in youth sport. Encouraging the athletes' intrinsic motivation should be the primary objective of the coach.

Because of their relatively short attention spans, young children often lose their self-motivation more quickly than do older, more mature athletes. The coach must help maintain high levels of motivation by making practice sessions interesting and fun, and by providing positive encouragement and reinforcement to the athletes. One way of doing this is by changing routine, as discussed in Chapter 6. Coaches should spend less time trying "gimmicks" in practice and more time changing the structure of the practice itself.

The youth sport coach should be wary of the excessive use of awards as extrinsic motivation. If a trophy becomes the child's only reason for participating, the inherent value of sport as a means of teaching competition and cooperation is diminished. In the syndicated cartoon series *Tank McNamara,* Jeff Mutlar and Bill Hinds use sport as a vehicle for social commentary. A recent cartoon series dealing with youth sport illustrated an unfortunate but familiar reality: coaches in such programs exhibit distorted values when they let winning become the sole objective of the program.

It seems that the young children in sport often have a better sense of values than the coaches, leaders, and administrators of sport programs. Thomas reported that a recent study found that the majority of children in a little league program would rather play regularly on a losing team than "sit on the bench" of a team that won the league [7]. For these and probably for most children, the real motivation is the love of playing, not the trophy or prestige that comes from winning.

In a further illustration of how the values of the young participants may differ from those of the league administrators, an unpublished study by Greenberg showed that 96% of the youth sport participants questioned said that the most important objective in playing sport was *to have fun.* Winning was important, but was not of primary importance to these participants [8].

COACHING GIRLS VERSUS BOYS IN YOUTH SPORT

How does coaching young girls in youth sport differ from coaching young boys? There are certainly many similarities as to the physical skills and strategies needed by girls and boys to play the sport. Although we have all heard the phrase, "throws like a girl," there is really no structural difference between the way a boy throws a ball and the way a girl does. There is a mechanically correct way to throw, which should be taught to boys and girls alike.

As discussed in Chapter 2, boys and girls differ in their patterns of growth and development. Experts agree that until the onset of puberty, boys and girls are similar in size and growth patterns. But girls mature both physically and emotionally an average of one to two years ahead of boys. Until puberty, then, many girls are equal to boys in strength, body size, and speed.

It is clear that in many youth sport activities, girls can compete successfully with and against boys. This has been illustrated in numerous instances of girls successfully playing little league baseball, basketball, soccer, and even football against and with teams of boys. In the youngest age groups for soccer, girls and boys usually compete on the same teams. Because of a recent court case, little league baseball, the cornerstone of youth sport, is also experiencing a rapid increase of coeducational participation. But it still disturbs many old-time baseball enthusiasts to find that girls are not only playing, but receiving team awards for outstanding performances.

It is the adult leaders of youth sport programs who have been responsible for the segregation by sex in the programs. The children themselves are certainly accustomed to competing with and against one another: in this country, the typical elementary physical education program is coeducational. Today, even the junior and senior high physical education programs are coeducational—because of the mandate of the HEW regulation interpreting Title IX of the Educational Amendments Act of 1972.

The issue of coeducational youth sport raises several interesting questions. Will it be helpful or harmful to the emotional and physical development of young girls and boys to compete together? Could the cultural myth that sport is a masculine activity be dispelled? Are boys and girls similar in their psychological makeup regarding sport participation and receptivity to coaching? How many of the assumed psychological and emotional characteristics of boys and girls are caused by cultural influences rather than sexual differences?

At least the first three questions can be answered by one general statement: girls and boys are beginning to play together in sanctioned programs and there seem to be no reasons, either psychological or physiological, why they should not continue to do so. The last question seems to occupy the experts at regional and national sport psychology conferences every year. There is some agreement that cultural influences are responsible for the overt behavior of girls and boys in sport. In our society, certain behavior such as aggressiveness, is accepted for boys but not for girls. There is evidence, however, that as more girls become involved in sport, they will be less susceptible to cultural influences. More girls have in fact begun to participate because of a gradual weakening of the sanctions against women in sport.

ANXIETY IN YOUTH SPORT

Anxiety is a natural part of competition at any age level. But in the case of young and immature athletes, anxiety can have a severely harmful effect on athletic performance.

The successful coach must know his or her athletes. Some athletes tend to be more anxious than others. The coach must try to build the confidence of anxious players by helping them develop their physical skills and their understanding of the sport. Yelling at these players for making mistakes during games or practices will only increase their anxiety. Every coach of youth sport should remember that these athletes are just beginners in their level of skill and in their knowledge of the sport. They will make many errors—both physical and mental—as they learn to play the sport.

Once the coach learns which of the athletes have low or high anxiety levels, he or she can plan the best strategy to enable the athletes either to become motivated or to calm themselves before participation. Young athletes must be comfortable in the sport situation. This can be achieved if they have become competent in the skills required for participation and are confident of their abilities.

Youth sport programs have built-in opportunities for young athletes to "test themselves." Perhaps all athletes at this age and level of competition should be allowed to face such a situation as coming to bat in the last inning with two outs. To meet challenges and to accept defeat are two lessons we must all eventually learn. There is certainly advantage to be gained by learning these lessons early in life, through youth sport.

It is likely that, whatever their level of skill, most youth sport participants are more anxious when spectators are present, especially when the spectators are the parents and relatives of the athletes. Singer's review of research on this topic shows that in the early stage of learning a skill the presence of spectators can have a harmful effect on performance. It is only at the highest levels of skill that spectators seem to be beneficial or have no apparent effect [9]. Since most participants in youth sport are at the learning stage, it is logical to assume that spectators would be harmful to the performance of the athletes. But this may not always be the case. The motivation of some young athletes may be heightened and their performances enhanced by the presence of their parents at the game. Since parents are a part of the child's home environment, there seems to be no reason why they should not be a part of the child's sport environment. But parents should be aware that their presence could be harmful rather than helpful to the child's performance.

The pressure of "scoring a goal for daddy" or "getting a home run for mother" adds yet another dimension to the anxiety of children in youth sport competition. Young athletes often equate success in these activities with parental love. They sometimes find it difficult to distinguish between their parents' natural desire to see them succeed in sport, and their parents' feeling for them as people. If the athletes feel they have disappointed their parents by making an error or striking out in a game, they may believe their parents won't love them any longer.

Youth sport coaches should try to ensure that parents do not exert undue pressure on the athletes at practices or games. The recent manual on youth sport published by AAHPERD has emphasized the importance of this issue. The manual suggests that to help counteract parental pressure, the coach meet with the parents before the season to discuss the subject. It is also suggested that

> the positive approach of encouraging and rewarding *effort* rather than outcome helps to reduce pressure. . . . If you can get the parents to understand and reinforce this approach, you can benefit both the player and the parent. [10]

SETTING GOALS

An excellent technique in coaching is to allow each athlete to set individual as well as team goals for the course of the season. Although this method can be applied to youth sport, the coach should offer substantial guidance at this age level to help the players set realistic goals. Once the goals are determined, the coach should help each young athlete strive to reach his or her individual aims. Young athletes can learn a valuable lesson in life as they strive to be the best they can be in sport.

The coach should take care to place more emphasis on striving to meet these goals than on the outcome or the goals themselves. It is possible in youth sport, as in few other endeavors, for success to be measured in a variety of ways. Young athletes should be made to feel successful if they have set and met realistic objectives.

What is the importance of feeling successful in youth sport? Experts agree that a feeling of success contributes to a positive self-concept. Establishing such a self-concept at an early age enables one to be confident and willing to accept challenges later in life. This is especially important for girls and women in our society, who have at times been made to feel inferior to boys and men.

A research study of highly successful American women in the fields of business, medicine, and education revealed a common trait: all of these women had been encouraged by their parents to participate in competitive and challenging activities in their youth [11]. These early experiences apparently helped develop a willingness to meet challenge and to strive for success in the face of defeat or failure. The development of a positive self-concept early in their lives undoubtedly improved these women's chances for success in later life. Sociological studies of former men athletes report similar results for successful men [12]. Sport can exert a positive influence on the lives of young men and women.

SUMMARY

We have discussed the psychological value of sport for youth. Youth sport is not and should not be merely a minor version of professional, collegiate, or scholastic sport programs. The primary goal of these programs is to strive to win; the primary goal of youth sport programs is to enable participants to have fun while learning the value of competition and cooperation. It does seem, however, that many coaches of youth sport are placing more emphasis on winning than on fun.

Tutko has identified this emphasis on winning as the crux of the problem in sport today. He believes that this unrealistic emphasis can be destructive for the young athlete.

> The years 6-12 are crucial in development of an individual's growth of self. The years 12-18 are the period of social adaptation, of how a person relates to his peer group. The obsession with winning can interfere with healthy growth and psychologically scar a person for life . . . [13]

It is clear that youth sport can either be a valuable experience or an unpleasant memory. It is up to the coaches and leaders of such programs to determine how the youth sport experience will affect the participants.

STUDENT LEARNING ACTIVITIES

1. .Observe a youth sport league for at least ten to fifteen hours. Record your observations, noting such things as the characteristics of the coach, the motivation of the players, and the beneficial or harmful effects of such a program on young children.
2. Volunteer to serve as an assistant coach or referee/umpire in a youth sport league.

NOTES

1. Jerry Thomas, ed., *Youth Sports Guide for Coaches and Parents* (Washington, D.C.: AAHPER, 1977), p. 8.
2. Personal knowledge of Jack L. Llewellyn, frequent participant at youth sport clinics.
3. Thomas, ed., *Youth Sports Guide for Coaches and Parents.*
4. Ibid., p. 111.
5. Jay J. Coakley, *Sport in Society: Issues and Controversies* (St. Louis, Mo.: C. V. Mosby Co., 1978), pp. 117-118.
6. E. L. Deci, "Work: Who Does Not Like It and Why," *Psychology Today* 6 (August 1972): 57-58.
7. Thomas, ed., *Youth Sports Guide for Coaches and Parents*, p. 99.
8. Jayne Greenberg, "Competition and Children: An Attitude Survey" (Paper, Florida International University, 1978).
9. Robert N. Singer, *Myths and Truths in Sports Psychology* (New York: Harper & Row, 1975), p. 19.
10. Thomas, ed. *Youth Sports Guide for Coaches and Parents,* p. 22.
11. Margaret Hennig, "Career Development of Women Executives" (Doctoral diss., Harvard University, 1971), cited in Eva Balazs, ed., *In Quest of Excellence: A Psycho-Social Study of Female Olympic Champions* (Waldwick, N.J.: Hoctor Products, 1975), p. 16.
12. Edward Litchfield and Myron Cope, "Saturday's Hero is Doing Fine," *Sports Illustrated* 17 (October 1962): 66-80; Randy Jesick, cited in James A. Michener, *Sports in America* (New York: Random House, 1976), p. 237.
13. Thomas A. Tutko, "Sport is a Microcosm of the Society as a Whole," *Athletic Purchasing and Facilities* 2, no. 4 (August 1978): 13-19.

Chapter 15

Coaching High School Athletes

In reviewing the literature on coaching, it becomes clear that most of it has been written by men for male athletes. There have been some notable exceptions to this; but those authors who have written guides to coaching girls and women have given little attention to the psychology of coaching girls and women [1].

From the earlier chapter on coaching girls and women, it should have become clear that organized sport programs for men and women in the United States presently have a different philosophical basis. The philosophical differences can be attributed for the most part to culturally derived psychological differences between the men and women in sport—both athletes and coaches.

In this chapter we offer suggestions for coaching both girls and boys in high school sport. Before such a discussion can have meaning to potential coaches, it is necessary to mention the differences between girls and boys with regard to their psychological motives for athletic participation.

In a 1971 study, Brian Petrie compared the reasons given by college men and women for their involvement in sport [2]. We can assume that the results for college men and women would be similar to those for high school men and women. Petrie found that women emphasized "intrinsic satisfaction" while men emphasized "personal achievement and other instrumental goals." This difference in motivation is probably based on cultural influences rather than on biological or genetic factors.

Whatever the causes, psychological differences presently exist between men and women in sport. Coaches must take these differences into account. This is especially true for men coaches who coach women athletes, because they do not have an innate understanding of the female psyche. The same reasoning would apply to the few instances in which women coaches coach men athletes.

There will probably be an increasing number of men coaches for women's teams, as the women's model of athletics becomes more like the men's model, and the major emphasis is placed on winning rather than on participation. In women's programs, as winning becomes the criterion of success, men coaches, who have had more experience in athletic participation, recruiting, and coaching, will be hired to ensure quick success. This has already begun to occur, particularly in girls' and women's basketball, where men have had more experience with the five-player game.

In 1967, the girls' and women's national basketball rules changed the game from a six-player game using two divisions of the court to the five-player full court game. There is in consequence a relatively small number of women who have had playing experience in the five-player style, when compared to the number of men athletes with playing experience. The number of women with substantial coaching experience in this type of basketball is also much smaller than the number of experienced men coaches.

It is ironic that Title IX, which has been the greatest single impetus to girls' and women's athletics since 1972, may also become the greatest threat to the future involvement of women as athletic coaches. By creating single athletic and physical education departments with single administrations for both men and women, Title IX has in effect promoted the hiring of men to teach and coach women. In the 1970s, a period of declining high school enrollment, few new teachers were hired. Before Title IX, the men's physical education staffs in high schools usually outnumbered the women's staffs because of the extensive coaching responsibilities of the male teachers in a large variety of boys' sports. Because of Title IX, girls' sports have been added, but because there has been no addition of teaching faculty, the girls' sports are staffed, in many instances, by men.

CHARACTERISTICS OF MEN AND WOMEN COACHES

Because of the differences in philosophy between men's and women's sport, there are observable differences between the coaching styles of men and women. This is illustrated by Tables 15.1 and 15.2, which describe characteristics of "typical" men and women coaches. Table 15.1 is based primarily on descriptions of male coaches given by Tutko and Richards [3]. Descriptions of typical female coaches are listed in Table 15.2 as presented by Voelz [4].

If we review the characteristics listed for both sexes, it becomes clear that there are many similarities. Coaches tend to coach as they were "coached": they base their methods primarily on their past experience as athletes themselves.

THE MEASURE OF SUCCESSFUL COACHES

Only in recent years have sport psychologists attempted to study coaching methods to determine successful coaching techniques. There are several reasons for this scarcity of research:

1. The field of sport psychology is in its infancy: there are few professional sport psychologists, and research in the field is still limited. The First International Congress of Psychology of Sport was held in Rome, Italy, in 1965 [5].

Table 15.1. Characteristics of Male Coaches

TYPE	CHARACTERISTICS
1. "Hard-nosed," authoritarian coach	1. Believes strongly in discipline 2. Usually uses punitive measures to enforce rules 3. Rigid about schedules and plans 4. Can be crude and sadistic 5. Not usually warm personality 6. Very organized and well planned 7. Does not like to get too close personally 8. Often religious and moralistic 9. Often bigoted and prejudiced 10. Prefers weaker people as assistants 11. Uses threats to motivate
2. "Nice-guy" coach	1. Usually liked by a number of people 2. Considerate of others 3. Uses positive means to motivate athletes 4. Very flexible in planning—sometimes chaotic 5. Often experimental
3. Intense or "driven" coach	1. Frequently worried 2. Overemphasizes or dramatizes situations 3. Takes things personally 4. Spends endless hours on materials 5. Always has complete knowledge of game 6. Always pushing himself; never satisfied with accomplishments 7. Motivates players by example
4. "Easy-going" coach	1. Does not seem to take things seriously 2. Dislikes schedules 3. Does not get rattled easily 4. Gives impression that everything is under control; at times appears lazy
5. "Businesslike" coach	1. Approaches the sport in a calculating manner; very well organized 2. Very logical in his approach 3. A cool person interpersonally 4. Sharp intellectually 5. Major emphasis on out-thinking the opponent 6. Pragmatic and persevering

Derived from Thomas Tutko and Jack Richards, *Psychology of Coaching* (Boston: Allyn & Bacon, 1971), pp. 17-39.

2. Coaching success in the past has always been measured in quantitative terms, such as win-loss records.

3. Coaches themselves have been hesitant to change or to accept new ideas from people outside the coaching profession.

4. The determinants of coaching success are diverse and difficult to quantify; they include the personalities of coaches and athletes, as well as levels of skill, motivation, anxiety, and aggression, just to name a few.

Table 15.2. Characteristics of Female Coaches

TYPE	CHARACTERISTICS
1. Presser	1. Knows win/loss records of conference 2. Demanding in practice 3. Up on state of teams but may not realize own players' injuries 4. Punishes physically
2. Pusher	1. Strict disciplinarian 2. Not emotionally involved but pushes team as needed to save face
3. Puller	1. Carries total leadership load 2. Takes loss personally 3. Is truly involved 4. Drives tough physically but sometimes can't bear to watch in crucial situations
4. Primer	1. Is on even keel 2. Organized 3. Knows individuals on teams 4. Friendly with other coaches 5. Takes team to extra functions for exposure to information 6. Student of game 7. Secure
5. Pro-er	1. Gung-ho 2. Looks forward to new challenges 3. Personally psyched in competition 4. Positive outlook 5. Innovator 6. Experimenter
6. Plooper	1. Carries many papers with her but can't find what she wants 2. Minimal personal goals 3. Relaxed spectator 4. Indecisive 5. Not well organized 6. Easy going
7. Player	1. Doing 2. Showing 3. Participates in warm-up and practice 4. Has "When I" stories 5. Stays with team during whole competitive day 6. Enjoys group and action
8. Plodder	1. Has slow pace 2. No experimental ideas 3. Does not use psychology of coaching to utmost 4. Reacts against aggressive coaches 5. Meek

From Chris Voelz, *Motivation in Coaching Team Sports* (Washington, D.C.: AAHPER, 1976), p. 5.

A recent study concluded that a psychological training program for youth sport coaches in little league baseball resulted in a "significant and positive influence on overt coaching behaviors, player-perceived behaviors, and children's attitudes toward their coach, teammates, and other aspects of their athletic experience" [6]. The evidence also showed that children who played for the trained coaches experienced positive changes in self-esteem. Although there were no significant differences between the win-loss records of the trained and untrained coaches, the children who played for the trained coaches evaluated their coach and the emotional climate of their teams more positively.

A logical conclusion to be gained from this study, and we hope from other similar studies in the future, is that coaches can be trained to be more effective and more successful in promoting desirable educational effects in every scholastic and youth sport program in the United States. With the development of coaches' training programs and of new evaluative criteria for sport programs, it is hoped that the emphasis on win-loss records as the sole criterion of success can be reduced. Only in the professional sport arena, where the goals and expected outcomes of sport participation differ considerably from those of youth, scholastic, or collegiate sport programs, should win-loss records have any validity.

Parents, fans, and the general public must be educated as to the innate differences in performance and expectation between our educational sport programs and our professional sport programs. It is also clear that many coaches in educational institutions need to be reeducated themselves as to the expected goals and outcomes of their own programs. An example is the college coach who recently proclaimed, "I'd give anything—my house, my bank account, anything but my wife and family—to get an undefeated season" [7].

At all levels of sport, this obsession with winning is having a harmful effect on the educational value of athletic participation. Coaches bend and break the rules in order to win. In many instances, sportsmanship and ethics are traded for increased win-loss percentages. Tutko discusses the change in standards:

> We'll take every means possible to win. It has almost nothing to do with performance, much less pleasure. I'd be willing to bet that if there was an illegal but, totally undetectable, means to increase the chances of winning, 97% of the coaches in this country would do it . . . [8]

Much of the pressure to win is placed on coaches by school administrators and the public alike. Sabock aptly describes the dilemma of coaches in educational environments who have to win games and satisfy an athletically uneducated public.

> Coaches live in a materialistic world in which success (winning) is the goal, but they work in a setting where academic and character development of students is supposed to be the primary objective of education. . . . If the coach felt secure in the knowledge that the [school] administration was sincere in its stated belief as to the value of athletics . . . that the administration would make every effort to convey this belief to the community, and that they would support the coach as long as the coach worked toward these beliefs, regardless of the scoreboard, the coach could truly become a valuable asset as an educator in this kind of professional climate . . . [9]

The athletic education of the public has begun in part with the publication of such books as *Youth Sports Guide for Coaches and Parents* and *Joy and Sadness in Children's Sports* [10]. In addition, the American Alliance for Health, Physical Education, Recreation and Dance has promoted a better public understanding of the educational role of sport through various publications, advertisements, and films. But there is still much to be done in the area of public awareness. One of the first steps in this process is the education of people who want to be coaches. Books such as this one are necessary to fill a void in the training of coaches who will be working in educational environments. This book is not a how-to manual of coaching techniques; instead, it gives the prospective coach the insight and understanding necessary to educate and to promote the emotional growth of athletes in a humanistic environment.

The psychology of coaching high school athletes differs considerably from that of coaching athletes in youth sport. It is natural to assume that the differences are caused, in large part, by the difference in age and in physical and emotional maturity.

MOTIVATION

Whereas younger children are highly motivated to perform in sport, this motivation decreases when students reach high school age. The change in motivation is greater for high school girls than it is for high school boys. High school girls tend to lose some of the intrinsic motivation that they had when they were younger. This occurs for several reasons. First, high school students are easily influenced by their peers and by social pressures. As noted earlier, our culture does not value girls' participation in sport—particularly that of girls beyond the age of puberty. In her study of female Olympic champions, Balazs compares society's view of girl athletes to its view of women athletes:

> [At an early age] girls together with boys are allowed to compete in school and athletics without significant negative consequences. The little girl is rewarded for these successes and evolves a self-concept that tells her she can be successful and competitive. If there are not negative feedbacks from parents and teachers and as long as her friends are similarly achieving, this little girl will also feel normally feminine. Until puberty! . . . Successful competing and behavior that were rewarded until now, suddenly become negatively regarded. . . . [The developing girl] also faces a new social role expectation . . . [11]

It is clear that the typical high school female athlete is openly defying cultural standards, and must be highly motivated to want to compete in sport. Cultural standards, however, seem to vary from one region of the country to another. A study of high school female athletes in Iowa reported that young women who excelled in athletics were highly valued by their peers [12]. It would seem that women athletes from rural or agrarian regions of our country are respected more than those in urban communities. Perhaps this is a carryover from the beginnings of the country, when women were equal partners in the hard work of the pioneers' lives. During that time, there was somewhat less distinction than there is now between "masculine" and "feminine" roles for work or play.

For boys, on the other hand, sport participation is regarded as a valuable part of high school life. To some young men, just to be a part of the team is of paramount importance. Sport participation for boys has also been a significant way to achieve the "macho" recognition that is valued by many young men. The rewards received by high school boys for athletic participation are bigger and more significant than those received by girls. Motivation for boys and girls in high school athletics consequently requires different considerations.

Based on the study by Petrie cited earlier, it is clear that both high school and college coaches should make a special effort to encourage intrinsic motivation in female athletes. Coaches could promote a social environment—perhaps a sport club—for team members and stage "fun" activities as part of the functioning of the team. An example would be scheduling a visit to Disney World at the end of a trip to a tournament competition at a Florida school.

Whereas extrinsic motivators such as trophies and recognition are more valued by male athletes, evidence indicates that female athletes place importance on intrinsic motivators such as self-satisfaction and enjoyment of the activity. It is important that the young women athletes enjoy the experience of being part of an athletic team.

The changing priorities of both boys and girls in high school are another important influence on motivation. Because of the high inflation of the past decade, many families have needed the financial assistance of their high school age children. High school boys and girls may also choose to work instead of playing sport in order to earn extra money for a car or clothes, items highly valued by those in their age group.

CHANGING CULTURAL VALUES

There seems to be evidence of a slow change in the traditional view of women's participation in sport. This change is being effected by the increasing number of female competitors of all ages, as well as by increased media coverage of women in sport. The present craze for physical fitness is also helping bring about greater social acceptance of active sportswomen. It seems to be all right for a woman to participate in sport if it is solely for reasons of physical fitness—as opposed to competitive reasons.

James Levering, an educational psychologist and former physical education teacher, offers an example of this growing acceptance: "Eight years ago, in my sixth-grade recreation programs, boys would never ask girls to play. In the last few years, they've begun to. And now that more girls are playing sports, it isn't a bad thing socially. Girls who are seen as athletes aren't considered masculine anymore" [13].

Perhaps in the future both boys and girls will be equally motivated to participate in high school athletics, as our society begins to value sport participation for all, regardless of sex. In the athletic profession itself, this has become a reality at recent coaching clinics where psychological variables such as goal orientation and aggression are being discussed without reference to sexual differences [14].

MOTIVATIONAL TECHNIQUES

What techniques can a coach use to increase or maintain the motivational levels of high school athletes? As we mentioned earlier, high school girls require a high level of intrinsic motivation to be willing to compete; boys are more likely to be influenced by material rewards. The role of the coach of young women athletes is consequently to maintain an already existing motivational level. The coach dealing with young men should try to instill strong intrinsic motivation and to de-emphasize the quest for material gain. At the same time, coaches must offer guidance to both boys and girls who have the talent and potential to play beyond high school.

The most obvious motivational techniques are the traditional methods commonly employed by coaches. These include pep talks, bulletin board or locker room motivational messages, and tangible rewards earned by practice or game performances. There are books available to assist coaches in their motivational techniques [15].

Less traditional motivational techniques have also been used successfully by coaches of both female and male high school athletes. Among these are goal setting, affirmation, visualization, and positive mental attitude. These methods, which are discussed in the following paragraphs, have been tested and promoted for female athletes by Voelz and for male and female athletes by Singer and by Suinn [16].

Goal setting is a means of fully involving the athletes in all aspects of the sport program. At an early preseason meeting, the athletes are asked to set their individual goals for the season in specific terms. In basketball, for example, a player might say that he or she expects to average fourteen points and ten rebounds per game. These goals can be decided on and shared only with the coach, so that they are the player's personal goals. In the course of the season, the coach can review the goals with each player for possible revision.

A review of the section of Chapter 6 that deals with goal setting is appropriate at this point. Coaches have cited instances demonstrating that when athletes set unrealistic goals for themselves, their desire to achieve may diminish as the season progresses. Easy goals may be more helpful to the athlete than impossible goals. When an easy goal is met, revising the goal upward is a motivator to the athlete; revision downward may be disastrous to achievement. High school athletes, whether male or female, must keep their goals at a level appropriate to high school achievement, not to that of their college or professional heroes.

The players should also be asked to determine, as a group, the team's goals for the season: these should include affective as well as athletic objectives. Examples could be: "Showing respect for each team member" or "Having a team spiking average of 80%."

As part of setting goals, the players could also be asked to help establish the social and conduct rules for the season. While these rules must be essentially compatible with the coach's personal philosophy, it is advantageous to every coach to have the athletes participate in this process. Athletes are less likely to rebel against rules they have helped set. Such participation also shows each athlete that he or she plays an important and responsible role as part of the team; this increases the athlete's motivation to participate fully in all of the team's endeavors. Although the coach should reserve the right to make the final decision in this process, it is interesting that high school coaches have said that when athletes are given the responsibility to establish training rules, they are unduly hard on themselves.

The second method, *affirmation,* is defined as "descriptive statements used repetitively to create a positive self-image" [17]. The idea behind the practice of affirmation is that "we tend to become what we believe we are." This technique is an extension of the concept in motivation theory known as *level of aspiration.* Repeating affirmative statements is one way of encouraging athletes to set high levels of aspiration for their performance. Coaches should remember, however, that unless the athlete believes in the statements, the process of repeating them will be meaningless.

The advertising slogan that claims "You Gotta Believe," is appropriate to athletics. Although the effects of believing in oneself are almost impossible to quantify, it is nevertheless an important variable in athletic competition, especially among less skilled or less experienced athletes. Based on more than twenty years' involvement in athletics, it is the authors' opinion that "believing in oneself" probably contributes more than fifty percent to the end result of performance. "Believing" is simply another way to describe a self-confident or positive attitude toward performance.

Every experienced coach will acknowledge the importance to athletes of a positive attitude. Supporters of the technique of affirmation believe that athletes can build their confidence by repeating affirmative statements [18]. Examples of statements made by individual athletes would be: "I look forward to the opportunity of scoring a go-ahead goal in overtime"; or "I would like to face the challenge of batting with two outs in the final inning of a close game." A team affirmation might be, "We will remain calm and efficient in all stressful game situations."

A third method of motivation is *visualization,* which relies on techniques similar to those used in mental practice. The coach asks the players to visualize various competitive situations so that whatever players have to face in a game will not come as a surprise. The situations visualized can be general, such as the outcome of an entire game, or specific, such as facing a full-court press in basketball or executing a foul shot under pressure.

The likelihood of improving athletic performance through visualization depends directly on the athlete's perception of the correct skill performance. The coach should ensure that athletes correctly visualize performance; visualizing incorrect performance is actually practice for making mistakes. It is therefore important that the athletes know what is correct and what is incorrect execution of a skill. Visualization and the realistic prospects of success can then be valuable techniques of motivation.

Development of a *positive mental attitude* is a fourth motivational technique. Athletes who are physically competent are likely to have a positive mental attitude. Although many athletes succeed in spite of their skill levels, few athletes succeed in spite of their attitudes. A positive attitude is a prerequisite to success in athletics. The coach can promote this attitude by helping each athlete build self-esteem. This can be better accomplished through techniques of positive reinforcement than through embarrassment or punishment. It is generally accepted that people perform at the level that is expected of them. If the coach and the athletes cooperatively establish a higher level of expectation, the athletes' performance will be likely to match the expectation.

The coach can also encourage a more positive attitude among the team members by putting losses in their proper perspective. Voelz illustrates this in his comments on a twenty-three to eight team record: "Twenty-three wins and eight temporary setbacks. We made eight other schools happy, is that a crime?" [19].

Another coach, this one in high school football, used a slightly different technique to develop a positive attitude. He would not permit his players to say the word "defeat." Over a three-year period, his teams had twenty-six wins, zero losses. He contended that by not saying the word "defeat," his teams did not consider being defeated and had a winning attitude. But the ending to this story is not as encouraging. His teams began to lose games; they were about .500 over the succeeding three years. His motivational technique had lost its effectiveness.

We can see from the preceding example that positive attitudes are easy to acquire and maintain as long as the team is winning. When the team begins to lose, the coach has a real challenge. How do losing teams maintain a positive attitude? One high school boys' basketball team in Tennessee lost over one hundred consecutive games. But at the hundredth game, there was so much enthusiasm you would have thought they had won the previous ninety-nine games. The coach was obviously a master at dealing with emotions. Of course, the team had reached the point where winning was not on their list of expectations. The emphasis was on being positive, believing that anything could happen on any given day, and achieving realistic goals—such as scoring more points than in the last game. It was as if the quest to win had given way to the quest for survival. The coach's problems began when the team finally won a few games. The taste of a different kind of success awakened dormant desires to win. Developing and maintaining positive attitudes then became a greater challenge for the coach.

Coaches who treat each loss as if it were the end of the world will find that this tactic will soon lose its effectiveness with the team. To some coaches, losing may eventually mean the end of a coaching career and, consequently, the end of the world. But coaches should remember that losing may not have the same meaning to the athletes. Young men and women in high school have other avenues of achievement, if sport is not going well. A good example of athletes' attitudes was reflected in a booklet produced by the Minnesota State Coaches Association. Athletes were asked questions concerning practicing and coaching standards. One response seems especially appropriate here: when asked about the emphasis on sport and winning, athletes responded by saying "The coach has to realize that football is not my whole life . . ." [20].

Coaches should also be aware that today's athletes will not unquestioningly accept the coach's statements. The coach who overdramatizes the importance of a loss will soon discover that the athletes will characterize *all* the coach's opinions as dramatizations—and therefore as meaningless. If this occurs, the coach may lose the respect of the athletes, and lose effectiveness as a coach whenever he or she has information to share. As was mentioned in previous chapters, there is no substitute for honesty on the part of the coach. High school athletes are responsive to honesty—and know how to recognize it.

AGGRESSION

Although aggression is defined as "an act of hostility or violence" in most dictionaries, it has a special meaning when used in reference to sport. *Aggression* and *aggressiveness* in athletic competition have come to mean positively asserting oneself.

Aggression, or at least overt aggressive behavior, can differ from men to women athletes. If in fact aggression is a necessary ingredient in successful sport performance, coaches of girls and women may have a different kind of challenge than coaches of men and boys.

The coach of a typical high school girls' team will have to be especially concerned with the effects of aggression on athletic performance, because in our culture, women have been viewed as naturally nonaggressive; men are seen as naturally aggressive. This difference was discussed by Zoble in a review of literature on women in sport. She found that girls are consistently more punished for aggressive behavior in childhood than are boys [21]. Girls consequently develop alternative means of coping with their aggressive feelings, such as withdrawal of friendship, verbal attack, seeking adult intervention, gossip, tears, and somatic complaints [22].

For coaches of girls, the specific implication of these findings is that female athletes must be taught the aggressive techniques necessary for success in sport. The coach will also have to learn how to deal with the ways in which girls tend to express frustration or anger. Girls who have not had much competitive experience before high school will be particularly unfamiliar with aggressive sport techniques.

This can be illustrated by the experiences of a high school girls' basketball coach in an urban Florida community several years before the advent of Title IX. The coach had twin sisters try out for the team. Because the sisters had grown up shooting and dribbling a basketball—both with and against each other—they were extremely skilled at handling the ball. But they had never played competitively on a team. The coach found that they were insufficiently aggressive in playing the game. All of the twins' basketball skills had been developed in a cooperative mode; they didn't know how to out-hustle an opponent for the ball or drive against an opponent in a closely guarded situation. The coach soon discovered that teaching aggressiveness is perhaps a more difficult task than teaching the skills and strategies of the game itself.

For coaches of young men, this is rarely a problem. Male athletes have always been rewarded for aggression in sport situations. High school men are often selected by colleges because of their determination and aggressiveness. No doubt, as more girls begin to participate in youth and elementary sport, aggressive behavior will become a natural part of their play as well.

In a recent article discussing girls in sport, Hammer asked whether girl athletes can be both aggressive and feminine: "Traditionally, we haven't raised girls to be aggressive. . . . Can a girl be aggressive on the field and feminine off of it?" [23]. In the same article, Dr. Dorothy Harris, director of the Center for Women and Sport at Pennsylvania State University, replies that aggressive behavior is specific to a situation. Girls and women can certainly be aggressive in sport competition and nonaggressive in other situations. This observation certainly applies to boys and men as well. Many high school male athletes are nonaggressive off the playing field. As was discussed in Chapter 9, aggression itself is often sport-specific.

It is clear to even the casual observer that aggressiveness is an essential component of success in athletic competition. It is perhaps more valued and necessary in some sports than in others. For example, aggressiveness is more important to the team games of football, volleyball, soccer, and basketball than it is to gymnastics or golf. Whereas a gymnast may need to be aggressive only to try a new routine during competition, the volleyball player needs aggressiveness to attempt a diving save during a point rally in the game.

How does a coach teach aggressiveness? For athletes who are not inclined to behave aggressively, the coach must design practice situations that stress aggressive skills needed in game situations. The coach should first specifically identify aggressive situations in the sport. Examples for basketball could include scrambling for a loose ball, rebounding, and driving for a lay-up when closely guarded.

Other considerations the coach should review include:

1. Taking valid measurement of the athletes' aggressive qualities through personality inventories
2. Defining aggression in sport as assertive behavior rather than violent behavior
3. Rewarding aggressive behavior in game and practice situations
4. Using aggressive athletes as role models in practice situations
5. When coaching young women, arranging open team discussions of aggressiveness as an area of conflict for girls and women in sport

PSYCHOLOGICAL MAKEUP

In order to make use of motivational techniques, positive mental attitudes, or aggressive behavior, coaches must be familiar with the attitude or psychological makeup of each athlete. During at least the first three years of high school, young men and young women are at an "in-between" age. They are no longer kids, but they are not yet adults. They are going through an infinite number of changes. Sport can help or hinder young people as they prepare to become adults. Ideally, high school sport should be educational and assist young athletes in making the adjustments necessary during the teenage years.

The characters and personalities of high school athletes are more fully developed than those of participants in youth sport. But the older athletes are still impressionable, and over a period of time, may, as a result of associating with a high school coach, demonstrate certain behaviors and suppress others. A coach must be a model to the athletes and must be flexible in working with the various personalities on the team. The coach who is dealing with teams of both young women and young men has the added challenge of understanding the different attitudes of the two sexes toward competition. A review of Chapters 3 and 4 will help coaches understand the influence of personality on performance.

SUMMARY

Every coach and prospective coach should be aware of the importance of psychology in coaching high school athletes. We discussed variables such as motivation, aggression, and attitude, and listed characteristics of coaches as well. The coaching types presented by Tutko and Richards and by Voelz were presented not to recommend a style of coaching but to review alternative styles. It should be kept in mind that each type of coach can be successful and that seldom does a coach fit neatly into one category. What is important is that coaches have a psychological understanding of their own actions in order to better interact with all athletes, whether they are young men or young women.

NOTES

1. Donna Mae Miller, *Coaching the Female Athlete* (Philadelphia: Lea & Febiger, 1974); Patsy Neal, *Coaching Methods for Women,* 2nd ed. (Reading, Mass.: Addison-Wesley Publishing Co., 1978); Hally B. W. Poindexter and Carole Mushier, *Coaching Competitive Team Sports for Girls and Women* (Philadelphia: W. B. Saunders Co., 1973).

2. Brian Petrie, "Achievement Orientations in Adolescent Attitudes Toward Play," *International Review of Sport Sociology* 6 (1971): 89-99.

3. Thomas A. Tutko and Jack W. Richards, *Psychology of Coaching* (Boston: Allyn & Bacon, 1971), pp. 17-39.

4. Chris Voelz, *Motivation in Coaching Team Sports* (Washington, D.C.: AAHPER, 1976), p. 5.

5. Robert N. Singer, *Myths and Truths in Sports Psychology* (New York: Harper & Row, 1975), pp. 2-3.

6. Ronald Smith, Frank Small, and Bill Curtis, "Coach Effectiveness Training: A Cognitive-Behavioral Approach to Enhancing Relationship Skills in Youth Sport Coaches," *Journal of Sport Psychology* 1 (1979): 59-75.

7. Institute for Learning Staff, "Teaching Sportsmanship and Values in Athletes," *The Athletic Educator's Report* (Old Saybrook, Conn.: Institute for Management, 1978), p. 8.

8. Thomas A. Tutko, "Sports is a Microcosm of the Society as a Whole," *Athletic Purchasing and Facilities* 2, no. 4 (August 1978): 13-19.

9. Ralph Sabock, *The Coach,* 2nd ed. (Philadelphia: W. B. Saunders Co., 1979), pp. 27-30.

10. Jerry Thomas, ed., *Youth Sports Guide for Coaches and Parents* (Washington, D.C.: AAHPER, 1977); Rainer Martens, ed., *Joy and Sadness in Children's Sport* (Champaign, Ill.: Human Kinetics Publishers, 1978).

11. Eva Balazs, ed., *In Quest of Excellence: A Psycho-Social Study of Female Olympic Champions* (Waldwick, N.J.: Hoctor Products, 1975), p. 10.

12. B. F. Fasteau, "Giving Women a Sporting Chance," *Ms. Magazine* 2, No. 1 (July 1973): 56-58.

13. Signe Hammer, "My Daughter, the Football Star," *Washington Post Parade,* 5 August 1979.

14. This has occurred at several clinics in sport psychology in 1979 and 1980 at which Jack Llewellyn, along with other notable people in sport psychology, has been an invited speaker.

15. Thomas A. Tutko and Jack W. Richards, *Coach's Practical Guide to Athletic Motivation* (Boston: Allyn & Bacon, 1972).

16. Chris Voelz, *Motivation in Coaching a Team Sport* (Washington, D.C.: AAHPER, 1976); Robert N. Singer, *Coaching, Athletics and Psychology* (New York: McGraw-Hill, 1972), p. 225; Robert N. Singer, "Motivation in Sport" cited in Richard Suinn, *Sport Psychology: Theory and Application* (Minneapolis: Burgess Publishing Co., 1979), pp. 40-55.

17. Ibid.

18. Ibid.

19. Ibid.

20. *Listening to Athletes,* Minnesota State High School Coaches Association publication, 1976.

21. Judith Zoble, "Feminity and Achievement in Sports," in A. Yianakis et al., eds., *Sport Sociology: Contemporary Themes* (Dubuque, Iowa: Kendall/Hunt Publishers, 1976), pp. 185-193.

22. Ibid.

23. Hammer, "My Daughter, the Football Star."

Chapter 16

Coaching College Athletes

Psychology plays an important role in the coaching of college athletes. This is only natural, since psychology and coaching are both concerned with the study of human behavior. A detailed study of successful college coaches would show that these coaches are adept in the application of principles of psychology.

Why does psychology seem to play a larger role in coaching at the college level than at the high school or youth sport level? The importance of psychology in coaching seems to increase in direct proportion to the age and level of skill of the athletes being coached. In youth sport, coaches must certainly consider psychological variables, but the physical variables of growth and skill development have an overwhelming influence on the child's athletic performance. An example can be found in gymnastics: an eight-year-old child can, for the most part, learn the same gymnastic stunts as a young adult can. The child's only limitations are physical: related to strength, growth, and development. In contrast, the young adult's limitations are more likely to be psychological: related to anxiety, fear of failure, and pain of injury. When it comes to athletic performance and competition, psychological limitations can often be more debilitating than physical limitations.

By the time athletes reach the level of collegiate competition, they have probably developed minimum levels of skill and have had considerable competitive experience. Their competitive experience could have affected the athletes in several ways: if the athletes have been successful, their athletic experience will have heightened their self-confidence and level of aspiration; the self-concepts of less successful athletes may have been damaged by their experience in sport.

How could an athlete who had been unsuccessful in high school sport reach the level of collegiate competition? One would assume that only students who were successful performers in high school would become college athletes. Although this is certainly true in men's athletics, it has not always been the case for women. In many parts of the country, the growth of collegiate athletic programs for women has preceded the growth and expansion of high school athletic programs for women.

A brief review of the growth of women's athletics in the state of Florida will illustrate this phenomenon. The majority of women's varsity college athletic programs in Florida began in 1969, after several years of club sport or extramural status [1]. But in Miami and Dade County, Florida's largest urban area, girls' varsity athletics were not officially begun in the high schools until 1974 [2]. This was probably true of many other Florida high schools as well. Consequently, from 1969 to 1974, many of the women college athletes in Florida universities may have had little—if any—varsity athletic experience in high school.

With the tremendous growth of high school varsity programs for women since the publication of the original Title IX Guidelines in June 1975, this situation is changing. But until women athletes entering college are likely to have had athletic experience as extensive as that of men, coaches of young women will have an additional challenge: to help such athletes develop a positive mental attitude toward performance.

PERSONALITY

The past competitive experience of a college athlete will have had a decided influence on the athlete's personality. It is also true that an athlete's personality will have had a decided influence on his or her competitive experience. Personality is an important variable in coaching and athletics. Consequently, much of the research on athletes has been an analysis of the personality traits of the participants. The reader may wish to review the summary of this research offered in Chapter 4.

A good coach will become familiar with the various personalities of the athletes and choose his or her coaching styles accordingly. Just as various coaching personalities have been identified (see Tables 15.1 and 15.2), the personality characteristics of athletes have also been identified and categorized.

Much of the work analyzing the personalities of athletes has dealt with male athletes. Tutko and Richards have identified a number of personality traits related to high athletic achievement for men: drive, determination, intelligence, aggression, leadership, organization, coachability, emotionality, self-confidence, mental toughness, responsibility, trust, and conscience development [3]. It should be clear to anyone who is knowledgeable about women's sport that these personality traits also appropriately describe successful women athletes. Much more research is necessary before it can be determined whether basic personality differences actually exist between men and women athletes.

RECRUITMENT OF SIMILAR PERSONALITY TYPES

The college coach has a decided advantage over the high school coach in that athletes with certain personality traits can be invited to play for the coach's team. Whereas high school coaches are usually restricted to accepting athletes only from a surrounding school district or geographical area, college coaches can be selective and recruit only those athletes whose personalities are compatible with the coach's own personality.

The governing association for women's collegiate athletics, the Association for Intercollegiate Athletics for Women (AIAW), has only recently sanctioned recruiting as a legal means of securing women athletes. But since 1974, when changes in AIAW national rules and procedures made athletic scholarships available for college women, college coaches of women's teams have been carefully selecting women athletes to join their teams, just as men's college coaches have been doing for years. It is only natural that these college coaches would select athletes whose personalities would successfully blend with those of the coach and other players.

It is likely that men college coaches and men athletes have been more selective in this matching and meshing of personalities than have women coaches and athletes. Because of the rules governing athletic scholarships and transfers, men coaches have less room for experimentation—or error—in selection of players. The governing association for men's collegiate athletics, the National Collegiate Athletic Association (NCAA), has a rule that forbids transfer students from participating in athletics without "sitting out" athletic competition for at least one year. In addition, the NCAA and AIAW both have an implied rule concerning the renewal of athletic scholarships from one year to the next. Under these rules, it is difficult for a coach to withdraw an athletic scholarship or fail to renew it.

As of 1980, AIAW does not have a rule prohibiting women transfer students from immediate athletic participation. But the association's rules do prohibit a transfer student from being eligible for athletic financial aid in the first year of transfer. Many college women athletes have taken advantage of this transfer rule to seek an athletic program and coach with whom they can be satisfied. Much of this satisfaction is probably based on personality factors.

There are some men athletes who would accept or ignore personality conflicts with their college coaches because they are afraid to endanger their chance of being drafted into professional sport. In contrast, others would not hesitate to give up their athletic scholarship to transfer to another school where they will be afforded a better opportunity for potential advancement to the professional ranks.

In the past and even now, college women athletes have not had the professional sport opportunities that men have had. Most women athletes have consequently viewed college sport as a means of securing a college education—not as a career. If these women athletes were dissatisfied with their coaches, they were likely to quit the team, but remain in college. A few women athletes have elected to transfer to other schools, giving up their athletic scholarships. It will be interesting to observe the effects of increasing opportunities for women in professional sport on the women's collegiate programs. More women athletes may accept personality conflicts with their coaches, if they feel their athletic experience will provide them with a professional athletic career.

COACHES AND PERSONALITY CONFLICTS

Severe personality conflicts between players and coaches often produce disastrous results in athletics. This is best illustrated by examples of actual situations. In the late 1960s, a college basketball coach who was rather reserved and calm was replaced by a coach who was a "screamer," and who punished players both verbally and physically. The new coach had difficulties not with the new recruits, but with the returning athletes. The returning athletes also had problems with the new coach. A player who had been all-conference the previous year was so intimidated by the methods of the new coach that he did not play regularly after the fourth game. A potential career beyond college was ruined. It could be argued that a really outstanding athlete would have been able to make the adjustment. A stronger case is made, however, for the importance of a good relationship between the coach and the players, one that will enable them both to give their best to the team.

Another example occurred on the men's basketball team of a Division II college. After three years of recruiting, the coach had a team of players whose personalities were almost identical to his own. A walk-on player of outstanding physical ability joined the team. He subsequently made All-American and was number two in the nation in scoring. But neither the coach nor the other team members got along with the new player. The results were disastrous. Winning would no doubt have been sweeter—and may have occurred more often—if the team had been free of the pressures created by personality conflicts.

A third example concerns not conflict as such, but the potential ability of a coach to influence the behavior of his players. It is believed by those familiar with this highly successful Big Ten basketball team that the coach of this program can break players psychologically and mold their behavior. This technique, based on building concern for the team as a unit while eliminating any concern for individual performance, fosters strong, aggressive team play.

Numerous other examples could be presented, using strong coaching figures such as John Wooden and Al McGuire. Successful college coaches place a high premium on the manipulation of the psychological makeup of players.

PRODUCTIVE RELATIONSHIPS BETWEEN COACHES AND PLAYERS

Once the players have been chosen for the team, how can coaches deal most productively with the various personalities of the athletes? Coaches with many years of experience know that human nature decrees that it is virtually impossible for all the athletes to "like" the coach—or for the coach to like all the athletes. Inexperienced coaches and teachers often mistakenly believe that it is most important for their athletes and students to *like* them. Women often make this mistake, perhaps because of cultural differences in the way men and women in our society view social relationships: women have been raised to be more attentive to the emotional aspect of relationships than have men. When compared with men, women have also had fewer female role models in athletics and much more limited athletic experiences. What is *most* essential is that athletes *respect* coaches, rather than like them. For the team to be most efficient, mutual respect between the coach and the players must exist. Without this mutual respect, the productivity of the team will suffer.

By suggesting that respecting a coach is more important than liking a coach, we do not mean to imply that the coach should be a cold, uncaring, or insensitive person. As noted in Tutko and Ogilvie's research on coaching personalities in Chapter 4, men coaches score low in those personality traits that contribute most to being sensitive and supportive in interpersonal relationships. Both men and women must strive to develop coaching personalities that most encourage the productivity of the team.

Among mature adults, respect can exist independently of personality conflicts or differences. One would reasonably assume that in a college environment, the athletes and coaches are sufficiently emotionally mature to recognize this. But people are not always ruled by reason. In such an emotional endeavor as athletics, emotions, rather than logic, tend to determine behavior.

How can coaches ensure that athletes respect them and each other? The following list contains some suggestions that will help foster a humanistic athletic environment.

1. *Be consistent and fair.* The coach should treat all athletes the same way. Rules of conduct should be established jointly by the team and the coach and should be familiar to both. The coach must apply the rules consistently and fairly.

2. *Do not prejudge the actions or attitude of a player.* Without jumping to conclusions, the coach should confer individually with athletes whose actions or attitudes seem inconsistent with the goals of the team. The coach should also be able to distinguish between the action and the person: "Sometimes beautiful people commit ugly acts" [4].

3. *Do not make hasty decisions.* Just as good coaches carefully plan the strategy for a game, they should carefully plan decisions about the behavior or attitude of a player. Never make a decision in the heat of a moment.

4. *Communicate openly and honestly with the players.* Coaches should share their ideas, their decisions, and the reasons behind them. They should communicate openly with the team, either individually or as a group. Unquestioning acceptance of coaching decisions is a relic of the fifties and sixties. College athletes are intelligent and eager to understand; they will respond better to communication on these issues than to silence.

5. *Confront team problems.* In group sessions with the team, the coach should acknowledge major problems such as morale. Just as strategy sessions are conducted with the offensive or defensive units of various teams, it is sometimes necessary to have a session for the acknowledgment and resolution of morale problems that can affect the entire team. Try to analyze the cause of the problem objectively, taking care not to allow the athletes to isolate or identify specific team members as the source of the problem. The coach should serve as the counseling leader and guide the team to a resolution.

6. *Deal with the performance of the team in a rational and realistic manner.* The coach should teach the athletes that striving to play their best is the goal in sport. Individual athletes should not be pointed out as the cause of a loss or win. Athletes should be taught to accept losing and winning as natural parts of both life and athletics.

7. *Be a model for the athletes.* Coaches should be examples of the behavior that they seek from their athletes. For example, coaches who espouse good training rules and health habits, but who smoke cigarettes, will confuse their athletes. If coaches say one thing and do another, isn't *everything* they say open to doubt and questioning? A popular humanist speaker and coach, Don Bethe, has put it this way, "Your actions are so loud that I cannot hear what you say" [5].

8. *Treat each athlete as a valued member of the team.* The coach can prevent jealousies and conflicts among the athletes by treating each athlete as a valued member of the

team. Although some athletes will be more successful than others, the coach should make each member of the team feel that he or she is worthy, both as an athlete and a human being.

Underlying these eight suggestions is the assumption that coaches have a genuine interest in and concern for their athletes as fellow human beings. Without this interest and concern, it is virtually impossible for coaches and athletes to develop mutual respect. Without this respect, coaches will be limited in their efforts to achieve true success in athletics. Such success is not measured by win-loss records, but by the coach's positive and lasting influence on the lives of the athletes who studied and played for that coach.

MOTIVATION

Motivation is another important psychological variable in coaching college athletes. Coaches should be aware that there may be differences in the role that motivation plays for men and for women college athletes. From earlier discussions (Chapters 13 and 15) of society's view of women in athletics, it is clear that unlike men athletes, women athletes at the college level need a high level of intrinsic motivation to choose athletic competition. Although extrinsic motivations for women athletes have increased in quantity and quality in the past decade, women athletes are still violating a cultural standard. It is clear that strong intrinsic motivation is necessary for women to make such a serious decision.

The extrinsic encouragements offered to college women athletes are now approaching what they have been for college men athletes for decades. Among these are a "free" college education through athletic scholarships, the chance to be chosen for international teams (College World Games, Pan-American, and Olympic teams), the chance for a professional career in athletics (primarily golf and tennis, with more limited opportunities in basketball, softball, and volleyball), the chance for increased financial benefits through participation in "super-stars" competition and commercial advertising, and future career opportunities as a coach, athletic trainer, sport commentator, or a member of any other sport-related profession.

MOTIVATIONAL TECHNIQUES

The motivational techniques that a college coach can use are similar to those used by a coach at any other level of competition. The means of motivating athletes are limited only by the imagination and creativity of the coach. Among these techniques are pep talks, locker room signs and visual aids, and behavior modification through rewards for meeting practice or game goals. Examples of typical locker room signs and visual aids are listed in Table 16.1. Each coach will have to experiment and choose whichever techniques have positive effects on the athletes.

Some motivational techniques are more successful with men than with women athletes and vice versa. Some of the motivational techniques described in the following sections are directed to encouraging the intrinsic motives usually associated with women athletes. Each coach will have to decide what is most appropriate and effective for his or her players.

One motivational technique that has been successful for college women is organized cheering. One might expect that athletes of college age would be too mature or sophisticated to be motivated by a "rah-rah" approach to athletics. But many successful college women's teams in a variety of sports have a number of songs and cheers that they use with great enthusiasm and emotion before, during, and after games. It seems that the larger the team and the more people at the bench to cheer, the greater the benefits of group cheering.

It is difficult to determine how such cheering actually benefits a team. Does the cheering rattle the opposing team, causing their performance to suffer? Or does the cheering actually motivate the team to perform at a higher level of skill?

Team cheering and singing seem to be excellent ways for young college athletes to vent their emotions in a positive way. It may also be a means of maintaining unity among the starters and substitutes on a women's team. If the substitutes are involved in cheering for the entire team, they can feel that they have had an active role in determining the outcome of the game.

Team cheering and singing, however, must be spontaneous. Coaches can do little—if anything—to promote cheering if the athletes are too inhibited or quiet to begin on their own. It usually takes only one player on the team to spark or lead the cheering. The coach can help by recognizing the leaders in this effort and encouraging them. The coach should also maintain some control over the cheers: coaches should prohibit any cheering that is at the expense of the other team's players, coaches, or umpires. Cheering directed against another team is contrary to the spirit of athletics and should not be tolerated by the coach.

Although cheering and singing are often viewed as a part of college women's athletics, they are not essential to success. Some women athletes are serious or introspective; a team composed of such women would probably find cheering or singing distracting during an athletic contest. Spectators of the finals of the 1976 AIAW Women's Large College Volleyball National Championships saw such a team in action. The University of Southern

Table 16.1. Typical Athletic Slogans Used In Locker Rooms

The difference between champ and chump is *U*—Let's be champs!!

Luck is what happens when preparation meets opportunity.

Don't make excuses—Make good!!

The first element of success is the determination to succeed.

Nothing great was ever achieved without enthusiasm.

Work will win when wishing won't.

If you've made up your mind you can't do something—You're absolutely right!

The time to take advantage of the future is *today*.

A winner never quits and a quitter never wins.

The dictionary is the only place where success comes before work.

The only exercise some people get is: *Pushing* their luck, *running* down friends, *side-stepping* responsibility, and *jumping* to conclusions.

Lead, follow, or get out of the way!!!

All men and women may be born equal, but it's what they are equal to later that counts.

California team—made up of six starters and only two substitutes—quietly and efficiently won the volleyball national tournament held at Austin, Texas, in December 1976 [6]. This was in contrast to most of the other teams at the Nationals, who had numerous songs and organized cheers.

Singing and cheering can be used to promote team spirit, maintain morale, and vent emotion. But coaches should be wary of allowing such external modes of motivation to become more important than less conspicuous forms of intrinsic motivation. If a team is losing badly and the cheering becomes muted, do the athletes have enough intrinsic motivation to keep trying?

It is unusual to see a team of college men cheering, although the players on the bench may shout encouragement to those on the court or field. It is difficult to understand the reasons for this difference between men and women college athletes. There is legitimate reason to suspect that it is simply another instance of cultural standards manifesting themselves in sport: "Men play and women cheer."

Other methods of motivation for college athletes are goal setting, affirmation, visualization, and positive mental attitude [7]. These methods and examples of their use were described in Chapter 15. The reader is encouraged to review that chapter, as the methods are certainly appropriate for college athletes as well as high school athletes.

GROUP COHESIVENESS

The cohesiveness of the team can affect the motivation of the players. In team sport, the "togetherness" of the unit will have a direct effect on the success of the team. This is especially true in sports such as volleyball, football, or soccer. In volleyball, for example, no one player can achieve success alone; the spiker is unsuccessful without a good set and the setter is unsuccessful without a good pass. In football, the success of a talented running back would be limited without the aid of an offensive line.

Personal disputes and jealousies among athletes can often disrupt the unity of a team, as in the example from men's basketball cited earlier. Disputes and jealousies may or may not have an effect on the measurable success of the team. But whatever its effect on the win-loss records, dissension can make both players and coaches miserable, and take the joy out of athletics. Coaches should plan ways to ensure that the cohesiveness of the team is not eroded by discord.

According to the personal observation of the authors, which is perhaps limited in its scope, college women athletes seem to be less willing to accept super-stars or a hierarchy among players than are men athletes. This could be traced to the philosophical differences between men's and women's athletic programs—the meritocratic versus the egalitarian models discussed in Chapter 13. Men athletes following the meritocratic ideology view inequality as inevitable; that is, the most highly qualified will "attain the most important position" [8]. According to the egalitarian model associated with women's sport, inequality is "an area of constant conflict." [9]

Women may be less willing to accept the identification of certain team members as "super-stars" because they see this as an example of inequality. Once one player has been afforded super-star status by the coach or the media, there is a greater possibility of jealousy and conflict among team members. If this happens, and the performance of the team begins to suffer, the coach must recognize the situation and attempt to resolve such conflicts.

One method that has helped promote group cohesiveness in women's collegiate athletics is an awards party. The awards party is usually an informal gathering of the team, perhaps combined with a dinner. At this gathering, each athlete is required to present an award to one other team member. Each team member's award illustrates her contribution to the team. The coach decides in advance which team member will present which award; this should be kept secret by the players. To ensure that the athletes take the awards seriously, each award must be original: it can be in the form of a song, a poem, a humorous skit, or a story. This awards meeting should be held whenever it will contribute most to the spirit and morale of the team. One possibility would be to hold it immediately before an important state or regional tournament. The feeling of unity created by the ceremony will probably carry over through the competitive event.

In almost every sport in men's collegiate athletics, there are several athletes who are afforded star status. The star athletes seem to be accepted by their team members because winning is the goal: anyone or anything that can contribute to that goal will be accepted by the team. It is also likely that women athletes will come to share this attitude as their athletic programs move toward the meritocratic model.

ANXIETY

Another psychological factor that must be considered in coaching college athletes is anxiety. As discussed in Chapter 7, whether anxiety is an aid or a hindrance to athletic performance depends on numerous factors.

By the time athletes have reached the age and level of skill necessary for collegiate athletics, they have probably had a variety of competitive experiences. They are likely to have learned to cope with the anxiety that is a natural part of athletic competition. If they had not learned to cope successfully with anxiety by the time they reached the college level, they would probably have dropped out of competition. This would not be true of those athletes who have exceptional talent and can perform well in spite of a high level of anxiety.

The role of the coach is to help the athletes find efficient ways to cope with anxiety. The coach can use select tests to validly determine the athletes' tendencies to anxiety (see Chapter 7). Once the anxiety levels of the athletes have been identified, the coach can help individual players "practice" anxiety-producing situations.

In basketball, for example, the coach could create a drill simulating the last minutes of a game in which the team is behind by a few points. The clock should be running and the game realistically staged. Both the offense and defense can then practice under pressures similar to those of a real game. Such situations can be staged for every sport and should be a periodic part of the regular practice procedures for all teams. Coaches can determine the specifics for simulating the most common anxiety-producing situations for their team and sport.

This method of "practice under duress" has been popularized on television through the two-minute drills of football teams and the four-corner stalling offense of men's collegiate basketball. When players learn to practice under pressure, they can then play successfully under similar conditions in actual games. Other useful methods for dealing with anxiety are discussed in Chapter 10.

AGGRESSIVENESS

For both men and women, participation in collegiate athletics requires a higher level of skill than participation in high school sport. The reason for this is the selection process used by most college coaches. Because the number of high school athletic teams is much larger than that of collegiate athletic teams, only the most skilled high school athletes are selected for college teams.

Aggressiveness is a basic characteristic of the highly skilled athlete. Most athletes at the college level will be aggressive players. If the coach notices that an athlete needs to learn to be more aggressive, there are techniques that can be used to help the athlete. Such techniques include charting and rewarding aggressive behavior in game situations, and using aggressive athletes as role models in practice situations. It will also be important for coaches of women's teams to openly discuss with the team the conflicts women may feel about displaying aggressiveness.

With both men and women athletes, the coach's basic role will be to direct and channel aggressive behavior toward the achievement of a goal. Unchanneled aggression is usually harmful to performance.

SUMMARY

Several suggestions for dealing with college athletes have been presented. For most effective use, this material should be related to the material in the first part of the text. We offered several examples to illustrate the role of personality conflicts in performance. A list of suggestions to promote mutual respect between coaches and athletes was proposed. We explained the psychological concepts of personality, motivation, anxiety, cohesiveness, and aggression—and the role of such variables in effectively coaching college athletes. Examples for the application of these concepts were offered.

NOTES

1. Personal knowledge of Judy Blucker, one of the original organizers of the Florida Association of Intercollegiate Athletics for Women (FAIAW).
2. Information obtained from Russie Tighe, coach at Miami Jackson Senior High School, Miami, Florida.
3. Thomas A. Tutko and Jack W. Richards, *Psychology of Coaching* (Boston: Allyn & Bacon, 1971), pp. 42-47.
4. Don Bethe, "Effective Teaching, Coaching, and Interpersonal Communication Processes" (Paper, California State University, Northridge, Calif., 1978).
5. Ibid.
6. Personal knowledge of Judy Blucker, volleyball coach of Florida International University at the 1976 AIAW Large College Volleyball National Championships in Austin, Texas.
7. Chris Voelz, *Motivation in Coaching a Team Sport* (Washington, D.C.: AAHPER, 1976); Robert N. Singer, *Coaching, Athletics and Psychology* (New York: McGraw-Hill, 1971), p. 225; Robert N. Singer, "Motivation in Sport," cited in Richard Suinn, *Sport Psychology: Theory and Application* (Minneapolis: Burgess Publishing Co., 1979), pp. 223-232.
8. Michael Malmisur, "Title IX Dilemma: Meritocratic and Egalitarian Tensions," *Journal of Sport Behavior* 1, no. 3 (August 1978): 130-138.
9. Ibid.

Index

Affirmation, 160
Aggression, 97, 162-163
   aggressiveness, 176
   theories of, 98, 103
   types, 99, 103
   sex differences in, 101
Agility, 16
Alderman, R. B., 24, 25
Ali, Muhammed, 78
American Alliance for Health, Physical Education, Recreation and Dance, 137, 138, 143, 148, 157
Anxiety
   competitive, 80
   definitions of, 77, 78
   in college sports, 175
   in youth sport, 147
   state (A-state), 79, 82, 84
   techniques to reduce, 84
   trait (A-trait), 79, 82, 84
Archer, Clifford, 35
Arnheim, Daniel, 11
Aronson, E., 97
Association of Intercollegiate Athletics for Women, 134, 137, 169
   volleyball national tournament, 173-174
Athletic Motivation Inventory, 29-31
Austin, Dean A., 120
Austin, Tracy, 135

Balance
   dynamic, 15
   static, 15
Balazs, Eva, 158

Bandura, A., 98, 103
Barsch, R., 17
Bass stick test, 15
Berger, Joseph, 111
Berkowitz, Leonard, 99
Bethe, Don, 171
Biddulph, Lowell, 44
Booth, E., 40
Borg, Bjorn, 43

California Psychological Inventory, 29
Caprio, Frank, 111
Carlson, Robert B., 44
Cattell, Raymond B., 24, 26, 31, 35
Cattell Sixteen Personality Factor Test, 27-28, 42, 79
Clark, L. V., 122
Coakley, Jay J., 144, 145
Cobb, Ty, 79
Cohesiveness of team, 174-175
Coleman, James S., 18
Comaneci, Nadia, 134, 135
Connally, Maureen, 133-134
Connors, Jimmy, 43, 78
Cooper, Lowell, 40
Corbin, C. B., 122
Counseling
   ethical issues in, 129
   problem athletes, 130
   techniques, 128
Cratty, Bryant J., 11, 50, 77-78, 81
Crenshaw, William, 42
Critical learning periods, 16-17, 20
Cross, T. J., 118

Czechoslovakia, 4

Davenport, Joanna, 135
Davis, E. C., 135
de Coubertin, Baron Pierre, 135
Division of Girls' and Women's Sports, 133, 137
Dunham, Paul, Jr., 120

East Germany, 4
Edwards Personal Preference Schedule, 28-29
Egalitarian ideology, 138, 174
Egstrom, G. H., 122
Eitzen, Stanley, 18
Ellison, Kerry, 40
Endurance, 14
Epuran, Mihai, 52
Evert, Chris, 43, 134, 135
Eysench, H. H., 58

Femrite, Arnold, 36
Flexibility, 15
Four o'clock player, 78
Freischlag, Jerry, 40, 66
Friedan, Betty, 134
Frostig, Marianne, 17

Gaither, Jake, 17, 97
Gale, C. K., 110
Gamesmanship, 78, 79
Getman, G., 17
Gilliam, P. W., 58
Goal setting, 73, 160
Greenberg, Jayne, 146
Griffith, Coleman R., 53, 70
Gruneau, R., 137
Guilford, J. P., 26

Hammer, Signe, 163
Hansen, G. F., 50
Harris, Dorothy, 163
Hartman, David, 36
Hartogs, R., 58
Heeschen, Richard, 15
Hellison, Don, 101
Hempstone, Smith, 135
Hendry, L. B., 36
Hinds, Bill, 146
Hollingsworth, Barbara, 82
Horghidan, Valentino, 52
Hutson, Margaret, 82
Hutton, Daniel, 43
Hypnosis, 108

Ikegami, Kinji, 42
Information processing, 90
Inverted-U hypothesis, 83

Johnson, B. L., 51
Johnson, Granville, 43
Johnson, Warren, 43
Johnson, W. R., 58

Kephart, Newell, 16-17
Killy, Jean Claude, 5
Kinesthetic awareness, 13
Kirkson, Arond, 99
Kistler, J., 41
Korbut, Olga, 135
Kroger, W. S., 110-111
Kroll, Walter, 42, 44

Langer, Philip, 82
Lawther, O. H., 35
Legron, Leslie, 108
Levering, James, 159
Llewellyn, Jack, 5, 113
Lopez, Nancy, 135

Malmisur, Michael, 137-138
Malumphy, T. M., 40
Martens, Rainer, 66, 78, 80
    Sport Competitive Anxiety Test, 80-81, 85-86
Maslow, A. H., 51
McEnroe, John, 43
McGuire, Al, 170
Meggysey, Dave, 138
Mental preparation, 107
Mental rehearsal, 4, 5
Meritocratic ideology, 137, 174
Minnesota Multiphasic Personality Inventory, 28
Mohr, Dorothy, 119
Motivation, 49
    definitions of, 50
    drives, 51
    extrinsic, 53, 59
    gimmicks, 64
    incentives, 52
    intrinsic, 53, 59
    needs, 51
    of college athletes, 172-174
    techniques, 63, 67, 159-162
Motor ability, 10
Mutlar, Jeff, 146

Naruse, Gosaku, 109
Nastase, Ille, 43, 78
National Association of Girls & Women in Sport, 137
National Collegiate Athletic Association, 137, 169
Neal, Patsy, 101
Nelson, D. O., 82
Nelson, J. K., 51
Niemeyer, R. K., 118, 119
Novaczyk, Todd D., 82, 83

Ogilvie, Bruce, 5, 29, 37, 170
Orlick, Terry, 99

Paulus, Paul B., 70
Pele, 136
Perception
    auditory, 11-12
    tactile, 11-13
    visual, 11-12

Personality
  and sport psychology, 9
  coach-player relationship, 37
  conflicts, 169-170
  definitions, 24
  importance, 23
  inventories, 26
  of coaches, 38, 170
  of college athletes, 39, 168
  traits, 25
Pestalosi, Robert, 11
Petrie, Brian, 153, 159
Piaget, Jean, 16
Polyphasic Values Inventory, 36
Positive mental attitude, 161-162
Practice
  distributed, 119, 120, 121
  massed, 119, 120, 121
  mental, 121, 122, 123, 161
  under duress, 175
  whole versus part, 117, 118
Psyched, 78
Psychometrics, 3

Reality therapy, 130, 131
Reflex development, 11
Relaxation, 4, 5
Richards, Jack, 38, 44, 154, 155, 168
Richardson, A., 122
Richardson, Deane, 41
Riggs, Bobby, 78
Robb, Margaret, 67
Rosenthal, Robert, 56
Rote, Kyle, Jr., 136
Ruebush, B. K., 58
Rushall, Brent S., 23, 40, 50
Ryan, E. O., 51, 58

Sabock, Ralph J., 127, 157
Sage, George, 36
Salter, Andrew, 108
Scott, Jack, 138
Scott, M. G., 120
Self-concept, 10, 18, 19, 51
Semeonoff, Boris, 25, 29, 31
Seymour, Emery W., 41
Shaw, Gary, 138
Shay, C. T., 118
Shick, Jacqueline, 122
Siedentop, Daryl, 50, 130
Singer, Robert N., 2, 24, 43, 50, 53, 56, 63, 66, 69, 73,
    83, 120, 148, 160
Skubic, Elvera, 66
Slevin, Robert Lee, 82
Soviet Union, 4
Spears, Betty, 134
Spielberger, C. D., 78, 79, 80
  State and Trait Anxiety Test, 82
  State Anxiety Inventory, 82
  Trait Anxiety Inventory, 82
Sperling, 40

Sport
  "big business", 138, 139
  early specialization in, 10
  educational, 138, 139
  egalitarian, 138
  growth of women's, 134-136
  humanistic, 138, 139
Sport psychology
  and Olympics, 4
  international, 4
Start, K. B., 122
Strength
  dynamic, 13-14
  explosive, 13-14
  static, 13-14
Suinn, Richard, 5, 112, 160

Title IX of the Educational Amendments Act of 1972,
    134, 136, 138, 147, 155, 163, 168
Tutko, Thomas A., 5, 29, 37, 38, 44, 83, 101, 149, 155,
    157, 168, 170

Ulrich, Celeste, 138
Ulrich, Richard P., 110
Unestahl, Lars, 110

Values clarification, 128, 129
Vanek, Miroslav, 81
Vaz, Edmund, 99
Vernacchia, Ralph, 135
Visualization, 161
Voelz, Chris, 160, 161

Wagner, C. O., 119
Walker, Eugene, 77
Wechseler, D., 58
Weinberg, S., 99
Whitley, Jim D., 120
Wickstrom, R. L., 118
Wooden, John, 36, 84, 170
Wrigley, Philip K., 4

Yerkes-Dodson law, 57, 83

Zaharis, Babe Didrikson, 133-134
Zalchkowsky, Leonard, 101
Zoble, Judith, 101, 162